PROUD SHOES

Black Women Writers Series

PROUD SHOES

THE STORY OF AN AMERICAN FAMILY

———

Pauli **MURRAY**

BEACON PRESS, BOSTON

To Caroline, Edmund, Marie, and the memory of Pauline Fitzgerald Dame

Beacon Press
25 Beacon Street
Boston, Massachusetts 02108

Beacon Press books
are published under the auspices of
the Unitarian Universalist Association of Congregations.

Printed in the United States of America

04 03 02 01 00 99   8 7 6 5 4 3 2 1

Library of Congress Cataloging-in-Publication Data

Murray, Pauli, 1910–1985.
   Proud shoes : the story of an American family / by Pauli Murray ; foreword by
Patricia Bell-Scott. —1st Beacon Press ed.
   ISBN 0-8070-7209-5
   1. Afro-American families—Biographies.   2. Fitzgerald family.   3. Afro-
Americans—Social life and customs.   Murray, Pauli, 1910–1985—Family.   I.
Title.
   E185.96.M96 1999
   306.85'089'96073—dc21   99–14164

The past is the key of the present and the mirror of the future, therefore let us adopt as a rule, to judge the future by the history of the past, and having key of past experience, let us open the door to present success and future happiness.

FROM DIARY OF ROBERT G. FITZGERALD,
JULY 26, 1867

Foreword

> Great art is not a matter of presenting one side
> or another, but presenting a picture so full of the
> contradictions, tragedies, [and] insights of the period
> that the impact is at once disturbing and satisfying.
> —PAULI MURRAY

On July 18, 1933, a young Pauli Murray scribbled a sketch in her diary that would eventually blossom into the family memoir *Proud Shoes*. Over the twenty-odd years that it took to write this story, she thought a lot about what it meant to be an artist. She was at times so pained by the process that she had to set the project aside. But a healing clarity always followed the pain, enabling her to paint life as she saw it. What she created is a compelling family saga that gives us two views of the American experience: one a close-up that follows her family—the Fitzgeralds—from the early 1800s to the beginning of the twentieth century, the other a wider angle that situates her ancestors' story on a larger cultural mosaic.

Although *Proud Shoes* was conceived as a children's story to be shared with her nieces and nephews, it became a defense of a personal and collective heritage that challenged the ethnocentricism of the 1950s. It spotlighted black achievements that had been ignored or denied. It exposed the "secret" of rape and voluntary interracial sex that so characterized the American South. It raised the lid on racial passing and on class and color conflicts within black communities. And it proved that a black woman could tell an honest story about slavery, the Civil War, and Reconstruction.

Given the boldness of its themes, it is not surprising that *Proud Shoes* met with a mixed response on its release in the fall of 1956. From many reviewers came praise and recognition. Writing in the *New York Times*, Henrietta Buckmaster called it "a gallant book" by "a writer of uncommon gifts." Bryon R. Bryant of the *San Francisco Chronicle* judged it "superior to most non-fictional works about the South." Margot Jackson of the *Akron Beacon Journal* said that it was history "told with an uncanny newness for now it is a Negro writing of slavery and the Civil War." And the former First Lady, Eleanor Roosevelt, wrote in her newspaper column that this was "American history which all American citizens should read."

But some reviewers read *Proud Shoes* as social commentary with far-reaching ramifications. Roi Ottley of the *Chicago Tribune* remarked that "Not so many years ago a distinguished white family, descendants of a Revolutionary war hero known to every schoolboy, paid a Negro family who bore his name a reported $50,000 to change its name. . . . There are thousands of such intertwined Negro and white families, particularly in the south. But until now . . . this aspect of Americana has been largely shrouded in mystery." Patricia Speights of the Mississippi-based *Clarion-Ledger & Jackson Daily News* saw the book as a disturbing omen: "The cause of miscegenation is herewith presented by a writer who has been actively associated with the cause of civil rights. . . . In these days of racial tension . . . a book such as this can serve no useful purpose."

Although there is no evidence that *Proud Shoes* fueled racial strife in 1956, this was unquestionably a period of significant social change. Indeed, it was the year the Supreme Court outlawed racial segregation on the Montgomery, Alabama, city buses; it was also the year that several legislators signed the so-called Southern Manifesto opposing the integration of public schools. Clearly, some Southerners saw a direct link between this book and the one thing they most feared—racial mixing. Many stores simply refused to stock the book, and the Southern press rarely mentioned its existence.

In short, the political climate of the late 1950s obscured the literary brilliance of *Proud Shoes*. Less than five thousand copies were sold and it languished for twenty-two years. In 1978 it was reissued in an

expanded edition, its publication undoubtedly encouraged by the phe-
nomenal success of Alex Haley's *Roots*. *Roots* was a historical novel
based on stories of Haley's African and enslaved ancestors, and nearly
every review of *Proud Shoes* invited comparisons between the two. Jack
Hicks of *The Nation* wrote that *Roots* "dwells most effectively on
African continuations . . . , [whereas] *Proud Shoes* traps the beast of
American slavery." But some savvy critics, like Larry Swindell in the
Philadelphia Inquirer, saw *Proud Shoes* for what it truly was—"not a
spinoff on *Roots* but a splendid forerunner."

This time *Proud Shoes* was not shunned by the Southern press, and
it was given a new reading that went beyond earlier preoccupations
with race. Readers were fascinated by the perseverance and character
of the Fitzgerald women. The public was also intrigued by its author,
the Reverend Dr. Pauli Murray, who had accomplished so much in her
own life.

Never rivaling *Roots* in the breadth of its audience, *Proud Shoes* did
find a home in many classrooms. For the next decade, there would be
a stream of reports from students who fell in love with these "flesh-
and-blood characters." Many saw, for the first time, a connection
between their lives and the nation's history. One student of German
immigrant parents revealed: "I have previously thought of the two
[family and U.S. history] as being totally separate, but I now understand that without one there couldn't be the other."

Knowing that contemporary readers might question the value of a
forty-something-year-old family memoir, I offer the following reasons it
still commands our attention. First, we need to read this book because
of who Pauli Murray was *and* for what she, nurtured by her family,
helped this nation to become. As a young civil rights activist in the
1930s, she confronted the exclusion of black students at the University
of North Carolina. In 1940 (fifteen years before Rosa Parks refused to
surrender her seat to a white passenger on a crowded bus), Pauli was
jailed in Petersburg, Virginia, for violating a state law requiring segregation on public buses. Three years later (almost two decades before
the college student sit-ins of the 1960s), she organized a series of
protests by Howard University students at segregated restaurants in
Washington, D.C. She later championed women's rights by challenging the exclusion of women students from the Harvard Law School.
She also cofounded the National Organization for Women, and

became the first black woman priest in the two-hundred-year history of the Protestant Episcopal Church. Surely these contributions, though often forgotten, have earned her a place in the American narrative. For without her activism *and* her literary genius, we would certainly be less than we are.

Second, we should read this book for what it is, an exquisite and groundbreaking work of creative nonfiction. Because it was written at a time when genre distinctions were for some sacrosanct, *Proud Shoes* became an archetype for a generation of writers who would later merge novelistic techniques and nonfiction.

Third, we ought to read this book for what it teaches about the healing power of narrative. That Pauli often spoke of its writing as an "act of growth" is testimony to the resilience which so pervades its voice and form. That countless readers have been emboldened to ask penetrating questions about their own family histories is testimony to its nurturing expanse.

Finally, this text should be read for the insights that it offers to a culture still struggling to find ways to talk about our connections to each other. Clearly the controversy caused by recent DNA evidence linking Thomas Jefferson to a son of his slave, Sally Hemings, demonstrates the need for a continuing dialogue about this social construct we call race.

Several years ago I asked the Reverend Dovie Roundtree, a longtime friend of Pauli's, what Pauli would want us to learn from her life. And Dovie replied that Pauli was most passionate about sharing what she called "the fullness of life." *Proud Shoes* is, I believe, the precious by-product of an artist's deepest yearnings. My hope is that we can finally appreciate the magnificent portrait she has left us.

PATRICIA BELL-SCOTT, editor of *Flat-Footed Truths: Telling Black Women's Lives* and *Life Notes: Personal Writings by Contemporary Women*, is working on a book about Pauli Murray. She is a professor of family and women's studies at the University of Georgia in Athens.

Introduction

When *Proud Shoes: The Story of An American Family* was first published, it reached only a limited audience. In 1956, family roots and black family life in particular did not excite public interest. While many black families had a rich oral tradition which they shared privately, few had the time or incentive to develop formal genealogies or to write family histories which were non-fiction.

Why, then, did I decide to write a family memoir? The idea began to grow in me from the time I was graduated from college in 1933, firmly set (I thought) on being a writer. I gathered notes and scribbled sketches, but the struggle to educate myself and to earn a living during the Depression, and then my law studies and practice, kept me from writing for many years.

Originally, I intended *Proud Shoes* for my small nieces and nephews, who had never known their Fitzgerald ancestors and were curious about their family. It was to be a children's story, as I remembered it through the eyes of the child Pauli. What changed my direction, and gave me a motive so compelling that I interrupted my law practice for four years to devote myself full time to researching and writing *Proud Shoes,* was the political and social climate of the 1950's. The civil rights movement was gathering momentum. At the same time, the country was gripped by the hysteria of McCarthyism. The fear of Communism was rampant; anyone who championed a liberal cause was vulnerable to the charge of disloyalty. "Communist-inspired" was the easiest way to label and discredit civil rights efforts. As a civil rights activist fighting against racial segregation when challengers of segregation policy were few and defeats were customary, I found it imperative to declare my American heritage. Not Communism, but the ideals and influences within my own family had made me a life-long fighter against all forms of inequality and injustice. The title *Proud Shoes* is from a line written by Stephen Vincent Benet in 1934 about Paul Engle's first book of poetry, *American Song:* "Here is a new voice—and the voice of a new generation... its clear incisive speech cuts deep into native ground. Here is somebody walking in America in proud shoes."

Proud Shoes is not fiction, although in a few instances I took liberties and drew conclusions which the facts seemed to justify. It is an attempt to give a coherent account of my forebears, based on tales told to me and facts discovered in my search of the historical record. I was able to confirm enough of the family stories to trust the credibility of our oral traditions. Throughout the narrative, I tried to distinguish between the facts and the legends which could not be substantiated.

My search began with my maternal grandparents and led back to their immediate antecedents and the places where they had lived. I traced the first three generations of my maternal ancestry, covering the period from 1808 to 1919. Essentially, however, the book is a biography of my grandparents, Robert and Cornelia Fitzgerald. I used genealogy primarily to establish their identities and to indicate ancestral influences on their personalities.

I like to think that while my grandparents' story is the centerpiece of the book, *Proud Shoes* is also the story of a people involved in a crucial turning point in our nation's history. Once I had located members of my family in a particular setting or at a significant moment, I often amplified their story by filling in the historical background of their community— the events which shaped their lives.

While the story focuses on the racial conflict within which the family had to work out its destiny, it also frames portraits of several remarkably brave and independent women. They were not conscious feminists, but in coping with the intolerable tensions of their time they assumed responsibilities and performed actions which quietly defied convention and transcended "a woman's place."

Authenticating black family histories has always presented problems. The most formidable barrier to the development of a continuous record of antecedents was the experience of slavery, which all but wiped out the identities of black ancestors. Symbolic of blanket anonymity is the way in which slaves were enumerated in the Census of the Slave Population. Before the 1870 Census, three separate census rolls were kept: the white population; free people of color; the slave population. In the slave census, only the name of the owner appeared. Slaves were listed by age, sex, and whether "Black" or "Mulatto" (designated by "B" or "M"). It was necessary to enumerate the slave population to determine the number of representatives in Congress from each slave state; a slave counted for three-fifths of a person. However, slaves seldom appeared by name in public records unless an owner mentioned them in a deed, will, court proceeding, or bill of sale.

After the Civil War, the energies of several generations of black Americans were absorbed by the sheer struggle for survival. Much of their pre-Civil War family history was lost. There were many reasons—the chaos of Reconstruction, the scattering of families through migration, the persistent illiteracy inhibiting writing and record-keeping, and the failure to preserve oral traditions while older people were still alive or their memories were still fresh.

In addition, among many Negroes in the South there was a self-imposed silence about the past. During my childhood, young adults were reluctant to discuss slavery as part of their personal history, although they were barely a generation removed from it. Some of the older people who had been slaves clammed up when they were asked questions. Others found that as soon as they began to reminisce, their children would change the subject. While this tendency was not universal, it helps to explain why so little has been written about black family history from the inside. When the former slaves passed from the scene, their descendants were apt to blot out the family experience: it was too painful to live with.

Throughout slavery, free black families lived in both the North and South, and their numbers increased during the decades before the Civil War. Many of these families had members who were literate and who developed strong traditions and lived surprisingly stable lives in spite of their hazardous position in the midst of the antebellum controversy over slavery. Among them were successful farmers and property owners, skilled craftsmen and craftswomen, and proprietors of small businesses. They could be identified in the Census of Free People of Color and in local property and tax records or business directories. Their significance lay in their stubborn determination to lead a normal existence and in their capacity to survive and event to make modest progress in the face of constant disparagement

My maternal grandfather's family was one of these clusters of free people of color. The Fitzgeralds of Delaware and Pennsylvania migrated to North Carolina during Reconstruction. Their family history coincided with the closing decades of the slavery controversy, the Civil War, Reconstruction, and the beginning of the twentieth century. Their restless search for better opportunities placed them at strategic points in the current of tumultuous events during these periods. They documented the Fitzgerald saga through a few business records and letters, numerous photographs, and the portions of my grandfather's diary which managed to survive. (These portions covered the years from 1864 to 1871.) The strong identification of the Fitzgerald family with the Union cause was important in the eyes of descendants living in the land of the Confederacy in the aftermath of the War Between the States.

By contrast, my grandmother's people, the Smiths of Chapel Hill, North Carolina, were a white slave-owning family of local prominence. Theirs was a story of deep sexual and emotional involvement with slaves, across the racial and social barriers. Whether it sprang from lust or devotion or sense of kinship or moral obligation, this involvement led the Smiths to act in contradictory ways and to be ambivalent about an institution that they were unwilling to renounce.

My dual family heritage made a deep impression on me as a child. I grew up in North Carolina, in the three-generation household headed by my maternal grandparents. I listened avidly to their family tales, which were the principal means of entertaining children before radio, movies, and television. These tales filled the void in my life created by death and illness, which had deprived me of my parents and had separated me from my brothers and sisters. And while the family stories created some inner tensions, they provided me with a sense of continuity. They certainly gave me a strong sense of personal identity to counteract the effect of the stereotype that Negroes had played no significant part in their nation's development.

This stereotype was contradicted by the history of at least four generations of Fitzgeralds that I could identify. The first generation, born in the early 1800's and contemporaries of Abraham Lincoln, were moderately successful farmers in Delaware and Pennsylvania. The second generation (my grandfather's generation) was born in the 1840's and 1850's. Its members were literate at a time when the ability to read and write was not yet widespread in the general population. Among them were school teachers, farmers, brickmakers, and small traders. The menfolk reached maturity in time to take an active part in the Civil War. The third generation (which included my parents, aunts and uncles, and older cousins) was born in the 1870's and 1880's; it had enough of a head start to be among the first group of young people to attend the colleges and trade schools for Negro freedmen established in the South during Reconstruction. From its ranks came carpenters, dressmakers, a graduate nurse, a pharmacist, a lawyer, a public school principal, and a large number of female elementary-school teachers.

The fourth generation (to which I belong) was born in the first two decades of the twentieth century, when black people in the United States had reached the lowest ebb of their fortunes since Emancipation. We came to adulthood during the Great Depression, but a number of us in the family managed to go to college and professional school. Some continued the tradition of teaching and nursing; some went into law, medicine, or university education; some went into business careers in banks and insurance companies. Many moved to cities in the North and lost their strong family identity.

Since the deaths of Robert and Cornelia Fitzgerald, two more generations have come into existence. The fifth generation (my nieces and nephews) reflects the broadening opportunities of their era; the members are found in government service, banking, electronics, public relations, and professional sports, as well as education. The sixth generation is still largely in public school or college.

The reconstruction of my family history has called for the intellectual discipline of biographical research in order to present family members as they actually lived. In 1952, when I began my concentrated research, my grandparents had been dead for about thirty years, and my own memory of them was the memory of a child of twelve. My most valuable resources in reviving their personalities and traditions were their three surviving daughters: Pauline Fitzgerald Dame, 82; Marie L. Fitzgerald Jeffers, 80; and Sarah Ann Fitzgerald Small, 76. They were all retired teachers, with active memories, a youthful zest for life, and the time and intense interest to give me the benefit of their own recollections. At first, they had some anxieties about the possibility that my disclosures would compromise the memory of their revered parents; soon they warmed to my project and threw themselves so enthusiastically into it that it became a joint family enterprise.

Fortunately, Aunt Pauline and Aunt Sallie lived with me. They were my daily consultants. To respect their sensitivities, and to test the accuracy of my characterizations, I read them portions of the manuscript and we had long discussions (and made some revisions) to "get it just right." Through Aunt Pauline's eyes, especially, I began to feel that I knew people who had died many years before I was born. As the oldest daughter, she had known all the members of my great-grandparents' generation who appear in *Proud Shoes* and who were still alive in the early 1870's. While I wrote, one or another of my aunts would interrupt with a recollection of an almost-forgotten incident or a diagram of a family homeplace no longer standing. My mosaic took shape under their vigilant eyes.

My great regret is that none of my aunts lived to read the published result. At least, in their closing years, they were part of its making. They shared in the findings of my field research and had a sense of significant undertaking which made them feel productive to the end. I know the story has a flavor which comes from the wealth of human detail they gave me; it could have come from nowhere else.

My field research had the thrill of detection when the clues panned out. Rigorous discipline was needed for the drudgery of sifting through masses of documentary material in search of one relevant fact or one confirmation of a family legend. The trail of the Fitzgerald family led me into nearly a dozen localities in several states. It took me into musty basements of old courthouses to pore over dust-silted and sometimes indecipherable handwritten entries in old volumes. I learned about the vast treasure of Americana in local historical societies, state archives, the National Archives in Washington, and school or church records. I found that each locality had its own captivating legends preserved in family papers; its traditions recorded in pamphlets and privately published little books; its stories printed in almanacs, newspapers, business directories. Almost every place had "the oldest living inhabitants" and their recollections. Most important, almost every locality had its own regional-history enthusiasts, who welcomed me into a fellowship of digging into the past. Some of them gave me expert guidance which improved the efficiency of my research and shortened my labors.

As my work progressed I gained a new conception of history. I was amazed to find that apparently anonymous men and women, living in ways that seldom attract public notice, leave behind them a personal record of activities which may illuminate the social history of a nation or an era as much as the activities of the leaders, the movers and shakers. These personal records live hidden away in old documents—deed books, tax declarations, court papers, applications for military pensions, church registers. One of the most poignant reminders of the human condition I found was a routine entry in the daily ledgers of the War Department kept during the Civil War period. It was a footnote to the assassination of Abraham Lincoln: the owner of the house to which the stricken President was taken after the fatal shooting had put in a claim for $5.00, the cost of replacing the sheets used during Lincoln's dying moments. (A later entry showed that payment of the claim was authorized.)

The conviction grew in me that one of the best ways to incorporate social and political history into one's own experience is to embark on a search into one's family history. In the process of trying to locate the names of members of my family, I amassed significant related knowledge about the communities, institutions, politics, and personalities which touched their lives.

My full understanding of the Civil War, for example—the war which I had known from textbooks—did not come until I spotted the names of my great-grandfather Fitzgerald and his sons in the successive payroll lists of the Quartermaster's Corps. Through these lists I was able to follow their movements; and by reading the detailed annual reports of the Quartermaster's Department, U.S.A., I gained insight into the hardships endured by the "ordinary" men upon whom the Union Army depended for food and supplies. Each document that I unearthed—my grandfather's military forms, filled out in his own handwriting; the regimental papers confirming the entry in his diary about his service as Company Clerk; the logs of the naval vessels to which he was assigned, that tracked his naval career—bound me more securely to my nation's history. It reassured me that the lowly as well as the great were an integral part of the record.

This merging of my personal past with the larger history was a natural outcome of my searches in public archives, which housed, in close proximity, the records of obscure citizens and of the country's leaders. Under the leveling influence of time, these ancient documents spoke to me of a common humanity and narrowed the distances between races, classes, and political positions. When I was going through records at the federal courthouse in Wilmington, Delaware, I accidentally saw the original copies of pardons signed by Abraham Lincoln. A century fell away: the man was more real than the colossus enshrined in the Lincoln Memorial. And when I found the decision, in carefully written long-hand, of Chief Justice Roger B. Taney of the United States Supreme Court holding abolitionist Thomas Garrett liable for penalties under the Fugitive Slave Law, the man whom I had met previously only in the printed accounts of his opinion in the *Dred Scott* case emerged as a living force.

In my journey back in time, I supplemented documentary research with real contacts. During the spring of 1954, I retraced the life of the Fitzgerald family in Delaware and particularly in Chester County, Pennsylvania, where they settled near Lincoln University from 1855 to 1869. This area was close to the borders of two slave states and rich in the traditions of the struggle between abolition and slavery.

Fortunately, I met two local residents—Dr. Horace Mann Bond, then president of Lincoln University, and Mr. L. C. Ficcio, a genealogist in Oxford—who shared an enthusiasm for the history of free Negro families who had settled in the county before the Civil War. They had already dug up considerable information on the Fitzgeralds and their neighbors before my arrival and were overjoyed to find a living descendant of one of those families whose history meshed with the beginnings of the University. We spent many hours exchanging data and unearthing new facts which made mid-nineteenth century Chester County come alive.

With the help of deed descriptions and an old map of the county that listed my great-grandfather's name beside a dot representing his farm, we were able to find the exact site of the Fitzgerald homeplace a short distance from the entrance to Lincoln University. We followed the legendary routes of the Underground Railroad to the houses still standing which had served as stations for runaway slaves. We tramped through the woods, retracing the movements of slave-catchers and kidnappers, and I was able to relive the notorious Parker kidnapping of 1851, through yellowed newspaper clippings which Mr. Ficcio gave me. I became so immersed in the past that for months after my visit I found myself dating correspondence 1854 instead of 1954.

Following this joyous romp through the early history of the Fitzgeralds, I had to face the difficult and painful decision of including my grandmother's "Smith side" of the family story—a decision with which I had been wrestling during the months of my research. The Smith story awakened long-dormant, unresolved questions of identity and intensely conflicting emotions. It also resurrected the ominous shadow of slavery which still hung over the South of my childhood.

So far as I knew, the Smiths had left behind no descendants except those of my grandmother and her three half-sisters. Thus I was in the position of having to acknowledge publicly a kinship which had not been recognized and which was laden with feelings of shame. It was not so much the fact of mixed ancestry which troubled me, since this was true of both sides of my maternal lineage. I could accept my grandfather's background because he was a product of voluntary intermarriage, his slave origins were more remote, and his family had experienced two generations of freedom before the Civil War. In my grandmother's story, I had to come to terms with a racially mixed ancestry linked with an immediate slave heritage which bore the dual stigma of inferior and illegitimate status.

It was one thing to recall my grandmother's view of herself: her insistence that she was free; her dismissal of slavery as a mere technicality in her case; her pride in her ancestry and in Mary Ruffin Smith's recognition of their kinship throughout her life as well as in her last will and testament. It was quite another thing to look at the full implications of that relationship in the cold light of the record a century later; to identify my grandmother by age and sex, listed anonymously as a "Mulatto" in the 1860 Census of the Slave Population. There could be no doubt about the place assigned to her in history. One had only to consult the Record of Baptisms in the Chapel of the Cross in Chapel Hill to find my grandmother, her half-brother, and three half-sisters listed by name and age on the register dated December 20, 1854, under the heading "Five Servant Children Belonging to Miss Mary Ruffin Smith."

My grandmother's father, Mary Ruffin Smith's brother, Sidney, was a lawyer, and Grandmother had absorbed a strong sense of the law from him. Yet she had been able somehow to transcend a degraded legal status, and to concentrate on the extra-legal reality of human relationships. I had loved my grandmother when she was alive, and in justice to her memory I had to try to see the people she loved through her eyes, if that were possible. I had to realize that in essence her story was a human story as old as the Biblical narrative of Abraham, his bondswoman Hagar, and their son, Ishmael; and that it pointed up the complex interrelationships within slavery that defied monolithic classification. In the telling of my grandmother's story I had to embrace *all* the tangled roots from which I had sprung, and to accept without evasion my own slave heritage, with all its ambivalencies and paradoxes.

Thus the writing of *Proud Shoes* became for me the resolution of a search for identity and the exorcism of ghosts of the past. No longer constrained by suppressed memories, I began to see myself in a new light—the product of a slowly evolving process of biological and cultural integration, a process containing the character of many cultures and many peoples, a New World experiment, fragile yet tenacious, a possible hint of a stronger and freer America of the future, no longer stunted in its growth by an insidious ethnocentrism.

This view was not altered by my later exploration of my African cultural roots during an eighteen-month sojourn in Ghana in 1960 and 1961. My experience in Ghana cleared my vision of whatever negative stereotypes had blurred my understanding of the African background; but it also strengthened my conviction that I was of the New World, irrevocably bound to the destiny of my native America.

The self-image which emerged from my exploration of my roots did not anticipate the intense Black Consciousness which developed in the decade after the publication of *Proud Shoes*, with its accompanying polarization of the races. It may be that I telescoped history, projecting my vision into the future, leaping over the intervening stages of pluralism and ethnic consciousness.

Yet *Proud Shoes* and its portrayal of the entanglement of the races is not a unique story. Over more than two centuries, enough criss-crossing of racial lines and recirculation of genes within designated races has occurred to make the notion of racial purity a highly questionable biological concept for many future Americans. Multi-racial origins of both blacks and whites are realities; they may be ignored but not wholly discounted. The acceptance of the possibility of relatedness would do much to defuse the highly charged discussions on race. Ultimately, it might help to ease the transition to a more humane society.

Proud Shoes does not explicitly state this conclusion. It ends on a note of rebellion and defiance which marked my early youth and made me cling to my grandfather's memory as a symbol of active struggle for liberation. Throughout those early struggles, however, my grandmother's tradition was always in the background: her acceptance of her relatedness to the dominant class and race; her view of her own life as a symbol of the possibility of reconciliation between races and classes, however fragmentary the symbol may have seemed.

In later years, it has occurred to me that my grandfather's impact on my life may have been responsible for my decision to become a civil rights lawyer, while my grandmother's influence may have led me finally into the ordained ministry. Certainly, it would be fair to say that these two traditions—each making its own strong claims—have been major determinants in my own development. And while sometimes the one and sometimes the other has been in the forefront of my consciousness, neither has yielded the field, and both must be the ultimate measure of my own existence.

PAULI MURRAY

Alexandria, Virginia
March, 1978

1

GRANDFATHER FITZGERALD marched slowly down the narrow stairs, one hand grasping the banister and the other whacking each step with his gold-knobbed cane. He wore his dark salt-and-pepper broadcloth suit, a white shirt and a loosely knotted black tie around his high stiff collar. Grandfather dressed up as if he were going to town, even when he was only going to sit on the front porch. From his height on the upper landing he looked very tall and invincible to me, although he was really a slender frail man and couldn't have been more than five and a half feet. He always stood erect, head up and chin thrust out from his scraggy throat, as if at attention. Grandfather had marched off to war when he was twenty-three and though he was now seventy-five he had never stopped being a soldier.

Down he came, the worn boards creaking under him, the crack in the plaster of the stairwell quivering like a torn scar. The twelve o'clock factory whistle had just sounded a long blast across the hills and Grandfather was late for our morning session on the porch. He never liked to be late for anything. In most things he was ahead of time.

The sun poured through the open doorway and motes of dust shimmered and danced along a golden shaft from the upper hall window. As I waited for Grandfather near the bottom landing, a cracked slate and the newspaper under my arm, a beam of sunlight fell on his furrowed dull-ivory-colored face. At that moment he looked like one of the stone figures in the cemetery behind our house. His high forehead, his thin nose that turned up slightly, his gaunt sensitive face, strong jaw and jutting chin were like tinted marble. But for the crisp black hair that sparkled with a few white strands, the bushy dark brows overhanging his deep-set eyes and the heavy black mustache flowing downward from his upper lip, he might have been a carved stone image. Even his eyes had the fixed and faraway look of a statue. They seldom looked directly at me but over my head into space.

He stopped on the bottom landing to sniff the air, then pushed open the screen door with the tip of his cane and went onto the porch. I followed him silently. It was late spring. The sky was deep blue and a breeze was stirring. Blue jays fought among the limbs of the tall elms in our front yard and an occasional feather floated to the ground. Down an embankment beyond the hedge, the blossoming pear trees in the field swayed slightly and white petals drifted through the air. The morning air was warm and laden with smells, heavy fragrance of wistaria vines which covered half of our front porch and climbed over the roof, whiffs of fresh manure, newly plowed earth and the odor of rotted weeds, stagnant water and pigpens which hung over the Bottoms.

Grandfather paused at his big green rocker, decided against rocking and moved stiffly to a sawed-off armchair without legs which hung on heavy chains from the porch ceiling. He often preferred the armchair swing to the rocker because it was behind the wistaria vines and almost completely hidden from the field and road in front of our house. I had lived at Grandfather's ever since Aunt Pauline had brought me to North Carolina three years earlier, right after my mother's death. I was now almost six. Whenever I heard the rusty chains complaining or the rocker thumping on the porch in the mornings, I knew Grandfather was ready for me to recite my lessons. I'd hear him banging his cane against the side of the house impatiently, a signal for me to come running with my slate and the morning newspaper. Grandfather had taught school in his youth and thought there was nothing like getting an early start on a good education. His first pupils had learned to read from newspapers, almanacs and pages from the

Bible and he was teaching me by the same method. He called it killing two birds with one stone.

"Are you ready to recite?" he asked.

"Just about," I said doubtfully, looking at my empty slate.

"*By an' by, when the morn-in' comes,*" came Grandmother Fitzgerald's voice from around the house. Grandfather stiffened and sat up suddenly. It was a bad sign when Grandmother began to sing that song. She was on the warpath again and the slightest thing would set her to puffing up like a wet hen. When Grandmother got mad she boiled over with a scalding tongue and Grandfather could stand almost anything except Grandmother's tongue when she got to fussing.

Earlier that morning she had gone outdoors and come tearing back into the house, banging the doors and slamming pots and kettles around in the kitchen so hard that the walls shook. She was now up in the stable loft singing at the top of her lungs. The old stable was almost falling apart from age and disuse, for our horse had been sold long ago and the cow had died, but Grandmother used the loft to store broken furniture, chipped dishes, rusted pots, baskets of rags and old clothes, bundles of newspapers and other castoff stuff. She saved it for a rainy day, she said. She never believed in throwing anything away, not even a piece of string. It might come in handy. Whenever she was upset about something she would climb the rickety ladder to a loft made of loose boards laid across the rafters and rummage around among the piles of junk she had put there.

Grandfather waved his cane toward me.

"Where's your grandmother, child?"

"Up in the stable loft, Granpa."

"I knew it! I knew it!" he stormed. "I've told Cornelia to stay out of that loft. That woman will break her neck on that old ladder one of these days. You go tell her I said to come down out of there."

I went and came back. "She says she'll come down when she good and gets ready to. And Granpa, she's piping hot about something."

Grandfather grunted. "That woman's mad about something

most of the time." He sighed. "No peace for the weary. Did the mailman come yet?"

"He passed long time ago, but he didn't come up here."

"Well, that's that. Let's get on with our lesson."

"*All the saints are gath-ered com-ing home,*" Grandmother's song floated down to us from the loft. Grandfather's long bony fingers gripped the chains, his mustache wiggled furiously, his throat jerked up and down as if he wanted to say something and was swallowing hard to keep it back. He sat tense with listening, his cane clutched between his knees, his colorless eyes flickering, his head tilted to one side.

"You see anybody on the road?"

I glanced hastily up and down Cameron Street, the yellow dirt road which ran down a short steep hill, over a wooden bridge, past our house and into Morehead Avenue and which separated us from the Bottoms on the other side. The road was empty.

"Nobody yet."

"So far, so good. You keep on the lookout and let me know if you see any goings on."

Grandfather relaxed in the swing and laid his cane across his knees. He took a square of Red Mule tobacco from his pocket and cut himself a plug with his pocketknife. One had to be around Grandfather a little while to discover he was blind. His hearing was so acute he seemed aware of my every movement and of everything else that went on about him. He sensed without seeing much that I missed with my two good eyes, but since the dirt road was beyond our wide front field and he could not hear that far away, I had to be eyes for him.

"Are you ready to read that list of words I taught you yester-day?"

My heart knocked as hard as if Grandfather could see the empty slate.

"I don't have them written down, Granpa. I rubbed off the slate to do the sums you gave me."

"All right. Say them from memory."

"I—I—"

"Well, do you know them or don't you?"

"Ye-s, Granpa, I know a few."

"How many times have I told you not to say 'yes' when speaking to an older person? Say 'yes sir' or 'yes ma'am.' It's more polite. And don't let me ever hear you saying 'yessuh' and 'nosuh' to anybody."

"But Granma says 'yes' to everybody."

"You're not Grandma. You'll start to school next year and I want you to have good manners and speak well. I don't want anyone to say a Fitzgerald is dragged up. Now, let me hear you pronounce those words."

I struggled with memory. Slowly I could see the words appearing on the blank slate.

"Am-m-mu-nit—nishun, pre-par-ed-ness, Al-Al-lies, sub-b-marine, con-con-scrip-p-shun—"

"That will do. That's pretty good for a little girl. You may make a fine scholar some day if you keep at it." When Grandfather said something was "pretty good" he meant it was almost perfect. He was very sparing with his compliments. He said he never wanted me to have a swelled head.

"We will tell-l-l the stor-ree-ee-ee how we over-come-m-m-me," Grandmother wailed. Her voice was louder. She must be coming down the ladder. Grandfather shrank deeper into the swing and huddled there.

"Anybody on the road yet?"

"A horse and wagon coming down Cameron Street hill." The wagon team rumbled across the narrow wooden bridge over the branch at the bottom of the hill and jogged along the road past our house. When the team had gone Grandfather sat up again.

"Did you get the *Morning Herald?*"

"I got it right here on the floor."

"Oh, such English. I *have* it right here," Grandfather corrected. "Start with the headlines on the front page as usual. Pronounce each word clearly and distinctly. If you don't know the word, don't mispronounce it. Spell it and I will pronounce it for you."

"Can I read the funnies when I get through the news?"

"You're getting so you speak just like that ignorant riffraff in the Bottoms. Pay attention carefully. When you ask permission to do something, you say 'May I,' and when you ask whether it is possible for you to do it, you say 'Can I.' You just asked permission to

read the funnies, so you should have said 'May I.' Do you understand the difference?"

"I guess so—but I hear Granma saying—"

"I've told you before, Grandma is old enough to speak as she
pleases. You're still a child and you have to make your way in life.
Nothing shows up *who* or *what* a person is as much as the way he
speaks. I won't have any grandchild of mine sounding as if he is
a nobody and came from nothing."

"Well, may I, Granpa?"

"No you *may* not read such foolishness. There's plenty to read
that's uplifting. Now stop fooling and proceed."

I unfolded the newspaper from the small square package the
newsboy had made of it to toss it over the hedge into our yard
without having to climb the brick steps in the embankment. I
spread it on the floor and lay flat on my stomach. Keeping one
finger on the comic page so I could snatch a quick look if Grandfather happened to nod, I began laboriously to read the headlines,
then columns of war news, spelling out the difficult French names
as I went along. It was tedious work, but Grandfather always
wanted to know every military detail of the world war in France
and I dared not skip over anything. In my anxiety, at times I got
the words so mixed up he would look puzzled, shove his hand
behind his ear, lean forward and command me to read that part
over again.

"*An' we'll understand-d-d it bet-ter-r-r by an' by,*" Grandmother
moaned. Her voice was so close now I had to shout almost so that
Grandfather could hear me above the high shrill notes that
wavered across the Bottoms to the opposite hill and back again. I
stumbled along but Grandfather was only half listening. He was
trying to tell what Grandmother was doing in the yard at the side
of the house. He soon wearied of my faltering over unfamiliar
phrases and waved his cane.

"At ease. Go ask your grandmother if she's almost through out
there. It's time to eat."

I went around the house. Grandmother was squatting on the
grass between the kitchen window and the wellshed, sorting old
scraps of cloth from a basket and spreading them about to sun.
How she had managed to get the basket down the ladder was more

than I could tell. From the cemetery fence to the front yard the lawn was strewn with strips of red flannel, blue serge, colored ginghams, ragged shirts, faded petticoats and brown stocking tops. Grandfather would have said the place looked like a buzzard's roost.

Like Grandfather, Grandmother too looked as if she had walked right off one of the cemetery monuments. She had the same sharp features, long sensitive nose, thin lips, prominent cheekbones, strong chin and pink-and-gray hue as the marble angels when sunset fell on them. But unlike the graveyard angels, she had fire in her dark eyes and a restless energy in her weatherbeaten hands. She was a plump little woman in her seventies, with a strong mobile face and soft white hair that blew about her head. She was almost never still and moved about with nervous quick gestures as if she were continually shaking off a restraining hand to get on with what she was doing.

"Granma, Granpa wants to know when you'll be through. He's getting mighty hungry."

"He'll just have to wait till I'm done here. Rome wasn't built in a day. I'll fix his victuals directly. It's always something to aggravate you."

"You mad about something, Granma?"

"I'm a short horse easily curried today, Baby. Anybody fools with me this morning, I'll be on 'em like a duck on a June bug."

"What's the matter? You don't feel good?"

"I'd feel better if I knew who turned loose that Bergins horse again last night. He got up there in my field and ate the tops off my young corn. I just wish I could have caught 'im. There'd be a dead critter in that alley sure as I got breath in my body."

"Oh, Granma!"

"I mean it! The devil's been busy bright and early trying to make me lose my religion. But don't you mind, child. Whatever goes over the devil's back sure got to come under his belly."

I looked toward the cornfield that lay between our alleyway to Morehead Avenue and the cemetery fence. The field stretched from our stable to the Bergins' high back fence and was Grandmother's favorite planting ground. I could see where the horse had trampled down some of the corn shoots. The Bergins family were our nearest neighbors and we got along pretty well with them except for two things. Their cottage was built on a slanted line and sat a few inches over on our alleyway. Grandmother was very particular about metes and bounds and was always complaining about the Bergins' house sitting over the line. She said it was trespassing and we ought to make them move it. The other bone of contention was the Bergins horse. Mr. and Mrs. Bergins worked in the factory all day and their fourteen-year-old daughter, Lucy, had charge of grazing the horse after school. Lucy was careless about tying the horse and sometimes he worked loose from his halter and got into our cornfield.

Grandmother's special fighting piece was trespassing. Otherwise she was a good Samaritan and regularly went about the neighborhood on her errands of mercy carrying food and little jars of liniment or salve to sick folks. She was so generous that my aunts would protest.

"We lug the food in and you lug it right out again," they'd say.

But let one of the neighbors or their cattle stray onto our property by an inch when they weren't coming to see us, and Grandmother was ready to preach a sermon. You could tell when somebody had provoked her and one of her preaching spells was coming on. She'd always start singing "By and By."

Grandmother had to have lots of space. She couldn't bear to be closed in. Our house sat far back from the road behind a hedge in a grove of elms and fruit trees. There had been no neighbors to plague Grandmother when Grandfather had the house built back in the 1890's. A wheat field used to grow on the steep hill behind it and a wide meadow in front of it rolled downward to a brook. On the other side of the brook, pine and cedar forests used to rise on the eastern hills as far as she could see. Now the town had moved in upon us. The forests were gone and all that was left was a clump of pines. Back porches faced us on two sides. Our house crouched on a narrow shelf of land between the cemetery, which had swallowed the wheat field, and the washed-out gullies of the opposite hillside. North of it two streams formed a branch that ran along the dirt road through a wilderness of tall weeds and weeping willows. We called this marshy low ground the Bottoms.

Grandfather had lost most of his land but had managed to hang on to the fields nearest the house. He no longer farmed them or made bricks from the clay in them. We were able to avoid very close neighbors but not even the fields between us and them could prevent ructions. Our yard was plainly visible from the back porches along Morehead Avenue and the neighbors on that side of the Bottoms kept up with everything Grandmother was doing in our yard. They'd shout across the lowland to the neighbors on Cameron Street hill and although they didn't mention her by name, Grandmother said they were "signifying" about her. They seemed to know just when she was ripe for a preaching and took delight in setting her off.

If the neighbors had seen Grandmother this morning they gave no sign. The back porches were quiet and the road empty except for an occasional wagon team and two or three small children who raced down Cameron Street hill rolling hoops and screeching with joy, their bare feet and the steel rims kicking up little squalls of dust as they sped by.

"Want me to help you finish up, Granma?" I asked, anxious to get her inside.

"No Baby, you go back and keep your Granpa company."

I went back to the porch.

"Granma's busy sunning rags. She won't be in for a while yet. That Bergins horse got into her corn again and she's a short horse easily curried, she says."

Grandfather chuckled. I knew I had tickled him but his face got solemn again before I could ask him to tell me a story. He sat staring into nowhere, brooding over his cane, his eyes filled with strange shadows. I always looked forward to Grandfather's story-telling when I finished my lessons if he was pleased. I never tired of Reynard the Fox, the industrious Little Red Hen and the wise animals of *Aesop's Fables*. I would follow intently, correcting Grandfather if he varied the tale by a word or a tone of voice.

When he was in an especially good mood he would tell me true stories of himself and his boyhood in Delaware and Pennsylvania, of the times before he went blind when he fought as a Yankee sailor and soldier in the Civil War and when he first came to North Carolina to set up schools for the Negro children. He would tell how the Ku-Klux Klan dressed up in bed sheets like ghosts and

rode around his little schoolhouse trying to scare him away and
how he always kept his musket loaded and ready to shoot. My eyes
bulged and my spine tingled. I loved these stories best of all. It
made me feel very proud to know how brave Grandfather was and
how he had fought for freedom, although I did not understand
then what freedom really was.

Today Grandfather looked so stony I dared not ask him for
stories. Nor could I risk going beyond speaking distance. He
brought up his own children on the rule, "Answer whether you
hear or not," and he had not changed. He had a reputation for
whaling the daylights out of grandchildren who did not move fast
enough when he called; he'd lash out at them with whatever he
happened to be holding at the time—his saber, a saw, a broom
handle or his cane. He had not struck me with the cane but I was
never sure when my turn might come. I sat squirming on the top
step, itching to run across the field and make friends with the
children rolling hoops. I knew that if I started off the step, he'd
sing out to know where I was going. I longed to call or wave to
them but they might wave back or venture toward our yard. That
would never do. Grandfather had given me strict orders about
playing.

"I don't want you bringing stray young'uns up here," he told
me. "I won't have every rag, tag and bobtail in the Bottoms clutter-
ing up my yard." I knew he would enforce his command with the
ever-present cane. So I sat hugging my knees and pretending not to
see the children and wondering how long it would be before Aunt
Pauline and Aunt Sallie came home from school.

As I look back on it now, I did not fully realize then what blindness meant to Grandfather. We accepted it so completely at home
that I found it no more strange than my being left-handed, a dis-
advantage one was expected to overcome like any other hardship.
We never spoke of it. It was a point of honor with Grandfather
never to ask someone else to do for him what he could do for himself. His blindness didn't seem to matter much anyway because he
could do almost anything. He was seldom idle. The house was full
of rag rugs he had plaited from the stocking tops and old scraps
Grandmother saved. On its rack in the center of the parlor
mantelpiece stood the three-masted model schooner which he had

made on one of his many visits to the National Soldiers' Home at Old Point Comfort, Virginia, complete with tiny intricate wire riggings and miniature white canvas sails. It rivaled in importance the gilt-framed painting by Miss Mary Ruffin Smith called "The Silver Fountain" which hung just above it over the mantelpiece and which Grandmother counted among her most treasured heirlooms. Each year Grandfather pruned the grapevines and trained them along the arbor which arched over the garden walk from our back door along the cemetery fence to the red-brick outhouse. He would cut the vines carefully with his pocketknife and tie up the stragglers with pieces of cloth. He often went by himself on trips to town a mile away, a solitary erect figure tapping an arc with his cane.

Grandfather was the family encyclopedia. He knew everything there was to know, I thought. Neighbors often came to him for advice and everyone who stopped at our house liked to linger and pass the time of day with him. He held a lone fortress of respect in a jungle of human relationships.

Perhaps the one thing he never mastered was how to handle Grandmother. The two of them were as different as chalk from cheese and it was pull-Dick-pull-Devil with them most of the time. If Grandfather said "gee," Grandmother would say "haw," and if she was on a rampage with the neighbors, he might as well try to stifle a volcano. Yet he was sitting there now in the swing listening with every nerve, as if by just sitting on the porch and keeping himself informed he could prevent what he knew was bound to happen.

As I sat there hoping my aunts would come soon, I noticed the children had suddenly disappeared. Down Cameron Street hill ambled Crazy Charlie, barefoot and bareheaded as usual, his ragged pants rolled halfway up his scaly brown legs. Every few steps he would shriek wildly, jump high in the air, land on his haunches, beat his breast and wave his clenched fists. Nobody seemed to know how old Charlie was or where he lived, but he had roamed the Bottoms ever since I could remember. The children fled when he came along, hid behind their houses and peeped at him. The grown folks laughed at his antics and he would go from house to house where the people would feed him and give him old clothes. Some folks called him crazy but Grandmother said Charlie had plenty of sense. He knew how to live without working. He wandered about singing a senseless little tune, terrifying the children with his shrieks but giggling with glee when he made the older folks laugh.

"Who's that coming?" Grandfather wanted to know.

"It's Crazy Charlie."

"Oh goodness! Where's he now?"

"He's crossing the bridge."

"Is he looking this way?"

"No sir, and he's in the middle of the road."

"Let's hope he stays there."

The back porches on Morehead Avenue stirred suddenly as if moved by a common electric current. People hung over the railings and began shouting at Charlie and at each other from porch to porch. Charlie danced about in the road singing his crazy off-key tune:

> Hoppergrass settin' on a sweet-pertater vine,
> Sweet-pertater vine, sweet-pertater vine,
> Hoppergrass settin' on a sweet-pertater vine
> A suckin' up dat juice.
>
> 'Long come a turkey gobbler sneakin' up behin',
> Sneakin' up behin', sneakin' up behin',
> 'Long come a turkey gobbler sneakin' up behin',
> An' knocked him off dat sweet-pertater vine.

As Charlie capered about in the road, a thin, youngish, brown-skinned woman named Bessie came out of the corner house near Morehead and started walking swiftly toward him. Grandmother said she was "one of those bad women of the Bottoms." A man's battered hat sat on the back of her head, her petticoat hung below her frowzy skirt and she hobbled along on high heels with her hands gripping the small of her back, her elbows behind her and her hips swaying from side to side. She whistled loudly and kept glancing toward our house. She needn't have taken such pains to attract Grandmother's attention for Grandmother could see everything that went on in the road. Bessie slowed down when she passed Charlie. She came back to him, said something and pointed our way. Charlie nodded, leaped in the air again two or three times and the last time landed on the edge of our front field.

"Hoppergrass settin' on a sweet-pertater vine," he began.

At the same moment Grandmother streaked across the yard to the hedge as if she had been shot out of a cannon. Her wispy white hair swirled about her head; her dark eyes flashed fire and brimstone; her whole body bristled and mobilized for an attack. She had a mattock in her hand.

"You get right off my property, you good-for-nothing tramp! You know better than that. Don't you let that swish-tail hussy get you into trouble!" she bellowed.

This was the moment Grandfather and the neighbors had been waiting for. It always started with somebody walking on our land. He got up and shouted through the wistaria vines at Grandmother.

"Cornelia, you come into the house. Don't go down there making a spectacle of yourself!"

"You mind your business, Robert Fitzgerald," Grandmother snorted over her shoulder. "You take care of your end and I'll take care of mine. The Lord gave me a mouth and I aim to use it whenever and wherever I've a mind to. I ain't going to let these dirty niggers walk all over me."

Grandfather was finished. He had done what he could. He couldn't stop her but at least the neighbors would see he had no part in it, so he stumped his way into the house slamming the screen and the door behind him. I could hear him climbing the stairs to his room and pretty soon the upstairs window banged shut. I knew he would not come out again as long as Grandmother was in the front yard.

"I told you to get off my land," she yelled again.

Charlie jumped up and down on the ledge, cut a buck and wing and giggled. He looked across the Bottoms to see if the neighbors were watching. Bessie told him something else and he yelled across the field.

"If you don't want your precious land walked over, why you don't put no fence round it?"

"I don't need no fence. Trespassing is trespassing. You got good sense. You better start using it. You ain't satisfied with the sixteen foot of land my husband give the city so's you could have a road 'stead of a cowpath to walk on. You got to come up on my property. I'll put the law on you if you don't get down from there right away."

"Ki-yah! Ki-yah! Ki-yah! Do your stuff, Charlie! Aw preach it, Miz Fitzge'l!" roared the neighbors from their back porches.

Charlie, taking the cue, began to shimmy along the ledge, but when Grandmother started down the embankment brandishing her mattock he hopped back onto the road and skedaddled toward Morehead Avenue. But he had lighted the fuse and Grandmother detonated against Bessie, who stood in the road where Charlie left her, bending over with laughter.

"You no-mannered slut! You spraddle-legged whore!" Grandmother bawled. "You put him up to it. I never had no trouble out of Charlie till you moved down there in the Bottoms. I don't bother him and he don't bother me, but you nasty, stinking wench, you don't like peace. You're a strumpet, that's what you are, a yaller-bellied, white-livered strumpet! A whistling woman and a crowing hen ain't never coming to no good end, you mark my words."

"Yuh maw!" Bessie bleated. Folks called that "slipping you in the dozens." They were fighting words.

"Don't you sass me, you little harlot. I'm old enough to be your grandmother. The Bible tells you those that don't honor gray hairs will be cut off and cast into hell's fire."

"Lissen to the Word! Glor-ee Hallelujah!" chorused the back porches.

"Hey Bessie, you better get ready 'cause your time ain't long."

"Watch out. She'll put a curse on you!"

The show was warming up. The neighbors were feeding the flames. It had happened many times before and the hullabaloo which followed seemed according to script. Grandmother planted herself midway across the field, close enough to the house to make a retreat in case Bessie rushed her, but in the open where she could see all the mischief-making neighbors roosting on their back porches. She took her text: "Right is right and right don't wrong nobody," and began her sermon. She blasted away, now at Bessie, now at the neighbors, her voice ringing to the hilltop, bouncing

back across the Bottoms to the tombstones behind our house and
sailing back to the hillside again in many voices. She stamped her
feet, shook her head, waved the mattock in the air and brought it
down to earth again with loud "Hanhghs" to emphasize her points.
She spat in Bessie's direction and Bessie turned her back and
flounced her rear at Grandmother.

"Shake your butt at me, you filthy prostitute. A cow's gonna
need a tail in fly time and yours is near 'bout rotten with the bad
disease."

"Let your jelly roll, Bessie. You won't have it long!" from the
back porches.

Grandmother waved her mattock toward the porches.

"I'm onto you wenches up there on the hill, sitting 'round all
day on your asses not doing a lick of honest work and meddling
with decent people's business. You're nothing but a bunch of
houts and your menfolks a passel of gamblers and bootleggers.
You're so mired in the devil's work you're on your way to hell and
torment just as fast as you can go. You ain't worth the dirt under
my feet. If a single solitary one of you hussies was worth your salt
you'd be out somewhere earning your daily bread. No, you're too
busy 'tending to what I'm doing. Don't think you can pull any
wool over my eyes. I see almost every move you make. I got eyes
in the back of my head. What's more you don't own a button, you
haven't got a pot nor a window, you got nothing now, you never
had nothing and you never will have nothing as long as you live."

The neighbors howled and guffawed and threw their aprons over
their heads. Bessie cavorted in the road, conscious of her audience
but being careful not to come up on the ledge. Grandmother
ranted up and down the field, keeping a strip of land between
herself and Bessie.

"You blaspheming South Car'lina darky, I know your kind. You
all come pushing in here lately, crowding out respectable folks
with nothing but a shoebox and the rags on your backs. You ain't
fitten to be among decent people. They've had you in slavery so
long you don't know how to act. You so ig'rant you can't tell piss
from vinegar and you don't wanta learn. You're so pore you live
piled up in rented shacks on top of one another like hogs in a
wallow. They'd have to put a saucer on your corpse to get the

money to bury you. Just keep on running your whorehouses and bootleg joints and you'll end up on the roads with a ball and chain around your ankle. You're lice, that's what you are. I got as much time for nasty, dirty, stinking, low-down, onery, mean, trifling, trashy, no-count niggers who ain't worth shittanmolasses as I got for an egg-suckin' dog or a rattlesnake. In fact, I got more time for a rattlesnake. It's more respectable."

Now Grandmother had drawn blood.

"Who do you think you are, you half-white bastard!" Bessie snarled.

"Humph! You think I'm insulted?" Grandmother retorted. "I'll tell anybody I'm a white man's child. A fine white man at that. A southern aristocrat. If you want to know what I am, I'm an octoroon. I don't have to mix in with good-for-nothing niggers if I don't want to. I don't like trashy folks whether they're black, white, blue or yaller. If you mix with the dogs you'll be bitten by the fleas."

"Whyn't you move if we ain't good enough for you?"

"I don't have to move. We own our property. We're not here today and gone tomorrow. I don't have no renting agent standing at my door every Saturday ready to set me in the street if I don't have my rent money. Possession is nine points of law, and I can have the law on anybody that puts one foot on my land without my permission. And I'll tell you another thing. My father was one of the best criminal lawyers in the South. He was in the North Carolina legislature. Before the Civil War he saved fourteen poor Negroes from the gallows free of charge. He got many colored folks out of trouble and kept 'em from rotting in jail, but a jailhouse is too good for trollops like you. You oughta be down under the jail."

People collected in groups along the road and on the hillside to listen to the harangue. The more scathing Grandmother's tongue the more the neighbors seemed to enjoy it. She raged back and forth in the field, knee-deep in briars and cockleburs which caught her skirt and hiked it over her bright red flannel petticoat. Her white hair blew about her face like dandelion thistles in the wind. The Bottoms rang with "Amens," catcalls and loud handclaps.

When Grandmother ran out of words and stopped to catch her breath, somebody hurled a tantalizing remark and the ruckus began afresh. She took a new text, quoted from the Bible and prophesied the doom of all the offending neighbors and their progeny.

When a stream of school children began to trickle down Cameron Street hill, I knew school was out and Aunt Pauline and Aunt Sallie were not far behind them. Bessie and the neighbors knew it too and Bessie sidled along the road and up the hill. The neighbors quieted down. They never liked to have my aunts catch them openly heckling Grandmother, but they liked nothing better than to see those two dignified schoolteachers walking down the road when Grandmother was in the middle of a fracas.

The school children began a singsong, the little ones repeating the big ones, "Hi-do, Mis' Dame—Mis' Dame—Mis' Dame! Hi-do, Mis' Sallie—Mis' Sallie—Mis' Sallie," and my aunts hove into sight marching together in rhythm and saying their howdies from side to side without bending their heads. They already knew what awaited them. Aunt Pauline, the taller and stouter of the two, moved heavily. She was a large stern red-faced woman in her middle forties who wore gold-rimmed glasses and drab subdued clothes. Aunt Sallie, several years younger and still unmarried, was stylish, peach colored, sprightly and full of bounce. She had a merry laugh that started in high key and ran the scale downward.

My aunts carried themselves with an uprightness befitting their high station as examples to the community. They had been teaching for many years as Grandfather had done before them and all the grown folks regarded them with deep respect. The children looked upon them with a mixture of fear and awe not unlike that accorded to a policeman. They told me once that when they were young girls, everybody could tell when Robert Fitzgerald and his daughters were coming along even when they were far away. They all walked like soldiers. Grandfather would stop suddenly, pluck at the sleeve of the daughter nearest to him and say, "Wait a minute, children. We're out of step. Now, *left*, right, *left*, right," and from two to five daughters would swing forward with him in military stride, flanking him on each side and stepping high, long voluminous skirts swirling about their ankles, shoulders back and heads up in the air.

They strode the same way now, while the children scampered from the middle of the road to let them pass and flowed around them again. Grandmother was still yelling to the hilltop and a few neighbors were cackling at her, but my aunts took no notice of it. They crossed the bridge, waved good-by to the school children and swung along the path through the field toward the house, walking archly through the hubbub as if they did not see or hear a thing out of the ordinary. They bent their heads slightly at Grandmother but the neighbors knew that not one of our family would interfere with her sermon. That would be swapping the witch for the devil. My aunts would scurry into the house, draw all the shades and stay hidden until she was so hoarse she was down to a whisper or got tired and came inside of her own accord.

Aunt Pauline spied me on the top step.

"What're you doing out here?" she scolded. "Didn't I tell you never to stay outside when your grandmother is preaching? You go right upstairs to my room, look on the bureau and bring me that little bottle of spirits of ammonia."

Aunt Pauline's usually strawberry-pink face was pasty white like the times when she had weak spells during thunderstorms. As I hurried upstairs I could hear the shades coming down. Aunt Sallie went into the parlor without even taking off her hat and began to play hymns on Grandfather's wheezy organ.

"Rock of Ages, cleft for me," she sang gustily, trilling the notes the way she did on Sundays in the St. Titus mission choir. Aunt Sallie had a strong beautiful voice and at times like this she pulled all the stops out and let it fill the house. I carried the bottle of ammonia to Aunt Pauline, who had gone to the kitchen and turned on the water faucet full tilt. As careful as she was about using water and running up the water bill most times, she did not care how hard it ran when Grandmother was yelling out front so long as it drowned out her voice. She took the bottle from me, poured a few drops into a glass, swished it under the faucet and drank it. Then she dropped into a chair and started fanning herself.

"Run outdoors and get me some kindling to start the fire. Have you had anything to eat?"

"Not since this morning."

"Papa must be starved. Hurry up. And don't you go near that front yard."

"No ma'am."

I was halfway to the crib for the kindling when I was aware of an awful silence in the front field. Grandmother had stopped yelling. I saw her sloshing through the weeds dragging the mattock behind her and headed for our alleyway. At the same time I saw the Bergins horse leisurely cropping tender green shoots in Grandmother's cornfield. Lucy Bergins was standing on her back porch watching the horse but making no move to catch it and tie it up. She was a short, squat, creamy-brown girl who looked old for her age. She had large buck teeth, eyes that bulged like a toad frog's and a little nose mashed into her face. Grandmother said she looked like the last end of pea pickings. Her parents were always very respectful to Grandmother and never joined in the laughter from the other back porches, but Lucy was a sassy one. My folks said she was feeling her oats.

"I caught you, you dirty little filly. I saw you turn that horse out for pure meanness," Grandmother shouted at her.

"I didn't do no such thing. He broke his halter and got loose by 'imself," Lucy shouted back.

"Don't you dispute my word, you low-down little hout. You're a liar and the truth ain't in you. I been watching you a long time and I don't miss much. Idleness is the devil's workshop. You come home every day from school and lay up there with other women's husbands while your pore mother's working her fingers to the bone to make something outta you. In my time, we tied little fastass wenches like you to a tree, turned their clothes over their heads and horsewhipped 'em right on their naked behinds. That's just what I oughta do to you right now, horsewhip you and teach you a lesson. You get that devilish horse outa my corn, you hear?"

Lucy surveyed the line of back porches. Dozens of eyes were following every move. The neighbors were waiting, listening. That horse had plagued Grandmother for a long time. Now she had caught both Lucy and the horse in the act. Lucy put her hands on her hips and tossed her head.

"You want the horse out, you catch 'im and put 'im out yourself."

Grandmother was already trying to catch the horse, but each time she got near it tossed its tail and frisked away just out of her reach. Grandmother flailed at the horse with her mattock; the horse pranced off trampling more shoots; the neighbors ki-yah-ki-yahed at her aggravation while Lucy was grinning and taking bows for her fine show. Grandmother stopped, winded, and leaned on her mattock.

"If you—don't come out here—and get this horse—I'm coming up there—and beat the living tar out of you!" she gasped.

"You just try it, you crazy old witch!"

Grandmother started for the Bergins fence. I didn't wait to hear more. I forgot all about the kindling. I rushed around the house and into the parlor and dragged the old family Bible off the stand where it always sat. Aunt Sallie was singing so loudly she did not hear me come in. I lugged the Bible to the front porch and put a brick on top of it to hold down the loose ragged pages. Then I lit out up the alleyway as fast as I could run. I could see Grandmother struggling with the lock on the Bergins gate. She couldn't open it. By the time I got to her she was astride the Bergins fence holding on to the wire with one hand and swinging the mattock with the other. Lucy was frozen with terror to her porch. Just as Grandmother was about to get her other leg over the fence I caught hold of it with both hands and held on fast. Grandmother hung there swaying on the fence, the mattock wavering dangerously near my head.

"Granma! Granma!" I screamed. "Come down quick. I got something important to tell you."

"Lemme go, child!" Grandmother was doing her best to kick free and hold her balance. Her leg jerked backward like a cow's hind leg at milking time. She dangled while I held on.

"Granma, I tell you it's important."

Grandmother tried to pull her leg up once more, then gave up and let it fall back, sending me tumbling to the ground.

"What on earth do you want, Baby?" she asked. However angry

Grandmother was about other things she was never harsh with me. She said I reminded her too much of her daughter Agnes, and that I had my mother's eyes. I was her weakness. I got up and yanked at her red petticoat.

"Bend down, so's I can tell you in your ear." I didn't want Lucy or the neighbors to hear me. Grandmother reluctantly climbed off the fence and bent down.

"Granma," I whispered, "I know it ain't Sunday but I got the big Bible on the front porch, the one Miss Mary Smith gave you. Come down to the house right now quick, and I'll read to you in the Psalms. I'll even try to read a little about 'Zekiel in the valley of the dry bones and Dan'l in the lion's den."

I had touched on Grandmother's two favorite Bible selections. And she treasured that ragged old Bible Miss Mary Smith of Chapel Hill had given her more than any other article in the house. She said she got it when she was a little girl and was confirmed at the Chapel of the Cross. It was over one hundred years old. It was the one book Grandmother tried to read herself, peering through her glasses and spelling out the Psalms a word at a time. I had learned to read some of the Psalms by now and every Sunday evening I would read to Grandmother some of her favorite passages. She seemed so proud of having me read to her from the big Bible that I loved it as much as she did. I liked the huge print and the way the verses were divided on the pages. I liked the sound of the words rolling off my tongue and I would let my voice rise and fall like a wailing wind just as I had heard Reverend Small chant the morning lesson at St. Titus on Sundays. Grandmother had utmost respect for the Holy Word.

She hesitated.

"You sure got me where the hair is short, Baby," she said. "Why would you want to read the Bible to me when I'm so vexed?" I could see she was weakening.

"You said any time was a good time to read the Scripture, didn't you? Please come on to the house. Aunt Pauline's going to fix supper and she's got the water running so she can make you some nice cool lemonade while I read to you. Don't you want some lemonade to cool you off?"

Grandmother considered. The sweat was pouring down her face and her clothes were soaked with it. Her face was flushed and she was panting hard. I pulled her gently toward the house. The Bergins horse had moved down the slope and was now grazing on the Bottoms. Grandmother picked up the mattock and took a step toward home.

"I've never been one to turn my back on the Word of God," she said.

Behind us Lucy snickered. Grandmother turned around. Lucy's grin faded.

"I'll tell you something, you little tramp. Just as sure as there's dead folks over in that cemetery and my name's Cornelia Fitzgerald, you're going to pay for what you said to me today. You're going to bring sorrow and shame on your people. That dumb animal don't know right from wrong, but you do. As the Lord is my witness, you and that horse is marked for a bad end. Vengeance is mine saith the Lord, and I will repay. You're born but you ain't dead and I'll live to see my words come to pass."

Without another word she flung herself toward the house, leaving Lucy and the neighbors gaping and wondering what had happened. I was up the front steps ahead of her and picked up the Bible. "Let's go inside to the dining room where it's quieter, Granma."

Grandmother let herself be led inside and flopped into a big armchair. I propped the Bible on the table and began to read from Psalms, letting my voice rise and fall like Reverend Small's. I could hear Aunt Sallie in the parlor pumping the organ and singing "Rock of Ages" for the sixth time through every verse. Grandfather was stomping about upstairs in his room, but outside everything was still. Pretty soon Aunt Pauline came in and set a glass of lemonade on the table near Grandmother's chair and went out again. I finished the passage and looked up at Grandmother for approval. The glass was empty, but Grandmother's head was on her chest and her lips let out a little snore.

That same afternoon after supper we heard a commotion in the Bottoms and then somebody fired a shot. The Bergins horse had fallen over an embankment and broken its leg. They had to shoot it. A few months later, Lucy's mother took her out of school suddenly. The older folks said it was a terrible thing to happen to poor Mrs. Bergins, who was so high minded and such a nice woman, but that it couldn't be helped. They said Lucy was going to have a baby. The neighbors never doubted Grandmother's prophecies after that.

2

IF GRANDFATHER had not volunteered for the Union in 1863 and come south three years later as a missionary among the Negro freedmen, our family might not have walked in such proud shoes and felt so assured of its place in history. We might have fought our battles with poverty and color troubles, thinking of ourselves as nobodies or not thinking of ourselves at all, dying out with nothing to remember of us except a few census figures. Grandfather's struggle made the difference, although Grandmother Cornelia supplied her share of pride. What he attempted—far more than what he finally achieved—made him our colossus and beacon light. Because of him we felt that we belonged, that we had a stake in our country's future, and we clung to that no matter how often it was snatched away from us.

As a child growing up, I was never allowed to forget that Grandfather had been a soldier and that I was a soldier's granddaughter. This knowledge carried a heavy burden of responsibility and permitted no betrayal of mortal weaknesses. A soldier's granddaughter must have courage, honor and discipline. I must stand tall and never indulge in the fears of other children. When Aunt Pauline wanted me to do something odious or frightening—like swallowing a dose of castor oil or facing the tombstones after dark to bring in the slop jar somebody left by the cemetery fence—she never threatened or offered reward.

"Now, you must be a brave little soldier just like your grandfather. He's not afraid of anything. He'd walk right up to danger and shake it by the hand," she'd remind me.

At such moments, my shrinking spirit might wrestle with Grandfather's stalwart one and I might wish I were anybody but a Fitzgerald grandchild, but I was honor bound to set my chattering teeth, stiffen my spine and walk in Grandfather's shoes. To hesitate or show fear after this injunction was a disgrace too shameful to endure.

Nor could one admit defeat around Grandfather. His struggle with blindness was a constant challenge to us. It had caused him many setbacks and heartaches and had snatched success from him time and again, but he had never given up. He and Grandmother started married life together in a two-room house. He could see then, and he had great dreams. As his eyesight faded he followed one trade after another as teacher, tanner, farmer, carpenter, contractor and brickmaker, until finally he could not see at all. Through all of this he and Grandmother had managed to bring up six children, give them some education and finally to own their own home. To them there was a world of difference between those who paid taxes and those who paid rent.

"Always have your own little patch of ground and your own house if it's nothing but a shack," I was taught.

It took Grandfather twenty years to achieve it. He lost his brick business and most of his land but he held on to one acre and built his house on it. He and Grandmother often went without food to pay for it and keep up the taxes. To his family it was more than a home; it was a monument to Grandfather's courage and tenacity.

There was something solid and indestructible about Grandfather's house. It wasn't very large—it had only six rooms—and it wasn't nearly so fine as his brother Richard's house, but it was free and clear of debt and Grandfather had supervised the laying of each board and brick and shingle although he could see the work only through his fingers. It was as if he had built himself into the structure, for it had his stubborn character. It was sparingly constructed and unpretentious like himself. It wasn't even a two-story house. He called it a story-and-a-jump because the two bedrooms upstairs were part of the steeply slanting roof and had only half windows and low slanting ceilings. Downstairs the small parlor and another bedroom were divided by the narrow hallway which joined the dining room and kitchen at the back of the house. The wall plaster had cracked from many settlings; the furniture was sparse and very plain; the rooms were small; but each room had a fireplace and in cold weather a fire blazed cheerfully on a hearth somewhere in the house.

It reminded me of Noah's Ark perched on a little slope, its back hugging the ground, its front high on latticed brick underpinnings, and at each end a tall brick chimney built from the ground outside and towering above the roof. The place had a ragged beauty. Honeysuckle and morning-glory vines flowed over the sagging fences and covered the old latticed wellhouse. A trellis of red and white rambler roses sheltered our back door from the cemetery. Rosebushes, jonquils, irises and violets grew along the walks, and at the foot of each elm tree was a round bed of pansies. Apple and pear trees rimmed the garden and blackberry vines fought with the weeds near the garden fence. When I was a small child Grandmother planted a young orchard of plums, peaches, cherries and pears just below the wellhouse. As I watched her setting out the slender twigs she told me,

"I won't be here when these bear fruit, child, but they're for your time."

Grandfather's homeplace was about a mile from the center of Durham in the Maplewood Cemetery section of town. When he had it built back in the 1890's, he was so proud of it he called it Homestead on the Hillside, for it sat on a broad shelf of land between two hills. But like much that had changed since Grandfather lost his sight, the hillside behind it had become a cemetery and the forest rising in front of it had given way to the Bottoms.

In fifty years, Durham had spread rapidly from a village to a bustling factory center, sucking in the rolling pine country around it. Shacks for factory workers mushroomed in the lowlands between the graded streets. These little communities, which clung precariously to the banks of streams or sat crazily on washed-out gullies and were held together by cowpaths or rutted wagon tracks, were called the Bottoms. It was as if the town had swallowed more than it could hold and had regurgitated, for the Bottoms was an odorous conglomeration of trash piles, garbage dumps, cow stalls, pigpens and crowded humanity. You could tell it at night by the straggling lights from oil lamps glimmering along the hollows and the smell of putrefaction, pig swill, cow dung and frying foods. Even if you lived on a hill just above the Bottoms, it seemed lower and danker than the meanest hut on a graded street.

Of course, my family would never admit we lived in the Bottoms. They always said we lived "behind Maplewood Cemetery," but either choice was a gloomy one. The cemetery was so close that only a chicken-wire fence separated us. We used to say we would hit a grave if we sneezed hard. It overshadowed our lives. To the west as far as I could see up the hill were rows of turfed mounds, stone crosses, marble figures, tombstones and vaults. The oppressive nearness of this silent white world of stony angels, doves, lambs, tree trunks and columns gave me the feeling that death was always waiting just outside our back door to grasp me. I was never free from the presence of eternity, the somber symbols of the unknown.

The steep hill so dwarfed our house that when one stood on the cemetery side and looked down our house seemed to shrink into the earth. It was like living under a mountain of tombstones that would break loose some day and come tumbling down upon us. There was also something sinister about the Confederate gun at the top of the hill—mounted on a square base and decorated by a pile of black cannon balls at each corner—which pointed downhill directly at our back door.

At times the cemetery was like a powerful enemy advancing relentlessly upon us, pushing us slowly downward into the Bottoms. Indeed, some of its death and decay had already encroached upon us. Grandfather's crib and stable, which hugged the cemetery fence, had sunk into a marsh of standing water. The wellshed had rotted and I could look through a gaping hole in the latticework and see the oily green scum of water below the crumbling floor boards. That well was a childhood terror. I was always afraid I'd stumble and fall through the hole into the water.

The cemetery was looked upon as an intruder by our family, and Grandfather had battled against it for years before it got the upper hand. When he and his brother Richard first came to Durham in

1869, the place was a small village of three hundred people and Main Street was a muddy roadway lined with wooden shacks, warehouses and livery stables. A mile west of the village on the Chapel Hill Road was a tiny graveyard called Maplewood. East of Chapel Hill Road a forest sloped downward to a wide meadow containing a vein of clay. Back in Pennsylvania Uncle Richard Fitzgerald had been a brickmaker and Durham seemed the right spot to start in business. The village was earning a reputation for "Durham Bull" smoking tobacco which later assumed the famous trade name "Bull Durham." The future tobacco kings, Washington Duke and his sons, were still relatively poor tobacco farmers and had not yet set up their factory in Durham, but the town was growing and needed bricks for more stores and factories.

Within the next fifteen years Uncle Richard became Durham's leading brickmaker. By 1884, he had a large brickyard on Chapel Hill Road and orders on hand for two million bricks. During the same period Grandfather had a smaller brickyard and made bricks by hand. My family could remember the time when the hillside behind our house was a meadow and wheat field skirted by a forest of oaks, pines, cedars and sassafras bushes. Grandfather had an option from the city to dig clay from part of the land and farm the rest.

The trouble started when the city decided to extend Maplewood Cemetery east of Chapel Hill Road and canceled Grandfather's option. Grandfather suddenly found himself facing a neighbor without heart or feelings. Before that time he had had difficulty protecting his own land from the underground springs which bubbled up on the city's side of the line, but he had handled the problem by digging a four-foot ditch on his side to drain the water northward to a stream and putting up a wooden fence between himself and the city to protect his ditch.

Now the city's workmen began making a roadway on the city's side of the line and knocked down Grandfather's fence. They threw wagonloads of dirt over the line and filled his ditch. Water poured down the hill into our yard. Grandfather had his ditch reopened at his own expense and warned the city, but the careless workmen ignored him and kept right on refilling the ditch. Grandfather was furious. He went from one city official to another and got nothing but shrugs and stares. He then hired a lawyer and sued the city for damages.

Nothing came of it. A local newspaper reported derisively that a blind old colored man on the outskirts of town was stubbornly trying to prevent the city's development but had little chance of success. Grandfather was so humiliated and so feeble by now that he dropped the suit, but Grandmother refused to be silenced. She walked the fence line all day long and railed at the workmen. She told them nobody would put a stopper on her mouth as long as she could breathe. She warned that the graveyard would be so full of mean white folks there'd be no place left to bury them. Her prophecy came true sooner than anyone expected for the town was hit hard by a flu epidemic not very long after that. Tombstones and fresh graves began to appear at the top of the hill. The forest was cut down and the tombstones began to march down the hill toward our back door.

As the graves crept closer and the water from decomposed bodies drained over our property, our well was condemned. For a long time the family had to carry water by hand from a great distance until money could be scraped together to install city water. In a few years Grandfather's Homestead on the Hillside was isolated on its ledge, a basin for drainage from the cemetery hill. During bad weather we were mired in from constant floodings which settled under the house and rotted the foundations of the stable and wellshed. We had to slosh about in boots most of the time. Our house sank lower and lower and the walls began to crack. Late at night you could hear the old place shifting and groaning as it settled like a restless sleeper. We were seldom free from the sickening odor of standing water and rotting weeds. Our yard was crisscrossed with tiny ditches to get rid of it but we never entirely succeeded. Of course, the city never paid Grandfather a cent for any of the damage.

The cemetery had won but there was something stubborn about Grandfather and his land which refused to knuckle under. True, the graveyard was now at our back door, but Grandfather would not sell out and it could not drive him an inch farther. He walled it out by planting trees and rosebushes along our side of the fence. He developed his longest grape arbor parallel to the fence along our garden walk. In late summer ripe clusters of blue grapes hung in bright defiance of the canopies of death just beyond.

I sometimes thought the family never acknowledged they had lost the use of the cemetery land but continued to treat it as an extension of our property. In summertime it was far more my playground than our front yard. My folks were polite but not overfriendly neighbors. Our front field was a kind of moat which kept everybody off unless someone had special business with us. Life flowed gustily through the Bottoms and there was a continual uproar of shouting children, barking dogs, bellowing cows and people hollering back and forth across the low ground, but we were never a part of it. I used to watch the stream of neighborhood activity enviously from my perch on the porch step, but I seldom got a chance to join it unless I was sent on an errand which took me along the dirt road.

The dead behind us were closer and seemed more friendly at times than the living neighbors in front of us. In fact, Grandmother used to say dead neighbors made good neighbors; they kept their mouths shut and weren't always meddling into other folks' business. I think she said this so often just to reassure herself that she didn't really mind living there. She knew how dead set Grandfather was against pulling up stakes again.

The cemetery haunted family conversations. There was constant talk about selling out and getting away from there. Aunt Sallie complained most about it. She said she didn't see the need of people dying before their time and living in the sight of death forever. But Grandfather was settled under his own vine and fig tree at last and nothing but death would dislodge him. This place was his own; he had built and shaped it and he knew almost every furrow in the earth about it. Blindness spared him from the daily spectacle of sorrow the rest of us endured. The thought of change unnerved him, for a new home would bring new neighbors and new quarrels with Grandmother. I also suspect he would not have anyone believe his family was afraid to stay so near a graveyard. It was a living denial of superstition to remain there.

I'm afraid Grandfather would have disowned me if he had known the strange dual life I led—the suppressed terror by night and the macabre fascination by day which the cemetery held for me. As soon as darkness closed down upon us and we were shut in with it, our house became a fortress against imaginary ghostly legions. No matter what my head told me, I was never free from them. Even inside the house with the doors securely locked and bolted and the lamps lighted, I jumped at every noise and shadow. The walls faded and I could see the ever-present formless gray and white shapes just beyond the door. I dreaded to go outside when there was no moon to distinguish the trees and tombstones. Our own trees were whitewashed every spring and looked as ghostly as the stone figures. Sometimes fingers of light from a street lamp swaying in the wind on the opposite hill would probe the darkness. The cemetery would come to life. Dancing ghoulish arms and legs and indefinable shapes made of wind and shadow would move slowly across the faces of the tombstones. The mournful hoot of a stray owl would send fingers of ice down my spine. In cold weather a few frozen leaves left on the trees would clatter like bones. The worst fright of all was when some prankster prowled the graveyard after dark and pushed one of the cannon balls off its pile. The cannon balls would thunder down a bricked alleyway and crash into the cement base of the wire fence with a terrifying impact that shook the house.

Morning transformed the cemetery into a beautiful park of birds, rabbits, squirrels and, in summer, flowers blooming everywhere. But daytime also brought funerals, and the solemn burial preparations were an inescapable part of our lives. Gravediggers would appear with picks and shovels early in the morning, rope off a plot and put up a canopy. Then they'd take turns digging the grave. The digger's head would get lower and lower in the earth until it disappeared entirely and all one could see was the end of a shovel rhythmically throwing little piles of red dirt onto a steep mound of fresh soil.

My folks pointedly ignored the tradition that Maplewood Cemetery belonged to white people and that colored people were not supposed to enter it at all. We used it for our goings and comings to our relatives' homes on Chapel Hill Road. I spent many hours running errands back and forth along its many paths and roadways. Emboldened by daylight and the living creatures which inhabited it in daytime, I would loiter along the flowered paths searching for new graves. I'd make a little detour to visit a plot whenever I found one. A new grave, bright and poignant under its blanket of fresh flowers, always seemed so lonely to me. In a few days the gravediggers would come along and remove the faded wreaths, leaving a new scar on the green hillside. The recent dead seemed closer to the living than to the turfed mounds. I thought it might be comforting to them that someone stopped to wish them well in their unfamiliar home. Strange, now that I think of it, but I was on better speaking terms with and knew more about the *dead* white people of Durham than I did about the *living* ones. There were no barriers between me and the silent mounds.

Death could lower the barriers but never really wipe them out for the living. People whose kin were buried close to our house often came to the fence to borrow scissors, a jar or a hoe to fix up their graves. We never refused them and often they would stand at the fence for a while talking of their dead as if it eased them to have a listener so close by the grave.

Then one day a woman came down to the back fence and called to Grandmother, who was hanging up clothes in the back yard.

"Aint-ee," she said, "kin you lin me a hoe?"

Grandmother didn't answer or turn her head although she wasn't ten feet away from the woman.

"Aint-ee over there, I say kin you lin me a hoe?"

Grandmother walked to the back door and picked up the hoe leaning against the house. She turned around and I saw that her eyes were blazing.

"Don't you 'aint-ee' me, you pore white trash. I'm none of your kinfolks!" she snapped as she went inside and slammed the door shut in the woman's face.

3

ONE couldn't be around Grandmother for very long without hearing all about the Chapel Hill Smiths and the University of North Carolina. It was an obsession with her. If a
stranger stopped in the yard long enough to pass the time of day,
pretty soon I'd hear Grandmother telling him who she was, who
the Smiths were and how they endowed the University. Out of
her own vivid memories and the tales she heard from her mother
and the older Smith slaves, she literally breathed their history.

"Child, you listen to your grandmother," she told me. "Hold
your head high and don't take a back seat to nobody. You got
good blood in you—folks that counted for something—doctors,
lawyers, judges, legislators. Aristocrats, that's what they were,
going back seven generations right in this state."

"Mama, don't fill that child's head with all that old stuff," Aunt
Pauline complained. "We'd all be better off if we'd never heard
it. It never did any of us any good."

"Mind your business," Grandmother retorted. "The truth's the
light and the truth never hurt nobody. I'm proud of my kinfolks.
Besides, I'm telling this child pure history."

"That's what's wrong with this family now," Aunt Pauline said.
"Too much pride and not enough money to back it up."

But Grandmother would have her say although nobody else at
home wanted to hear about the Smith philanthropy. She talked of

33

the University as if she were one of its chief benefactors. She never forgot that a great-uncle of the Smiths on their mother's side, the younger Tignal Jones, had offered five hundred acres of his estate in 1792 to get the school located in Chatham County. His offer was rejected in favor of a better location in Chapel Hill, but eventually most of the Smith land passed to the institution.

Grandmother related this fact half proudly, half resentfully, and her proprietary attitude toward the University arose out of her feeling that it had received her inheritance. Mere mention of it aroused only bitter anger in Grandfather and my aunts. Education was a household god at home, yet none of us could attend the University or share the benefits bestowed upon it by Miss Mary Ruffin Smith. When Grandmother began harping on the subject, Grandfather got up disgustedly and stormed out of the room. My aunts started humming and banging things around so they wouldn't hear her. So she made me her wide-eyed audience.

Many a night she sat by the fireplace chewing on her snuff brush and conjuring up the old days at Hillsboro and Chapel Hill before the Civil War. She would trace the Smiths' ancestry back to their maternal great-grandfather, old Tignal Jones, who descended from English settlers in Chatham County during colonial days. Old Tignal's two sons, the younger Tignal and Francis Jones, the Smiths' grandfather, owned thousands of acres of fine timber land and a good many slaves. Francis Jones was something of a local hero around both counties because he had served as a lieutenant in Sharpe's Company during the Revolutionary War. When he died in 1844—the year Grandmother was born—his lands passed to his grandson, Dr. Francis Jones Smith.

Years later when I looked up the records I found Grandmother's family history to be remarkably accurate. But there was one haunting story she told me about the Smiths and Great-grandmother Harriet which did not appear in the records. I don't think she realized it but she repeated this story again and again with such passionate single-mindedness it was like the recounting of a long-buried wrong which had refused to die and which she expected me to right somehow. I did not hear it all at once. Some of it I found out on my own, but most of it I pieced together from what I heard her say and the stories she had told her own daughters when they were very young.

When Grandmother spoke of Great-Grandmother Harriet her face saddened and she shook her head sorrowfully. Sometimes she would break off in the middle of her tale and sigh as if to say what that poor woman went through was too painful to put into words. She would forget I was there and sit nodding her head and rocking back and forth, her eyes fixed on the red embers, as if she were caught up in some strange ritual of memory.

After a long while she would say, "My mother was a good woman and did the best she could, but she couldn't help herself." And then, as if summing up the whole thing, she would quote the Bible: " 'The fathers have eaten a sour grape and the children's teeth are set on edge,' " and add, "How true! How true!"

But it was a different story when she talked of her father. Remembered joy shone in her eyes and her whole being changed and quickened with excitement. An uncontrollable pride in blood welled up in her as she described the ruddy-faced, sharp-eyed, wiry little man with a long bullet-shaped head and quick catlike movements.

"My father walked like he was strung on electric wires and he had a voice that could hold you spellbound for hours. He could make a judge break right down and cry in the courtroom when he was pleading a case." Remembering how Grandmother's own voice rang over the hillside and held the neighbors, I could believe her.

Grandmother referred to the three Smiths of her story as "Miss Mary Ruffin," "Dr. Frank," and "my father, Lawyer Sidney Smith." They belonged to a leading Orange County family which lived first in Hillsboro and later near Chapel Hill. Their mother, the former Delia Jones, came from an old landholding, slave-owning family of Chatham County. Their father, Dr. James S. Smith, a descendant of Scotch-Irish Protestants who settled in Orange County, was one of North Carolina's most distinguished citizens. During Monroe's administration he served as a Democratic Congressman for two terms and later as a member of North Carolina's House of Commons.

The three Smith children were born and reared in Hillsboro.

Later the family moved to Price's Creek, a fourteen-hundred-acre plantation three miles from Chapel Hill on the old Pittsboro Road. By 1850 their land stretched for miles and they owned thirty slaves. Few Orange County families owned more than that. The large white, Doric-columned Smith house sat off the road beyond a great iron gate in a grove of giant oak trees. Grandmother said that when she was a little girl one of her duties in the fall was to rake the oak leaves into great piles and burn them. Dr. Smith was a trustee of the University of North Carolina for many years and his home was a center of political and cultural activity.

Mary Ruffin Smith, the oldest child, was a remarkably intelligent girl and, after the fashion of southern young ladies, was trained by a thorough-going governess, Miss Maria Spear, from New York. In another era, Miss Mary might have had a professional career like her brothers, since she had great ability, was a good manager, read widely on political affairs and maintained a deep interest in medical botany throughout her life. But in her time southern young ladies were not expected to earn a living or have a career. They were trained to become the mistresses of large slave plantations. So she learned music, art, literature and needlework and spent much of her youth painting with water colors and composing songs and ballads. Miss Maria Spear, the governess, was a warm, gentle, compassionate soul whose Yankee heart was opposed to slavery. Mary Ruffin admired and loved her and kept her in the family until her death around 1881, but she never absorbed her gentle ways. She grew into a proud, stern, inflexible woman.

Her two brothers, Francis Jones and Sidney, attended the University of North Carolina. Francis followed his father's profession and studied medicine while Sidney, the younger boy, was attracted to law and politics. He was a fiery orator and developed into one of the county's most effective stumpers. His father turned Whig in 1841 and was defeated for Congress, but Sidney became a leading local Democrat and went to Raleigh in 1846 as a member of the General Assembly.

Folks thought it was a shame that none of the three Smiths married, considering their talents and the fine family they came from. It was taken for granted that Miss Mary Ruffin would make one of the best catches in the state and that the boys would marry well and have distinguished careers like their father. Everything pointed that way. But as years passed and the Smith men were still bachelors, people hinted darkly that Frank and Sid had wild blood in them. They said their devilment just about wrecked their own lives and drove Miss Mary into a lonely spinsterhood.

Of course some folks said that Harriet was at the bottom of all the trouble, as if she were to blame, although she was the one person who never had any choice at all. Folks claimed that if she just hadn't come to the Smith home, Frank and Sid might have settled down to solid respectable married lives. Nobody would have condemned them too harshly for doing what many southern men of high standing had done—bred two lines of children simultaneously and on the same place, one by their lawful white wives and the other by a slave concubine.

It happened in the best families all the time. It was a sickness of the times which everybody talked about but nobody stopped. The southern lawmakers spent their energies arguing that there was an impassable social gulf between blacks and whites and slavery was therefore the natural condition of the blacks. Yet while they argued, their wives at home secretly hated slavery for the oldest of human reasons. The southern woman was never sure of her husband's fidelity or her sons' morals as long as there was a slave woman in the household. The slave woman's presence threatened her sovereignty, insulted her womanhood and often humiliated her before her friends. She was confronted with a rival by compulsion, whose helplessness she could not fight. Nor could she hide the mulatto children always underfoot who resembled her own children so strongly that no one could doubt their parentage.

It was to Dr. James Smith's credit that he had kept free of this sort of thing. Until he bought Harriet, the slaves he owned were listed as Blacks and there were no mulatto children on his place. In 1834, when Mary Ruffin Smith turned eighteen, she had her coming-out party. The family lived in Hillsboro at the time and kept only a few household slaves on their place. The boys were away in school at Chapel Hill. Dr. Smith was deep in a political campaign to win election as a delegate from Orange County to the state constitutional convention. The Smiths entertained frequently and now that Miss Mary Ruffin was of an age to go about in society, it seemed fitting that she have her own personal maid to accompany her and to serve her at home when she received guests. So that fall Dr. Smith bought Harriet, a fifteen-year-old beauty, paid $450 for her—a tidy sum in those days—and congratulated himself on getting an unusually good bargain.

Even then Harriet was known to be one of the most beautiful girls in the county, white or black. She was small and shapely, had richly colored skin like the warm inner bark of a white birch, delicate features, flashing dark eyes and luxuriant wavy black hair which fell below her knees. She was shy and reticent but her eyes talked. I never knew whether she had any Negro blood. Grandmother always said she was three-fourths white and one-fourth Cherokee Indian. It was not uncommon to find Indian mixtures among the slaves. Indian girls were frequently kidnaped and forced into slavery as concubines during colonial days when white women were scarce and the white settlers raided the Indians. There were many skirmishes between the settlers and the Cherokees of western North Carolina before the Cherokee tribe was driven out and made its sorrowful pilgrimage over the Trail of Tears into Oklahoma. The Indian women lost their identity, were listed as mulattoes and were often used as breeders. Their children brought high prices in the slave market. This may have happened to Harriet's Cherokee grandmother.

At the time, Mary Ruffin Smith considered herself most fortunate to have such a handsome young slave girl. She showed off her new maid to her women friends as one displays fine furs or jewelry. She was not beautiful herself—she was a tall, angular, dark-haired, sallow-skinned young woman, inclined to be stiff and awkward—but she commanded another's grace, which was the next best thing to being beautiful. Harriet was a well-mannered, reserved, devoted servant who apparently accepted her lot without question and was unconscious of the striking contrast between them. She waited on Miss Mary hand and foot, and for the first few years of her service she slept on a straw pallet just outside Miss Mary's door where she could waken at her mistress' slightest call. She went with her almost everywhere and was an unobtrusive figure in the background to attend Miss Mary's needs in public.

As Harriet grew older she grew more lovely, and her striking looks drew attention to her wherever she went. Miss Mary noticed that in public her slave girl far more than herself was the object of quick admiring glances from strangers. It was the same way at home when the Smiths entertained. Their guests could scarcely conceal their open-eyed admiration. The women were frankly envious while the men, young and old, stared at Harriet without restraint when she came into the room. They'd leave the most weighty conversation hanging in mid-air to appraise her from head to foot. No one could deny that they knew a good thing when they saw it. After all, these experienced plantation owners were accustomed to judging good horseflesh or sizing up prize cattle at a glance. They did the same with slaves. Dr. Smith's associates tried to outbid one another with handsome offers to buy Harriet, but while he enjoyed all the fanfare he did not need the money and told his friends she was not for sale. Not to be outdone, some of them tried to hire her out for breeding, but Dr. Smith only chuckled and said his daughter could not spare her.

Harriet was around twenty when she expressed the desire to marry young Reuben Day,* a free-born mulatto who lived and worked around Hillsboro. Dr. Smith readily gave his permission. It was a good match. He cared nothing for free Negroes generally —he had helped to change the state constitution in 1835 to take away their vote and bar them from education—but he had no objection if one of them wanted to marry his slave girl. It was good business. He had no obligation to the husband, and every child by the marriage would be his slave and worth several hundred dollars at birth.

Grandmother thought mighty well of the Orange County Days. They were a near-white family who had been free for several generations. The older ones had purchased themselves or been emancipated by their white kinsfolk and most of the younger ones were "free issue," or born free. They were hard working, thrifty and proud as tom turkeys. They had good reason to be proud, because they owned a little land and kept themselves afloat in spite of the hard times which faced all free Negroes in a slave state. The slaveowners were so afraid their slaves would revolt if they saw

---

*In official records, William Day; probably Reuben William Day.

the free Negroes get ahead that they made the laws especially oppressive against free colored people.

Grandmother never knew her mother's husband, Reuben Day, but she used to talk a lot about his brother, Tom Day, who was well known in ante-bellum North Carolina.*Tom was a fine cabinet-maker who had his own business. Wealthy white people came to him from all over the state to have their furniture made to order. By 1860 he was so prosperous he owned three slaves himself whom he used in his business. Grandmother said that when his wife died many years later he made her a rosewood coffin with his own hands.

Reuben Day was not so fortunate. He was a farm worker with no special trade. Reuben and Harriet could not even live together. They had to share brief visits in a little cabin on the Smith lot when Reuben was given permission to see her. When their son Julius was born around 1842, he was a Smith slave like his mother. Reuben did not like this arrangement, of course, and often talked of buying freedom for Harriet and her child, but they were high-priced slaves and it would take many years to save up the purchase money.

That was the way things stood when Francis and Sid came home from school and began practicing their professions around Hillsboro. They had not seen much of Harriet during their school days, but now they found a mature woman just a little younger than themselves and good to look at. Each had the same thought when he saw her and each read the look in the other's eyes.

Sidney had always been a hot-blooded, impetuous little fellow who hurled himself with single-minded fury into whatever caught his interest. Francis was by nature more cautious and restrained. Sidney exploded and spent himself, but Frank knew how to wait and bide his time. He was a tall, dark, brooding man who seemed withdrawn much of the time. While he said little and seemed calm and self-possessed at all times, he had a terrible temper beneath his quiet exterior.

Before long everybody in the house knew that a storm was brewing between the brothers and that Harriet was the cause of it. Francis watched her furtively from a distance, but Sidney was open with it. From the moment he returned home he could not

*Grandmother believed Reuben was Tom Day's brother, but I have been unable to confirm it.

leave her alone. His eyes followed her everywhere when she was in the room. He seemed to be always just behind her when she went out the door or standing in the shadows when she went to her cabin at night after her work was done. He would confront her suddenly on the stairs or in a hallway, block her passage and try to talk to her. She began to dread the sight of him and evenings when she finished her duties at the Smith house, she fled to her cabin, nailed the door from the inside, put sticks across the window and lay trembling for hours.

One day Sidney cornered her in the study and tried to kiss her. She fought him off and ran screaming from the house. Francis heard the fuss and that night the brothers quarreled about it after supper.

"Why don't you leave the girl alone, Sid?" Francis asked.

"That's my business," said Sid.

"Listen, you bullheaded fool," roared Frank. "If I ever catch you on that woman, I'll beat the hell out of you. You won't live to tell the tale."

There was an uneasy truce for a while after that, but Harriet felt like a hunted creature. When Sidney wasn't following her around, Francis' eyes were on her with an unmistakable look in them. Each brother was biding his time. She grew thin and haggard and Miss Mary frequently caught her weeping. Miss Mary was nobody's fool. She had watched her brothers and seen what was coming. Her mother was a meek, delicate little woman who had never taken a strong hand in her sons' affairs and only wrung her hands about it. She spoke to her father, but Dr. Smith seemed strangely unconcerned. He said the boys had to sow a few wild oats and they'd get over it. Miss Mary hoped desperately Frank and Sid would get interested in some of the eligible young women in their social set, but neither of them showed the slightest inclination to take a wife. They had eyes for no woman but Harriet.

Then one evening Sidney walked up to Harriet's cabin as she was saying good night to Reuben.

"Say boy, what're you doing on this place after nine o'clock? You're not one of our slaves," he said.

"You know me, Marse Sidney," said the astounded Reuben. "I'm Reuben Day, Harriet's husband."

"Husband!" Sidney exclaimed as if it were the first time he had heard such a thing.

"Yes sir. Me and Harriet got married more'n two years ago."

"Somebody's been fooling you, boy. Don't you know slave marriages aren't recognized in this state?"

"Oh, but you see Dr. Smith fixed it up for us. He gave us permission and the preacher said words over us. We're married all right."

"Can't help what the preacher said. You're up against the slave law."

"But Marse Sid, I'm free born and—"

"Then it's too bad you married a slave woman. You'll have to get yourself another wife."

Reuben was stunned. Harriet clung to him wordlessly. Fury and frustration boiled in him but he was helpless. Behind the evil little man who leered at him in the darkness was the oppressive weight of southern law and custom.

"And besides," Sidney was saying, "we don't want you on this place. You're a trespasser and if you come back, I'll have you whipped and thrown in jail."

Reuben started to say something, but Harriet clapped her hand over his mouth and pushed him through the door.

"Do like he says, Reuben," she pleaded. "Don't say no more. It'd only make it worse. Just go now."

Reuben had to leave without a word to Harriet. That was the last she ever saw of him. He tried to slip back to see her once more, but Sidney caught him on the lot before he reached her cabin. Frank was into it too. The brothers beat Reuben with the butt end of a carriage whip and when they finally let him go they told him if he ever came back on the Smith lot they'd shoot him on sight. He disappeared from the county and nothing was heard of him again.

Harriet had no one to turn to now. The other slaves on the place had watched this little drama and knew how it would end, but they kept their distance. They had learned that a slave was a marked woman when she got mixed up with the men in the Big House. Her own men were afraid to have anything to do with her and it wasn't safe for her to have a husband of her own. Look at what had happened to Reuben Day, a free man. The women felt sorry for Harriet, of course, but it was an ill wind that didn't blow somebody some good. If Marse Frank and Marse Sid wanted Harriet and got used to her, it might save their own skins for a while.

It was inevitable that Sidney should be the first to break the truce. It happened right after Reuben was run off the place. Harriet had nailed up the door as usual and put barricades against it. Later that night, after everyone had gone to bed, the other slaves heard Marse Sid break open Harriet's door. Ear-splitting shrieks tore the night, although he stuffed rags in the door and window cracks to muffle Harriet's cries. They heard little Julius screaming and Harriet's violent struggle before Sidney had his way with her. Nobody interfered, of course.

That was only the beginning. After that first night, Harriet went into fits of hysterical screaming whenever Sidney came near her. The more she reviled him the better he seemed to like it. He raped her again and again in the weeks that followed. Night after night he would force open her cabin door and nail it up again on the inside so that she could not get out. Then he would beat her into submission. She would cry out sharply, moan like a wounded animal and beg for mercy. The other slaves, hearing her cries, trembled in their beds and prayed silently for her deliverance.

It came one night when Francis laid for Sidney and caught him just as he was coming out of Harriet's cabin. The brothers had it out once and for all, and there was a terrible fight. Early the next morning one of the slaves found Marse Sid lying unconscious in the yard, his clothes soaked with blood and an ugly hole in his head. He got over it but it was a long time before he was up and about again. The Smiths never talked about what happened that night; they hushed it up and told some cock-and-bull story about Marse Sid falling off his horse. The slaves knew, however, that Marse Frank had carried out his threat.

Sidney was only twenty-four at the time and had a bright political future ahead of him, but he was never quite the same after that beating. He took to drinking and brooded his life away. He went down to Raleigh for one term in the legislature and there were flashes of brilliant success here and there when he was sober, but in the end he turned out to be one of the worst drunkards in the county.

He learned his lesson. He never touched Harriet again after that night. She was at last free to come and go unmolested, but for months afterward there was a wild look in her eyes as she carried Sidney's child and she went about with a silent smoldering hatred against him to the end of her days.

4

EVERYBODY around Hillsboro had heard how Frank and Sid Smith had run Harriet's mulatto husband out of the county and fought over her themselves. The family tried to laugh it off as ignorant slave gossip, but it was no laughing matter when Grandmother was born on the Smith lot in early February, 1844. Here was the proof of the pudding. She was indistinguishable from a white child and she had Sidney's features. What was more, he was gleeful over her birth. He refused to keep quiet about it and went around boasting to his friends about his fine little daughter.

Dr. Smith was frankly ashamed of his son but had long since ceased to have any influence over him. Luckily he had retired from politics after his defeat a few years earlier or this might have been used against him publicly. Mrs. Smith was heartbroken over the whole thing and some folks thought the shock of it hastened her to her grave. Francis, of course, had already gotten his revenge and said little about it except that he'd kill Sidney and hang for it if it ever happened again.

Mary Ruffin Smith was mortified. She had a strong conscience and deep family pride. She felt Sidney had disgraced them all. Not that she had ever seriously questioned slavery as a way of life or the foundation of her family's wealth and privilege. Nor had she ever disputed a master's absolute right over his slave's person even when it included assault and rape. She had heard her father and

Judge Thomas Ruffin expound these views too often to believe otherwise.

The whole thing fell on her shoulders because Harriet was her servant. She was too valuable to get rid of and, besides, the damage was already done. What was to be done with her little bastard? Put it in the slave quarters, of course, and try to live it down. Here was the rub. It was not so easy to act according to fixed ideas when something happened in one's own family. Try as she might to avoid the truth, it struck her with shattering clarity that this was Sidney's child, a *Smith!* She couldn't get around it. Slavery had produced its own monstrosity in Miss Mary's home as it had done elsewhere. Smith progeny had been born into slavery. It could be bought and sold like any other property and in time this girl child of Smith blood could be bred to other men no better or worse than her own father. Miss Mary Ruffin realized with horror that this bastard slave child was also her own flesh and blood—in fact, her niece.

Thus she warred with herself. There were no heirs in the house to soften the blow or conceal her dilemma. The very family pride which made her feel so disgraced by Grandmother's birth also made it impossible for her to let her own kin grow up like a slave. As Grandmother said, blood was thicker than water. Grudgingly, Miss Mary Ruffin brought the baby into the Smith house and kept a private nurse for her until she was six years old. It was the first of many such battles in her soul in which Miss Mary would be torn between conscience and pride. The decision set her on a course of action from which she could not retreat for the remainder of her life. Like Harriet, she was drawn deeper and deeper into a quagmire. She was to experience a common bondage with Harriet which transcended the opposite poles of their existence as mistress and slave.

Not long after Grandmother was born Francis Smith came to Harriet's cabin. She did not cry out; she had been expecting it. Perhaps she was resigned. Or perhaps in her wretched loneliness she was grateful to him and even flattered by his attention. She had been cast adrift between two irreconcilable worlds. No colored man in the vicinity would dare show interest in her as long as she belonged to the Smiths. She was a mere pawn in her masters' world, desired but not recognized, safe from the predatory Sidney only so long as Francis remained her protector. And while Francis was kinder and more patient than his brother, he was no less determined to possess her exclusively.

It soon became known around the place that Harriet was Frank's woman—and that was that. Theirs was a distant relationship, barren of all communication save that of the flesh. In the Smith house Francis was the silent, remote master who scarcely noticed Harriet's presence. And she waited upon him with the same impartial deference she showed the other Smiths, giving no sign that she was his mistress. Yet, over the years Harriet was silently devoted to him and no one ever heard of his having another woman.

Within eight years after Grandmother's birth, Harriet had borne Frank Smith three daughters—Grandmother's half sisters, Emma, Annette and Laura. Shortly after Emma was born, the Smiths moved to Price's Creek. It almost seemed that Dr. Smith pulled up stakes to get away from the glare of Hillsboro society and clacking tongues. First Sid, then Frank laying up with a slave wench and refusing to marry their own kind like decent people. And the Smiths were upholding them in their dirt, bringing their little bastards right into the home and raising them up as if they were part of the family.

If Dr. Smith had sold Harriet and her children the talk would have been worse. Then folks would have said the Smiths sold their own blood into slavery. Conscience is a ruthless master and the Smiths were driven into an enslavement no less wasteful than Harriet's. They were doomed to live with blunted emotions and unnatural restraints, to keep up appearances by acting out a farce which fooled nobody and brought them little comfort.

It was a life of baffling contradictions and ambivalences, of snarls and threats and bitter recriminations. Everybody blamed everybody else for what had happened. It was dog eat dog with Sidney and Frank. They quarreled all the time and the family never knew when one of them might murder the other. Yet neither would give ground and move out. Harriet never spoke to Sidney or came near him unless compelled to do so in the course of her duties. Her sullen anger expressed itself in every gesture when he was anywhere around.

She was now the mother of five children by three different fathers, all growing up on the same plantation but treated according to their fathers' positions. Julius, the oldest, was almost ignored by the Big House. Like any other slave he came up willy-nilly in the quarters. His mother was almost a stranger to him. She was absorbed by the Smiths and had little identity of her own. She must serve them at the Smith home all day and at night she must hurry Julius off to one of the other cabins so he would not be around when Marse Frank came. He was a sweet, lovable boy, but ill luck overtook him. When he was around thirteen, he got lost in the woods during a heavy snowstorm. They found him almost frozen to death. He was severely crippled for the rest of his life.

The four Smith daughters were brought up in the Smith house. They were aware of Harriet as their mother, but their loyalties divided according to their fathers and they looked up to Miss Mary Ruffin for everything. Harriet hovered anxiously in the background, completely overshadowed by the superior authority of her mistress. Miss Mary decided what the girls should wear, where they should go, whom they should play with, how they should be trained and what duties they should perform. She meted out their punishments and their privileges. Until Miss Mary's death Grandmother looked upon her as one looks upon a parent and she seemed to have more pity than daughterly affection for Great-Grandmother Harriet. Indeed, the two older women had shared a strange motherhood in which neither could fully express her maternal feelings. The same overpowering forces which had robbed the slave mother of all natural rights had thrust them unwanted upon the childless spinster.

The Smiths were as incapable of treating the little girls wholly as servants as they were of recognizing them openly as kin. At times the Smiths' involuntary gestures of kinship were so pronounced the children could not help thinking of themselves as Smith grandchildren. At other times their innocent overtures of affection were rebuffed without explanation and they were driven away with cruel epithets.

The family carefully preserved a thin veneer of master-servant relationship for the unbelieving public but the children's very presence betrayed them. They were so white skinned and looked so much like the Smiths nobody was taken in by such pretenses. Sidney would go out of his way to mortify his family. He'd call Grandmother when company was around.

"Come here, Cornelia. This one's my daughter. She's smart as a whip, too," he'd say, partly out of fatherly pride and partly out of revenge against Frank. The implication was clear that the other three girls were his brother's children.

Naturally, the girls grew up feeling themselves more Smith heirs than Smith servants. Emma, Laura and Annette were more subdued about it than Grandmother. Frank shrugged them off and treated them as part of the surroundings. They kept a respectful distance from him and addressed him as "Marse Frank." Their daughterly feelings were reserved for their own private conversations among themselves.

There was nothing subdued about Grandmother. She blurted out exactly what she thought and was afraid of no one. She never called anyone "Marse." She had the Smith pride and refused to regard herself as a slave.

"We were free. We were just born in slavery, that's all," she always said. And to her, there was a difference.

She was the most vivacious and high spirited of the four girls. She had inherited much of Harriet's beauty, was quick witted and alert, but high strung and difficult to manage. Miss Mary Ruffin had her hands full. Sometimes she'd complain to Miss Maria Spear, "I don't know what I'm going to do with that headstrong Cornelia. She takes the bit in her mouth and goes sailing off with it just like—" and she'd catch herself before she said "Sidney." In spite of herself, Miss Mary liked the girl's fine intelligence and spirit and was deeply drawn to her. From the first Grandmother was Miss Mary's favorite and knew it.

Sidney Smith gloried in her. He was an outcast in the family, tolerated because he was blood kin but detested because he aired a scandal. He lived in a guilt-ridden world. His little slave-daughter, Cornelia, was an extension of himself upon whom he could shower the love he had not been permitted to give anyone else. She was the one person in the household who adored him, accepted him completely and was fiercely loyal to him at all times. She followed him about the premises like a devoted dog and when she grew older she became his personal servant and confidant.

He was a creature of paradoxes: a man of unrestrained passions and deadly pride, yet tormented by idealism. He had come under the anti-slavery influence of liberal professors at the University when a student there. He was fully aware of the degraded position of the slave in his society. Grandmother said that when he was full of liquor he would tell anybody how he hated slavery and that he was a "Union man" even though a Democrat. Yet he had perpetuated the very evil he secretly deplored.

Grandmother's uncritical love for her father was intensified by her urgent need for acceptance and for an identity of which she was not ashamed. Her father and his people represented everything desirable in life—power, wealth, privilege and respectability. All her life she would strive to identify herself with the best of her father's world and reject all associations which linked her to slavery.

Sidney encouraged this attitude. Grandmother was the only person he allowed to enter his study. Whatever formalities she was required to observe elsewhere in the house, they were equals behind that study door. He dropped the restraints imposed upon him by the slave code and was as tender and kind as any loving parent. He was proud of her quick-witted ways and her drollery. She seemed old beyond her years and instinctively understood his loneliness. She would amuse him with sayings she had picked up from the older slaves. When he was sober he would teach her to read a little. She was his rapt audience when he prepared a case for court. She would listen intently as he expounded strange legal theories to her just as if she were the judge or a member of the jury. She drank in eagerly every gesture, every tremor in his voice as he moved toward a final stirring plea, the rapid changes on his mobile face, his nervous stride back and forth across an imaginary courtroom. When he had gone to court she would imitate him, pleading her case to his empty chair.

She spent every spare moment in his study, lovingly dusting his books and peering into the mysterious legal volumes with something akin to idolatry. She knew just where he liked to keep his pipe on his desk and when he was home she'd jump to light it for him. When he was away she'd sit at the desk, light his pipe and puff away at it reflectively as she had seen him do. He would come in from court after winning a big case and hand her a roll of bills as big as her arm. He trusted no one else with his money.

"Here, Cornelia. Hide this for me till I need it. And don't tell anybody about it," he'd say.

Many times Grandmother forgot where she had hidden the money and she used to say that if the old Smith house were torn down piece by piece, they'd find many a roll of money stuck between the chinks of the walls.

Although a slaveowner himself after his father died, Sidney nurtured in his own daughter a rebellion against everything Negro slavery encompassed. He instilled in her that she was inferior to nobody. He gave her pride in her Smith-Jones ancestry. She said he told her that she was an octoroon and could therefore marry into either race if she chose. He tried to protect her from the wounds of slavery by making her believe the one-eighth nonwhite ancestry was Indian instead of Negro. He made it impossible for her to adjust to her later Negro status and yet he could not offer the recognition to support the notions he planted in her fertile mind.

Sidney told Grandmother she was to have all his money when he died, but he died suddenly when she was around sixteen and whatever he had intended to do about her future perished with him. Dr. James Smith had passed on a year or so previously and left most of his real estate to Miss Mary Ruffin. Grandmother said Miss Mary took the money Sidney had left for her. She refused to believe that he had failed to provide for her.

This contradictory little man had had a compassionate streak in him. While he made most of his money defending the property rights of slaveowners, he often represented without charge free Negroes accused of crime. It was unpopular to defend them in the courts but he never turned them down and won many an acquittal for them. Grandmother told how once her father came home from court after having saved from the gallows an old Negro man accused of stealing a mule. The slaves met "Marse Sid" at the gate, picked him up and danced about the yard with him on their shoulders. She said his idea of celebrating a legal victory was to come home, turn his coat inside out, knock the top out of a jug of apple cider and go on a big drunk. In spite of his faults, I couldn't hate Sidney Smith when Grandmother talked about him.

Of all the Smiths, Miss Mary Ruffin had the heaviest cross to bear. She had to hold up the family name against Sidney's drinking spells, Frank's notorious consorting with a slave woman and a houseful of illegitimate girls whose Smith characteristics tormented her as they grew older.

It was too late to turn back now. What was done was done and she must do what was right according to her lights. She could not send them back to the slave quarters or let Smith kin grow up heathens. She must keep them in the house at all costs. Nor could she let them be sold as slaves. The only way to make sure this would not happen was to buy them herself. I don't know how she managed it, but by 1860 she owned Harriet and her five children. Grandmother said Miss Mary worked in her garden many a night by the light of the moon to earn the money to buy them. She may have raised medicinal herbs to get the cash. After she bought them she told the girls they were free, but she never manumitted them outright. She listed them as property until the Civil War freed all the slaves, and she valued them at more than a thousand dollars apiece.

They were the only daughters she knew and she clung to them, but her feelings of kinship collided with her sense of propriety as their mistress. She shuttled between indulgence and spitefulness, alternately mothering them and ordering them around. She had them trained in housework, sewing and embroidery, but scrupulously avoided giving them an education. She allowed Miss Maria Spear to teach them just enough to read some of the Bible.

Grandmother was not one to respect barriers and Miss Mary found it difficult to keep her at arm's length. She emerged as Miss Mary's strong right arm. She was entrusted with the keys to the Smith place, the great smokehouses and granaries, and Miss Mary relied upon her to report on the other slaves' doings. This last was not an easy role for Grandmother. As slave life went, the Smith servants were not badly treated. They had their own surnames and were allowed to marry and raise their families on the place. They were well fed, well clothed and thought a good deal of themselves. They even had their own plantation preacher, Uncle Ned Cole, who could read and whose moving sermons attracted blacks and whites alike from neighboring plantations.

But generations of distrust had built up a wall of enmity between the darker-skinned field hands and the favored mulatto house servants. Color had been used to fasten bondage upon the blacks and was now used to divide and weaken the slaves. Even slavery had its bitter rivalries for meager advantage and mulattoes were traditionally set against the other slaves to inform on their misdeeds. Grandmother had watched the overseer beat field hands for some trifling offense until the blood ran and then rub salt in the lacerated flesh. She hated cruelty. She could no more deny her sympathies for the cabins than she could renounce her bonds with the Smith household. She never betrayed the other slaves and Miss Mary was often exasperated by her shrewd concealment of what she knew.

The most striking aspect of Miss Mary Ruffin's conflict about the girls was in her attitude toward their religious instruction. She might have left them to be "converted" at one of Uncle Ned Cole's revivals on the plantation. Instead, she elected to send them to the Chapel of the Cross on the University campus in Chapel Hill to be trained in the Episcopal faith. Grandmother said that when she was twelve years old she was confirmed at the chapel along with the daughter of ex-Governor David L. Swain, who was then president of the University.

Every Sunday morning the four attractive girls were seen riding along with Miss Mary Ruffin Smith in her beautiful white family carriage on their way to the Chapel of the Cross. People seeing them pass nudged one another and said, "There goes Miss Mary Smith and her girls." To keep up appearances, Miss Mary sent them upstairs to the balcony in church while she sat alone or with Miss Maria Spear downstairs in the Smith pew. This only heightened the curiosity of the congregation.

Grandmother said the young men downstairs could never keep their eyes forward and were forever craning their necks to gawk at the four Smith girls who sat by themselves in the balcony. Like her mother, Cornelia had rosy skin, raven black hair and sparkling dark eyes. She wore sixteen long thick curls that fell below her waist and the curls whipped and lashed like sixteen long black snakes when she swung them. She said that the boys in the pews below would fairly drool when, out of mischief, she acted sassy and tossed her curls from side to side when she caught them looking.

Church members often asked Miss Mary, "Who are those beautiful girls up there in the loft?"

The answer was always the same, as they knew it would be.

"Oh, they're my maid's daughters."

As far as Miss Mary was concerned that ended it. Her lips snapped shut as if she'd bite their heads off if they asked anything further. She never let the remarks touch her. When church was out, she looked straight ahead as if she heard nothing, gathered up her girls, piled them into the carriage and drove off.

Because our house had such a strong Yankee tradition and Grandfather had fought to end slavery, it was many years before I could fully understand why Grandmother clung so desperately to memories of a world which had collapsed and disappeared so long ago. Now I know she fed upon her memories to appease a deep unsatisfied hunger. She embellished them and found solace to ease the frustrations of her later years—the barrenness of her existence near the Bottoms and the blighted life she led in a world where she had no place. The Smiths were her legacy made more tangible by sheer repetition of the facts which linked her to them. They justified her. She told their story with unabashed candor, and while sorrow and pride warred in her eternally, pride always won out. She had been robbed of her birthright, but nobody could rob her of her pedigree.

5

GRANDMOTHER'S SMITHS had nothing on the Fitzgeralds when it came to haughtiness and family pride. Grandfather's folks had not come south empty handed in 1869. Before
the Civil War they owned their own farm and had been in the
brickmaking business in Pennsylvania. Now four generations of the
Fitzgerald family spread out over the Maplewood section of Durham like the branches of a great oak. Not counting the in-laws, I had
two great-aunts, a great-uncle, seventeen second cousins and thirty-
eight third cousins, most of whom lived within a half mile of my
house and all of whom thought there was no one on earth better
than a Fitzgerald. Some people thought they were stuck-up and
others thought they were born aristocrats. No matter how threadbare or down at the heels they might be at the time, you seldom
saw any of them bent or cowed. They walked with their heads in
the air and they all talked back, even the little ones.

In my house, of course, Fitzgeralds and Smiths pulled us two
ways at once. It was a continual tug of war between free-born
Yankee and southern aristocrat. Grandmother was on one side
reminding us that her bluebloods had owned thirty slaves in their
heyday, while Grandfather was on the other letting us know his
folks were of equally good stock if not better, and besides, he had
fought for the Union to end slavery. While Grandmother clung
to her Smiths, the rest of us took refuge in our Fitzgerald heritage,

which was legitimate and which we could talk openly about. We prized our Irish name and free status long before the Civil War; both were distinctive in a small southern town dominated by names like Smith, Jones and Brown and haunted by grim ghosts of the slavery past.

For we lived in the evil shadow of the Confederacy although more than fifty years had intervened and two generations had come along since emancipation. There were still white people alive who had owned slaves in their youth and they refused to bury their Confederate corpse. Nothing pleased them more than to describe colored people as ex-slaves and nothing pleased us less. We'd rather have been called ex-convicts. Colored people grasped at any distinction to put distance between themselves and slavery. If one couldn't fall back on the amount of white blood he had in him, as Grandmother did, he'd rely on a free parent or free grandparent. And I could talk of free *great-grandparents*, something truly to be proud of in those times.

My Fitzgerald great-grandparents' portraits hung in the parlor at home, and it seemed to me they still presided over the affairs of the Fitzgeralds from their heavy gilded frames as they had done when they were alive. Grandmother Cornelia said once that when people died their spirits hovered about their pictures, and I believed her. When I'd go into the parlor to dust or practice my music lessons, living and dead Fitzgeralds of all ages stared down upon me from every wall. No matter where I moved in the room their penetrating eyes followed me.

There was Great-Grandfather. Charles Thomas Fitzgerald, a rugged, bushy-browed, heavy, mustached old gentleman wearing a Chesterfield coat and soft black bow tie which were stylish in the 1860's. He had the same rough-hewn features Grandfather had —high forehead, square jaw, strong chin and cavernous eyes—but where Grandfather Robert's face was stern and resolute his was gentle and wise. Beside him was Great-Grandmother Sarah Ann Burton Fitzgerald, his wife, tight lipped and prim, her long white face the essence of severity and gloomy determination.

I knew, of course, that Great-Grandmother Sarah Ann was a white woman of Swedish and French descent and that Great-Grandfather Thomas was a half-Irish mulatto. This seemed very natural to me, although our town rigidly enforced the separation of the races and had signs WHITE and COLORED everywhere to remind us stringently of this injunction. Before I was old enough to understand the full meaning of segregation I knew there was something woefully wrong about those signs, since there could not possibly be anything wrong with my Fitzgerald great-grandparents!

Great-Grandfather Thomas held the honored place in the short history of the Fitzgerald family. He was the revered father of Grandfather Robert's stories of childhood and the grandparent Aunt Pauline idolized. She made him seem as real to me as if he had been living in my time, although he was born a hundred years earlier. Whenever she spoke of him the stern lines in her face dissolved and her eyes grew soft like those of a little child, as if she were reliving the happiest moments of her own youth.

She remembered him as a robust farmer in his sixties who walked with a spring in his step and his broad shoulders thrown back as if he had always depended upon the good Lord and himself for whatever blessings he had in life. He was tall and bronze colored, had straight features and soft reddish-brown, kinky-curly hair. His smile was infectious; everybody who knew him liked him. Even the die-hard white farmers of Orange County, who hated only one creature more than they did a damnyankee and that was a Negro damnyankee, had to respect him. Folks said he could make friends with the devil and not give an inch on principle. He was a devoutly religious man but he never preached. He said the best way to convince people of anything was by example.

Since he could read and write, he handled all of his own business affairs. His rule was: "Never be beholden to anybody if you can help it." When he bought property he paid cash for it, and although he had bought and sold several farms during his lifetime, I never found a mortgage listed against any of the land he owned. He was scrupulous about paying his debts and equally scrupulous about collecting what was owed to him. And he trained his children that way. He dealt with them just as one deals with a bank, signing notes when he borrowed from them and keeping strict records when he advanced them money.

He'd use the latest farming methods, get the newest implements and have only the best quality of seeds, plants, cows, horses, chickens and turkeys on his place. Farming was his business and he made a success of it. But he never boasted about himself or what he could do. Humility was as great a virtue to him as independence.

This remarkable man, who combined courage with humor and seemed to live without rancor among the embittered, was born in Delaware July 28, 1808, which made him approximately the same age as Abraham Lincoln and Jefferson Davis. We knew very little about his early life. It was a subject on which he was extremely reticent. He never talked of his mother and we did not even know her name. He said only that a man named Lodge took care of him when he was a boy.

His father was a different story. Great-Grandfather Thomas steadfastly maintained that he was the mulatto son of a Lord Fitzgerald from County Kildare, Ireland. He didn't talk much about his father either except for the bare statement of who he was and where he was from. There was talk in the family that he deeply resented his father and that he had been too proud to take money left for him by that gentleman. But while he rejected the circumstances of his birth, which may have seemed to him dishonorable, he clung to his Irish name and his belief that he was of noble blood. The legend was plausible enough to have some vitality. The Earls of Kildare were Fitzgeralds who got their large Irish landholdings from the British Crown during the eleventh century. And in the long line of earls was a Thomas Fitzgerald, Tenth Earl of Kildare, who distinguished himself in the sixteenth century by being excommunicated and hanged for his participation in a rebellion against English rule. And there were Thomas Fitzgeralds in Pennsylvania and Delaware from the mid-eighteenth century to the early 1800's. One of them was a merchant who served in the Delaware legislature as late as 1804 and came from New Castle County, where my Great-Grandfather Thomas lived.

How much of his claim was fact and how much fancy is unknown, but his children were nurtured upon his legend. It started something of a tradition in our family. Grandfather Robert took it very seriously. I heard it all the time at home, and knew anyone of Fitzgerald blood was expected to act under all circumstances with dignity and courage befitting the name he bore. My aunts, who were the soul of correctness and the most law-abiding folk I knew, would tell you animatedly what Great-Grandfather Thomas said about his ancestry. Their eyes sparkled as they added they didn't know how true it was, of course, but one could tell they considered themselves a part of the Irish Fitzgeralds' tradition of rebellion against tyranny. Some of the younger descendants who knew almost nothing of Great-Grandfather Thomas and only casually brushed against his tradition would sometimes laughingly call themselves "the brown Irish" and wear a bit of green on St. Patrick's Day.

As I was growing up, Great-Grandfather Thomas' legend pushed back the narrow boundaries of my life and linked me to a romantic faraway land untouched by the humiliating hand of slavery. That it was devastated by famine and poverty was unknown to me. It was something concrete, a name and place I could see and touch on the globe. By default I had lost my African roots and knew nothing of my African ancestors, and the very fact of African ancestry had been shrouded in shame. Fitzgerald ancestors from County Kildare, Ireland, was a lilting and magical phrase which sounded well in my ears. It strengthened the growing shell of pride used to protect the soft underbelly and wobbly legs of a creature learning slowly to navigate in a cruelly segregated world. But more than anything else then, it kept me from acceptance of my lot. I would always be trying to break out of the rigid mold into which I was being forced. I would always be in rebellion against crushing walls until people no longer needed legends about their ancestors to give them distinctiveness and self-respect.

Long after I had grown up, I had the thrilling experience of having stories I had heard at home confirmed by documents in the historic Archives of the United States in Washington. Everybody's family, of course, is listed in the United States Census and there is nothing spectacular about seeing a census record, but it was a moment of high personal significance for me. No other experience gave me quite the feeling of belonging as the discovery that the shrine which holds the original copies of the Declaration of Independence and the Constitution of the United States also houses the family record of an obscure citizen like Great-Grandfather Thomas Fitzgerald, and that I could go there and read these documents for myself. Here was the tangible time-honored evidence that in 1850 he lived in Delaware, a Free Person of Color and a farmer worth several thousand dollars.

Flushed with this added dimension of citizenship, I thought it would be interesting to find out whether Great-Grandfather Thomas had earned his money by his own efforts or whether he had received it by will from the mysterious Irish ancestor whose name had such a marked influence upon our family. And so I stopped by the county courthouse in Wilmington to have a look at the records. I found no will, but I stumbled upon one deed to Thomas Fitzgerald, dated August 8, 1832, and duly recorded. The deed read:

I, George Lodge, for divers reasons and considerations have manumitted, discharged and forever set free from servitude of myself, my heirs, Executors, administrators from and after they [sic] date hereof a certain coloured man named Thomas Fitsgirls, aged Twenty-four years and eight days old who fell to me by will of my father, Samuel Lodge.

One hundred years of family tradition cultivated so carefully through four generations of Fitzgeralds crashed down on my head as I read the deed of manumission which freed Great-Grandfather Thomas at the age of twenty-four. It took me some while to comprehend fully what I had read. We had often gloated privately that in the Fitzgerald branch of our family tree, at least, there was no hint of slavery, and we had clung to the romantic notion of high birth for further support. All the while without our knowing it this simple document which would have toppled our proud pretensions had been a matter of public record!

Nagging questions tugged at me which I could not avoid. Why had Great-Grandfather Thomas, a thoroughly honorable man, concealed his past as if he had committed a crime he never wanted brought to light? And why had we been so eager to believe that not one of our Fitzgerald ancestors had been a slave?

Further probing into this mystery yielded the Lodge family papers in Wilmington, which suggested that Great-Grandfather Thomas had escaped the extreme brutalities of the slave system. The Lodges were a Quaker farming family of Brandywine Hundred just north of Wilmington and had never been large slaveowners.

Their faith forbade them to deal in the slave trade. George Lodge, the great-grandfather of novelist Anne Parrish, became a master involuntarily when he was twenty-two by inheriting from his father's personal estate in 1819 three young slave children, the oldest of whom was eleven-year-old Thomas Fitzgerald. Lodge never represented them as slaves to the census enumerator but only as Free Persons of Color and members of his household. According to Quaker custom, he manumitted each of them as they reached twenty-four (for they could not be recognized by others as free without a deed of manumission). He must have taught Great-Grandfather Thomas to read and write and treated him as a ward. There is good reason to believe that Great-Grandfather Thomas did not look upon himself as a slave at all and always had the promise of emancipation when he should reach maturity. George Lodge may even have compensated him for his labor as Quakers often did their slaves upon emancipation.

The cause of his concealment went deeper than his outward circumstances. It lay in the nature of slavery, and it laid bare an inward wound. No matter how humane George Lodge might have been as a master or the degree of freedom Great-Grandfather Thomas had enjoyed while in his service, under the law my great-grandfather was a piece of property without identity or any power of choice as to his future. All his hopes and aspirations rested upon the slender thread of another man's life, for should his master die before completing all legal steps of emancipation, Thomas Fitzgerald would pass into the estate to be disposed of like a mule or ox. During all of his formative years he was tormented by the conflict between his human attributes and his status as property. Initiative, learning, independence and nobility of being were all incompatible with a state of enslavement.

Against this background, Great-Grandfather Thomas' stature increased rather than diminished. I marveled that he had not let slavery stunt or embitter him and that the very qualities which it suppressed had triumphed in him. He was not a crusader, but he had shown what a freedman could achieve at a time when such proof was crucial to the cause of freedom. For thirty years he stood in the shadow of slavery, a solid argument for universal emancipation, until the issue was finally settled by civil war.

As I moved back painfully through memories of my own childhood and peeled off the layers of pride which had encrusted me, I came to see how those who have been crippled by damaging experiences seize hold of any crutch to help themselves along. I realized we are as anxious to hide our spiritual scars as our physical disfigurements. Slavery had done such violence to the human spirit that the very memory of it was intolerable long after people had outlived it. Even in my time many were trying to grow without roots at all, plucking their sustenance from the air about them. We Fitzgeralds had choked off part of our roots and hidden our deep scars beneath a lopsided pride.

It was just as well I had not stumbled upon Great-Grandfather Thomas' secret until now. I lived too close to the blight of the slavery past when I was a child, and there were no vaccines to protect me. It was still too threatening and the future too uncertain to risk looking backward with critical eyes. It was only as an adult living in the shrunken world of the mid-twentieth century and from the vantage point of present-day knowledge of human experience that I could now see a fragment of personal history in proper perspective. It had taken me almost a lifetime to discover that true emancipation lies in the acceptance of the whole past, in deriving strength from all my roots, in facing up to the degradation as well as the dignity of my ancestors.

Great-Grandfather Thomas' own life had contributed greatly to this realization, but he did not have this century of accumulated experience to draw upon. He had grown up during a period in which ignorance and cruelty were more common than learning and humaneness. Few people could read and write in his time and the only local journal in his state was the *Delaware Gazette*, which came out once a week. Dueling and random gun fights were frequent in the Wilmington streets and petty offenses were punished by the stocks, pillory and public whipping post, the last surviving in Delaware to the present day. Travel was perilous and when someone contemplated a trip to Philadelphia, twenty-six miles away, all his friends and relatives came to see him the night before the stagecoach left to bid him farewell and wish him a safe journey.

Slavery was an established institution in Delaware, but the little state swung back and forth like a sensitive needle between the growing anti-slavery views of Quakers in her north county, Quakers whose Pennsylvania cousins had already abolished it, and the strong pro-slavery sentiment of settlers in Kent and Sussex counties to the south whose ancestors had come from Maryland and Virginia. The result of this ambivalence was that in 1832 Great-Grandfather Thomas had the status of a Free Person of Color in a state which still held three thousand slaves.

What a miserably small portion of freedom was this heritage we had gloried in! How hazardous was the journey from the state of a freedman to that of a free man! Great-Grandfather Thomas could now come and go at will; he could marry and have legitimate children; he could receive the wages of his own labor and buy and sell property. But Delaware law left him like a man on the edge of quicksand; a misstep and he would be sucked back into servitude. The law declared that free Negroes and mulattoes "are idle and slothful, and often prove burdensome to the neighborhood wherein they live, and are of evil example to slaves." It excluded him and his children from state-supported education and denied him the right to vote. In fact, if he were caught within a half mile of a polling place on election day without an acceptable excuse that some unforeseen emergency had brought him there, he would be thrown into jail for twenty-four hours.

The one thing he must not do was to run afoul of the law in any way. He could not testify in court on any matter unless no competent white witness could be found. A staggering fine would be imposed upon him for a minor offense and if he could not pay his fine he would be sold at public auction back into slavery for periods up to seven years. If he left his native state for more than two months the law declared him a nonresident and he could not re-enter it to live, since Delaware barred free Negroes from coming into the state.

Ironically enough, the law valued the person of a slave as property more than it did Great-Grandfather Thomas as a free Negro. If a slave was convicted of a crime and executed, the state paid his master two-thirds of his assessed value, but Great-Grandfather Thomas had little or no protection. Gangs of kidnapers had replaced pirates as public enemies and engaged in a brisk trade

of Negro snatching in open defiance of the law. They preyed upon
free blacks and mulattoes; they would seize them at night, drag
them across the Maryland line a few miles away and sell them
south for large sums. Or they'd hold them prisoners in some
desolate spot and eventually ship them south by boatloads from
a place north of Wilmington on the banks of the Delaware called
Grubbs Landing, now known as Arden.

My great-grandfather could not even carry a weapon for his
own defense like other men unless he made special application to
a justice of the peace for a license and presented a certificate
signed by five judicious, respectable white citizens of the community. Nor could he join with other free Negroes for mutual
security without grave difficulty. Meetings of more than twelve
colored people after ten o'clock at night, whether religious or
otherwise, were unlawful unless continued under the supervision
of three respectable white men. Considering the narrow limits of
his freedom, it is no wonder that Great-Grandfather Thomas
shrank from admitting a more servile status. He could not shed the
mark of his color but at least he could shed the stigma of servitude
by moving away from the place where he grew up and keeping
quiet about his past.

Another reason for his silence may have been that he married a
white woman without a slave background and, having children of
mixed parentage, needed to maintain a position of respect in their
eyes. I don't know whether Great-Grandmother Sarah Ann shared
his secret, but I doubt it would have made any difference to her if
she had known about it. She was what she was, a rawboned,
homely farm girl who made no claims to high birth, who could
neither read nor write, but who had a shrewd head on her
shoulders and a mind of her own. She was a Burton, and everybody in those days knew that if you were either a Rodney or a
Burton in Delaware you were related to almost everybody else in
the state. The Burtons were legion and had freely mixed their
blood with Indians and Negroes.

As I heard the story from Aunt Pauline, who was a young
woman when Great-Grandmother Sarah Ann died, my great-
grandmother was the oldest of three daughters and a younger son
of a farming family named Burton who lived a few miles south of

Wilmington in the township of Christiana Hundred. Great-Grandfather Thomas worked for the Burtons as hired man and coachman and they thought highly of him. He was literate, had fine manners and was a hard worker who never wasted time. But he was not too busy with his chores to fall in love with eighteen-year-old Sarah Ann, a girl about eight years younger than he. Around 1834 they ran off together and got married. Her parents never forgave her, but her younger sisters, Mary Jane and Elizabeth, who adored her, kept furtive contact. Eventually they followed her example, married the handsome mulatto Valentine brothers of Wilmington and joined the broad corridor of mixed bloods between the races.

If Great-Grandmother Sarah Ann had any misgivings about marrying a colored man, she never voiced them. Once she had made her choice, she did not look backward. Aunt Pauline said she was a tall, fierce-looking, blue-eyed, black-haired rosy-cheeked woman who exuded competence and severity from stem to stern. She was as fierce as she looked. She seldom smiled and her eyes were like twin darts that went right through you. Everybody about her walked a chalk line. She was a domineering matriarch who ruled with an iron hand and a vitriolic tongue. Everything about her was plain. She parted her hair in the middle and carried it back austerely in a tight bun, exposing the whole of her long dour face and unusually large ears. She generally wore a dark simple frock, narrow at the waist, with huge pockets, a billowing skirt, a little white lace or muslin collar pinned about her throat and on her head a black bonnet tied under the chin with long ribbons.

"I guess she needed her sharp tongue," Aunt Pauline explained. "She was always betwixt and between, getting it from both sides of the fence. You see, everybody was so mixed-up and messed-up in those days you couldn't tell which was which."

It certainly seemed that way. Though my great-grandparents had leaped the race barrier they were not as unique as might be supposed. Race prejudice was present but it had not hardened and become the terrible bugaboo of later years. Wherever there was slavery, north or south, there were mulattoes. And wherever there were mulattoes there was an increase in intermarriage because white people maintained close ties with their colored kin. Not even a slave background was a bar to intermarriage. The memory of white indentured servants, who were bound out to masters upon their arrival in the New World to repay their passage by serving for a term of years, was still very recent among immigrant groups. Negro household slaves often married their masters' daughters.

In my great-grandparents' day intermixture was so common that the states passed laws against miscegenation, but the laws were like buying insurance after the house had burned down. There already existed such a large number of mixed bloods which defied identification that it was virtually impossible in some areas to draw any boundary line between the races. One-third of Pennsylvania's people of color were near white and it was almost the same among the free colored people of northern Delaware. The law recognized this group as "Mulattoes" and sometimes favored them slightly more than the blacks.

People traveled back and forth through this corridor of mixed bloods as they chose, depending upon their appearance and the strength of their ties. In the border states race lines were so blurred that often pure-blooded whites were kidnaped and sold south into slavery as mulattoes. The free colored population was a transmission belt, constantly receiving mixed bloods through the emancipation of mulattoes, quadroons and octoroons by their conscience-stricken white kinsfolk and constantly feeding the white mainstream by fair-skinned colored people simply disappearing from the colored race and emerging as whites.

It happened all the time and since racial identification was ultimately a matter of appearance, one didn't have to go far from his birthplace or sever his family relationships to do it. The census enumerators had a hard time of it because in many cases they had to take a person's word as to which race he belonged to. When women like Great-Grandmother Sarah Ann crossed the line in reverse, married Negro men and had children of mixed blood, they turned up in succeding census returns in the Mulatto column following the designation of their children. Nobody knows how much of this changing of labels went on in those days, but from my knowledge of the "lost boundaries" of my own family, I daresay it was a common occurrence.

From all that I could find out about Great-Grandmother Sarah

Ann, she had no Negro blood, but she simply refused to countenance race lines. This is not to say that she had an easy time of it. Wherever this blue-eyed, red-faced woman went in public with her copper-skinned husband she was confronted by insinuations or repeated efforts to probe her identity. By the time she came south, she was an old hand at shutting people up. She neither admitted she was white nor denied that she was colored. She let folks think what they pleased, and as Aunt Pauline said, she didn't give a hoot because she lived at home and boarded at the same place. She had a cryptic answer which made short shrift of meddlers and she passed it on to her near-white grandchildren growing up in the South.

"If they ask you what you are, just tell 'em that what they see with their eyes, they can't carry off on their noses," she'd say, snapping off her words like pistol shots.

Being caught "betwixt and between" the races, she was always doing battle. When the colored folks got to talking about "old poor white folks," she'd redden and remark that "Folks are folks and they all look the same in the privy." And when a Rebel neighbor came on her property one day and asked, "Aint Sary, has any of the niggers been stealing your chickens or your pigs lately? If they have, just let us know and we'll take care of 'em for you," she replied, "Yes, Uncle, to tell the truth some of my chickens have been missing. The only trouble is, I don't know whether it's *white* niggers or *black* niggers that's been taking them."

My aunts said Great-Grandmother Sarah Ann was as tightfisted as Great-Grandfather Thomas was generous. They'd laugh and say that she could milk mice running or skin a mosquito and use it for tallow. She was always looking for a profit and could drive a hard bargain with the best of traders. She'd haggle over a penny as quickly as she would over a hundred dollars. Back of this penny pinching was the history of a long struggle to get a toe hold, and years of wrangling in the marketplace. I gathered that until my great-grandparents moved to Pennsylvania in 1855, Great-Grandmother Sarah Ann had to wear the pants and hold the Fitzgerald family pursestrings.

They didn't talk much about those early years, but from the few things they said, one knew their path had been rugged. They stood almost alone. It was said that some of the Burton men were out for Great-Grandfather's blood and had made threats as to what they'd do if they caught up with him.

Money was scarce in those times, and with farmers everything depended upon the crops. My great-grandparents had no land and had to rent or farm on shares. They had to weather a depression and two severe crop failures in the first few years of their married life. They dared not borrow or get in debt. Delaware law held a Negro or mulatto man subject to imprisonment or servitude for debt long after it had abolished this penalty for others in the state. Great-Grandmother Sarah Ann had to endure the hardships of farm life while having babies almost every year. In the twenty years it took them to save enough to buy a farm in Pennsylvania and move there, she lost six of her twelve children in childbirth or from tuberculosis in their early infancy.

Hard times, sickly babies, bad crops and fear of family reprisals were bad enough, but her chief worry was over Great-Grand-father's safety. He wasn't the kind of man you could keep tied down and he seemed to have no fear. He said the Lord would take care of him, but Great-Grandmother Sarah Ann did not profess such faith in the Lord. She didn't join a church until she was an old woman and late in life she confessed to Aunt Pauline that she did not even know how to pray. She had only her instincts and her loyalty to guide her.

She never knew when Great-Grandfather Thomas left home whether she'd see him alive again. His tall bronze figure was an open target when he went to Wilmington. Negro snatchers prowled the streets on the lookout for quarry and the more up-standing and intelligent a colored man looked, the higher price the kidnapers could get for him. Of the two of them, I think she suffered more. She had to stand by and watch her husband thread-ing his way through the barbed-wire wilderness a person of color must travel. She knew the sharp difference in treatment when she was alone and when they were together in public. When they drove into town on business, drunken white men jeered at them and hurled threats at Great-Grandfather Thomas. There were limits to his restraint and the one thing she couldn't afford was to let him get mixed up in a street brawl. White men had been

known to provoke a colored man into a fight, bring him into court
where he couldn't testify and get themselves a slave cheap.

Great-Grandmother Sarah Ann held her peace for a while and
then she put her foot down. She took over the family trading
while Great-Grandfather Thomas stayed behind and looked after
the farm. This was their pattern for years and even after they came
south they went their separate ways in the business world. Great-
Grandfather learned not to argue with her. It would have done
no good and besides it had its advantages. In the marketplace she
was a white woman among other white traders and was not
penalized in prices on the basis of color.

Twice a week, as was the farmers' custom in Delaware, Great-
Grandmother Sarah Ann drove to town to sell their produce and
do the family buying. On Wednesdays she went to Wilmington
and on Saturdays to Philadelphia. The trip to Philadelphia was a
long, lonely one and there was always the danger of being waylaid
by a robber on the way home as Great-Grandmother Sarah Ann
drove her wagon through stretches of desolate woods.

She prepared herself for this emergency. She never displayed her
wealth in public and her plainness of dress made her inconspicuous. When she finished her trading she put her bills inside her
stocking in her shoe. She had a big pocket in her skirt which she
called "the World." Just behind this pocket was a long slit
through which she could reach a second pocket sewn into the
folds of her voluminous petticoat. She carried a few small coins in
the outer pocket, wrapped her hard money in a cloth and dropped
it into the inner pocket. Whenever she was stopped on the road
and ordered to hand over her money, she'd run her hand into her
skirt pocket and pull out the small coins, turning the pocket
inside out.

"Mister, I'm a poor woman. This is every cent I have *in the
World.*"

These were Grandfather Fitzgerald's roots. Looking back both
ways from the arch my grandparents formed, I came to a junction
of the races and slavery complicated by kinship on both sides of
the hotly contested issue. At each end of the arch a strong woman
shouldered much of the burden of the conflict. Great-Grandmother Sarah Ann Fitzgerald and Mary Ruffin Smith, who had

gone into the making of my grandparents, were born about the same time and each grew up in a slave state. Each lived through the Civil War and the Reconstruction era. Each spent her last years in Orange County only a few miles apart from the other and both passed off the scene within a few years of one another.

Here the similarity ended. Great-Grandmother Sarah Ann had none of the privileges of wealth and none of the social graces. She was a peasant who never read a book or painted a picture or had a personal maid or house servants. She had to struggle for everything she got. She claimed no religion and joined no societies for uplift. She was more like a field officer leading a charge than a mother of tender sensibilities, but in my eyes she outshone the more gifted Mary Ruffin Smith, whose philanthropy won her a marble plaque of honor in Memorial Hall at the University of North Carolina.

From the moment Great-Grandmother Sarah Ann married Great-Grandfather Thomas, she was enlisted in a cause which called for raw courage and no retreats. Her children were free born, but she watched them grow up on a battleground tormented by the pull and tug of their dual identities. Since they inherited heavily from their white ancestors in appearance, they had the choice of "going white" or "staying colored." Having observed how heavy a load was the burden of color, Great-Grandmother might easily have steered her children toward the white race. It would be all the harder for them to withstand the temptation to escape when the pressures were heavy. Too many white women have married men of Negro blood only to discover that they would rather their children be dead than have to endure what Negroes have had to endure. That Great-Grandmother Sarah Ann did not waver in her choice revealed a rare quality of strength. She threw her weight in the direction of remaining in the Negro race. And the delicate compass which kept her family pointed in that direction was a sickly, nearsighted boy with a thirst for knowledge, one of the children she almost lost in those early grim rounds with death. She and Great-Grandfather Thomas named him Robert George Fitzgerald.

6

GRANDFATHER ROBERT FITZGERALD, the third oldest of twelve children, was born in New Castle County, Delaware, October 24, 1840. During the first twenty years of his life, the threat of tuberculosis hung over his family and there was seldom a time when the home was free of sickness or death. The four oldest children—Elizabeth, William, Grandfather Robert and Richard Burton—survived, but there was a long period in which my great-grandparents buried six of their young who weakened and died before they got past infancy. Only two of those later children outlived the threat—Mary Jane, who was born when Grandfather was fourteen, and little Agnes, who came when he was eighteen.

He was one of the puny ones who had escaped death only because of a stubborn will to live. Delicate and frail from birth, he struggled through one sick spell after another. The doctor told his mother he had only one good lung and would probably never reach thirty. Moreover, he was nearsighted and as he grew up he suffered from attacks of night blindness. If one of these attacks came on while he was away from home alone after dark, he'd lose his way, stumble off the road and crawl about on his hands and knees in the woods for hours trying to find it again.

Continued hardship and grief had made Great-Grandmother Sarah Ann harsh and tight lipped over the years, but she reserved a tenderness for her "Robbie, dear boy," which she rarely revealed

to her other children. He was her favorite, partly because he
seemed wise beyond his years and partly because he represented
her lone victory over the plague which had wiped out half her
brood. She kept him close to her, made him her house and stable
boy and her companion to market. When he grew older, she relied
upon him for advice in most weighty matters and whatever course
he chose she could be counted upon to swing the family behind
his decision.

From early childhood, Grandfather was the most thoughtful
and sensitive of the Fitzgerald children. His brothers were sturdy,
rough-and-tumble fellows who could work hard but cared more
for good times than they did for deep study. Billy Fitzgerald, the
oldest boy, was more happy-go-lucky than his brothers. A handsome olive-skinned, hazel-eyed, wavy-haired lad, he had a droll
sense of humor and a great liking for the ladies as he grew older.
Fiery, red-faced, blond Richie had the same sharp blue eyes and
shrewd trader's head as his mother. He was quick to drive a hard
bargain and even quicker with his fists. His hot temper led him
into many skirmishes and even as an old man in his seventies he
used to laugh and say, "By golly, if I was dying and somebody
made me mad, I'd stop dying long enough to fight about it."

Robbie was shy, reserved and devoutly religious. He flowered
under a word of praise and could be flattened by an angry look.
If nature had robbed him of robustness it had generously endowed
him with tenacity. He was a slow, painstakingly thorough worker
who seldom gave up on anything he started out to do. His philosophy was summed up in a little story he used to tell me.

"Two frisky little frogs used to chase one another about a
springhouse where a farmer kept his milk. One night they jumped
into a large can of milk standing in the water to cool. They
paddled about trying to jump out again, but the neck of the can
was narrow and the cream was rising fast. Each time they made the
leap they fell back again. Finally they were both exhausted. One
little frog said mournfully, 'We'll never get out of here,' and with
that he sank into the heavy cream and was drowned. The other
little frog kept kicking feebly but with all his might. By morning
he felt something solid above him and found his kicks had made
a tiny lump of butter. He crawled on top of it and jumped out

of the can. So never get discouraged when you're in a fix. Just keep on kicking till you come up on butter."

Grandfather's earliest memories were of family prayers, which his father led on Sunday evenings before they went to bed. Great-Grandfather Thomas' religion was not the shouting kind; it was a quiet partnership with God, who was the senior member of the Fitzgerald household. The weekly accounting with the Lord was thorough and complete, and as regular as milking the cows or hoeing the corn. Everyone sat quietly while Great-Grandfather Thomas read slowly from the family Bible, pausing now and then to study a difficult word. That he could read at all made him a slender bridge over which his children could walk with heightened self-respect.

When he had finished and closed the Bible, everyone got down on his knees and bowed his head on his chair. Great-Grandfather Thomas began his prayer, talking easily and naturally to God as if He were in the room and deeply involved in every detail of the family's affairs. The prayer extended from the family circle outward to close and remote relatives, to friends and to all sorts and conditions of men. Nobody was left out, not even one's enemies. At the close everybody joined in to repeat the Lord's Prayer. This ritual which came down through the family over several generations seemed its greatest resource in time of trouble. Each member of the household was made to feel important in the eyes of the Almighty and that he had his place in the universe.

Great-Grandmother Sarah Ann's religion was less mystical than Great-Grandfather's but just as thoroughgoing. She had a passion for cleanliness and orderliness and she trained my grandfather rigorously along these lines. This training was a major asset in later years when he went blind and had to find everything through his fingers. He loathed harum-scarum ways and he'd fume if his inquisitive cane stumbled upon a broom or dustpan I'd forgotten to put away after I'd used it.

I can hear him now saying, "Everything has a place and belongs in it so that you can put your hands on it in the dark of night."

As if to drive home the point he told me how he had learned this lesson as a little boy.

"I left a pitchfork lying in the hay one afternoon and forgot about it. That night at supper we heard a loud commotion at the barn and I was sent down to see whether a blacksnake was after the chickens. I ran down to the barn and leaped through the doorway without thinking. I landed on top of the upturned pitchfork, which went right through one of my bare feet. My mother had to come and hold me by the shoulders while my father yanked and yanked at the pitchfork to pull it out. For weeks I had to hobble about with my foot all wrapped up in raw-meat poultices. I came near losing it, but I can tell you one thing: I never left tools lying about carelessly after that."

Another time his careful training had strange consequences. He was taught never to do anything by half measures. Whatever he tackled must be done right or not at all. This principle worked well until the day he hired out to Farmer Hoskins, a shriveled, crotchety soul who lived alone in a hollow near their place and farmed a few acres. Great-Grandmother Sarah Ann was against the idea from the start. Old Hoskins was known to be the stingiest man in New Castle County and one who couldn't keep hired help. Besides, it was rumored he had once owned slaves and she wanted no son of hers working for a slaveowner. Great-Grandfather Thomas couldn't see any harm in it. Robbie was a well-mannered boy and a good worker who was eager to please. Hoskins should have no complaints. So Grandfather hired out to Farmer Hoskins.

From the moment he arrived on the place Hoskins began shouting at him and hurrying him from one job to another. He milked the cow, lugged slops for the hogs, chopped kindling and dug potatoes while Hoskins ran behind him screaming in his ear that he wasn't working fast enough. He sawed firewood, stacked it neatly in the shed and was putting his saw away when Hoskins descended upon him bellowing that he wasn't going to pay him good hard money to poke along like frozen molasses.

Grandfather laid down the saw and looked Hoskins straight in the eye.

"I'm trying to do my work right, sir, and I'm doing the best I can. If you keep shouting at me I won't be able to do anything at all."

Hoskins whipped off his leather belt and struck the boy a terrific blow across the shoulders. Grandfather was too shocked to feel the pain. Automatically he began to run and did not stop running until he reached home. Great-Grandmother Sarah Ann took one look at his blanched face and did not need to ask him what happened. She pulled up his shirt and saw the long red welt on his back.

"Damn his soul! Damn his blasted slaver's soul!" she screamed.

It was the only time Grandfather ever heard his mother utter a curse. She swore she'd never let him hire out again as long as they lived in Delaware, and she kept her promise. She sent him to school in Wilmington instead. As for Grandfather, he never got over that experience. Throughout life whenever he was frightened or upset, great red splotches jumped out on his body as if he had been beaten with a lash.

Grandfather thought of Wilmington as his native town, since he was born in Christiana Hundred a few miles from there. Although he often said he was ashamed of having been born in a slave state, he had a fierce attachment for Wilmington. He spent much of his early youth in its busy streets, loved its boats and waterways, had learned to swim in the Delaware, went fishing with his father and brothers along the river banks and heard Great-Grandfather Thomas tell many tales of digging for pirates' treasures along the sandy marshes near the river's mouth. He attended his first school in Wilmington and as a young man taught there for a while.

The Wilmington of his boyhood in the 1840's and 1850's was a bustling little stagecoach and shipping center of twenty thousand people of whom three thousand were free people of color. It was on the mail route from Maine to Georgia and was a great port through which immigrants from Europe had poured for many years. In colonial days the town was settled by Swedish, Dutch and English groups. In Great-Grandfather Thomas' youth, it was a refuge for the French who fled the Napoleonic wars. When Grandfather Robert was a boy, refugees from the German Revolution of 1848 and the Irish Potato Famine swelled the growing town. By that time there was only a handful of Negro slaves left in New Castle County. Most of Delaware's two thousand slaves were found in the southern part of the state.

Built on high ground between two streams, Wilmington sloped

gently southward from Brandywine Creek north of the town to Christiana River. Gristmills flourished along the Brandywine while fishing sloops and schooners pushed upstream on the Christiana to the wharf just east of the Market Street drawbridge. Smaller vessels could continue upstream for about four miles. The Brandywine and Christiana joined a little east of the town and emptied into the broad Delaware two miles away.

Twice a week in season, Great-Grandmother Sarah Ann drove to market. She liked to get to town by six o'clock and have her stall set up before her competitors arrived. Everything was gotten in readiness the night before. They'd gather the fruits and vegetables, tie up the chickens and ducks and churn the milk. Grandfather said that in those days they made butter by pouring the cream into a huge barrel with large paddles attached to a long shaft. He'd hitch the horse to the shaft and drive him round and round in a circle until the butter came. Then Great-Grandmother Sarah Ann salted it, placed it in pound and half-pound molds, kneaded and squeezed until all air holes disappeared, then weighed and tested each print to make sure she was selling a "solid pound." She told her grandchildren proudly that in all her years of going to market the town authorities never once confiscated her butter because of short weight.

On days they made the long journey to Philadelphia, the entire family was up by midnight. They hitched the horse to the big, black-covered Dearborn wagon, loaded in the butter, eggs, baskets of peaches and apples, garden vegetables, and chickens, geese or turkeys tied together by the legs. They hung a lantern on the side and by one o'clock Great-Grandmother Sarah Ann and Robbie were jogging off into the night amid the screeching of excited fowls and howling of the Fitzgerald dogs which were left behind.

Grandfather had a particular fondness for Bags, a disreputable looking bulldog on the Fitzgerald place, but Great-Grandmother Sarah Ann wouldn't hear of taking him along.

"The market is no place for a barking dog and that's the word with the bark on it," she said.

So Bags had to be tied up every time they left home, much to his and Grandfather's chagrin. Great-Grandmother Sarah Ann usually rode up front alone and drove the horse while Grandfather curled up in the rear with the produce and often fell asleep. Once he fell asleep while they were bumping along early one morning and woke suddenly to find the wagon had stopped.

"If you know what's good for you, Mister, you'll take your hands off that bridle," he heard his mother saying. She sounded more annoyed than frightened. Grandfather scrambled up and peeped through the canvas in time to see the robber draw a bowie knife and start for the wagon seat. At that moment a growl came from underneath the wagon and Bags leaped at the robber's throat. The dog had the man on the ground and was about to chew him to pieces before Great-Grandmother Sarah Ann and Grandfather could jump down and pull him off. The dog had broken his chain and trotted along quietly behind the wagon for miles without either of them knowing he was there.

"That robber nearly scared me out of a year's growth," chuckled Grandfather, "but at least Bags got his chance to go to market for once in his life."

In Wilmington, Great-Grandmother Sarah Ann rented a stall near Market House on High Street (now Fourth) between Market and Shipley streets, which ran north and south the length of the town. Like other farmers, she backed her wagon against the curb, unhitched the horse and sent Grandfather off to water and graze him, arranged her goods attractively in her stall and sold directly to passing customers. The Wilmington curbstone market is an old tradition, and farmers from outlying parts of Delaware and near-by Maryland and Pennsylvania have been coming to town twice a week since William Shipley built the first market house on High Street in 1736. Today if you visit the city on market days, you will see the farmers' vehicles lined up along the curb on one side of the street for blocks. They now use King Street, one block east of the old market site, and they bring their goods to town in jeeps, station wagons, small trucks or the luggage compartments of their cars, but little else has changed. Each farmer has his own little stand on the sidewalk and sells to passersby as farmers did in Great-Grandmother Sarah Ann's day and long before that. If you talk with some of them today, you'll discover that the same family has had a stand in Wilmington for three or four generations.

Grandfather remembered market days as the most exciting of his boyhood. When selling was brisk, he'd weigh up and measure out for customers and count change for his mother. When trade was slow, he'd wander about the streets and down along the wharves, or sometimes visit his Valentine cousins on French Street, not far from the marketplace. There was much for a curious boy to see and hear. Most information passed along by word of mouth and the market was a natural place for the exchange of news and opinion. On the south side of Market House near Shipley Street was the Swan Hotel, where the Philadelphia stagecoaches came and went twice a day. Soldiers drifted back from the Mexican War talking of gold which had been discovered in California. Sailors hinted darkly of mysterious cargoes which never came into port but which were landed on a desolate strip of beach down the Atlantic Coast on dark moonless nights. Negroes were still being captured in Africa, smuggled into the country and sold south to traders for handsome profits. But there were times when sailors returned empty-handed from these strange voyages, for their ships had run across the path of government patrol boats and they had dumped the Negroes overboard and left them to the waves. There were other horrible tales told in the marketplace by people who had survived the great famine in Ireland. They talked of desperate men who beat little children to death to get a pound of meat and of those who ate the flesh of people who had already starved, to keep themselves alive.

Grandfather loved to stand on the wharves and watch the boats coming and going. On clear days he could see the white sails of vessels moving up and down the Delaware. Wilmington had a fleet of whaling ships, some of which were called "temperance ships" because they sailed away for periods up to three years with men aboard who had been sent by their families to cure themselves of drinking. It was like a holiday in town when one of these ships returned after a long absence bringing beautiful shells, whalebone and other treasures from foreign lands. When the oyster schooners came in from a big haul the townspeople flocked down to the Market Street wharf to go aboard and buy oysters. One could buy a half peck with salt and soda crackers thrown in for about five cents, and everybody would open and eat his oysters on the spot.

The docks were piled high with watermelons, baskets of potatoes, fruits, vegetables and grain for shipment to northern cities. Schooners brought in loads of lump plaster from Boston and Newport which the farmers hauled away to the mills, where the plaster was ground for use on the land. Watching the heavily laden boats moving down the river bound for distant ports, young Robert Fitzgerald dreamed of going to sea someday.

Once a year after the harvest the Fitzgeralds joined their Burton and Valentine relatives and drove about to the big camp meetings in Pennsylvania and northern Delaware which brought together people from three states. The crops were in and the farmers were enjoying a brief holiday. It was a time for family reunions, visiting among friends and feasting as well as praying and repentance.

The most famous of these was the Big Quarterly Meeting, which took place in Wilmington on the last Sunday of August every year. Like other families, the Fitzgeralds dressed in their best clothes, packed huge lunches into the Dearborn and drove to Wilmington to take part in the festivities. The Big Quarterly was held at the African Methodist Union Church located in a small grove on the west side of French Street between Eighth and Ninth. It had been a meeting place for people of color ever since Peter Spencer organized the little Union of Africans back in 1799. From fifteen to twenty thousand people attended the annual meetings. Slaves mingled with free persons, for the Big Quarterly was the one large holiday masters gave to trusted servants after the crops were in.

While the meeting itself began at six o'clock on Sunday morning and ended around eleven that night, from early Saturday morning Negro farmers began arriving in town with their families. Teams of every kind lined the streets for blocks, and since the little church could hold only a fraction of the multitude, services were kept going all day by relays of ministers and singing bands—roving groups of itinerant singers who followed camp meetings from place to place each year.

Other services were carried on outside the church in a corner of the grove, but the main business of the Big Quarterly was

m dawn until the last team rumbled homeward long
ight, it was the duty of everyone who came to stuff
ong tables covered with flowing white cloths stretched
from cnd to end of the grove. Eating stands packed closely
together lined both sides of French Street for several blocks and
overflowed into the side streets. Tables and stands sagged under
piles of fried chicken, roasted beef, barbecued pork, smoked ham,
meat pies and dumplings, pickled pigs' feet, fried fish, sausage
puddings and scrapple. There were great slabs of golden cornbread
soaking in butter, pans of yeast rolls and crusty brown yeast loaves,
pots of steaming corn rigged up on little campfires, greens and
cabbage, crocks of coleslaw, tomatoes and spiced cucumber pickles,
preserves, pies, cakes, watermelons, lemonade and even ice cream.
Hawkers yelled themselves hoarse to attract buyers for their food.
Almost as many white people came to observe the gaiety and buy
meals from the stands as did colored people. It was the one time of
the year when slavery and hard times were forgotten, and for a day
at least even slaves felt like free men.

It seemed to me only natural that Grandfather should go to
school as a boy. Actually, it was very unusual for a child of color
to receive any formal education in those days, especially in a slave
state. Free public schools were just getting under way in the
northern states and Negro children were not encouraged to attend.
Throughout the slave states education was prohibited. Most laws
made it a criminal offense to teach a Negro to read and write.
Assemblies of slaves, free Negroes or mulattoes held for the purpose
of receiving mental instruction were unlawful and punishable by
fines, imprisonment or flogging. Delaware did not go that far; it
merely earmarked all school funds for white children and left the
colored children to get education the best way they could. Only
187 of more than 18,000 free people of color in the state—one out
of every hundred—were attending school in 1850.

The Quakers of New Castle County had worked persistently to
develop schools for colored children since 1801, and by the time
Grandfather came along they had two excellent elementary schools
in operation—one for boys and one for girls. He received his first
formal instruction at the African School on Sixth Street in Wil-

mington. Had he been a more robust boy he might not have gotten any schooling at all. Farming folks needed every hand at home to help out, but Grandfather had an eagerness for knowledge and his parents also felt he'd never be strong enough to earn his living on the land so they encouraged his efforts to become a "scholar." At that it was an uphill struggle, interrupted by periods of illness and the necessity to stay home during the planting season, but he went as often as he could and studied hard in between times to keep up with the work.

Despite irregular attendance, he got a strong foundation in the three R's. The Quakers were thoroughgoing schoolmasters and dedicated to their work. They believed that emancipation and education went hand in hand and worked fervently toward both goals. Every child of color properly fitted for an occupation was further proof that Negroes were capable and worthy of freedom.

Grandfather's Quaker schooling was a great boon to the Fitzgerald family. Before long he was reading almanacs and newspapers and explaining what they meant. As he progressed he began teaching his brothers and sister what he learned in school. Evenings after supper, Great-Grandmother Sarah Ann would clear the kitchen table and Lizzie, Billy and Richie would gather around the lamp sharing a primer while Robbie assumed the manner of a stern schoolmaster and had them recite the ABC's. In time they were reading a little, learning to write and do sums in arithmetic. Great-Grandmother Sarah Ann did not attempt to learn, but sat near by with her patchwork, pleased that her children were getting some book knowledge.

Grandfather absorbed other influences at the African School in Wilmington which shaped his later development but which were less communicable to his family. It was a natural training ground for Abolitionism and the pupils learned of the growing struggle for emancipation along with their lessons. They were regularly examined by a committee of Quakers who visited the school to maintain high standards and get firsthand information in their work of raising funds for its support. Most of these were men and women whose anti-slavery activities were well known to people of color.

Chief among them was Thomas Garrett, a tireless member of

the school committee whose concern for education was rivaled only by his labors on behalf of fugitive slaves. Portly, rosy-cheeked, red-haired "Father Thomas," in his wide-brimmed hat and long black Quaker waistcoat, was a familiar figure about the school. Grandfather had known him ever since he could remember. He was an edge-tool maker and iron merchant whose house and store was on Shipley Street near the marketplace. The Fitzgeralds traded there and often brought their tools to Mr. Garrett to be mended.

A zestful man of bubbling good humor, Father Thomas inspired confidence and affection in young and old. He seldom missed an opportunity to talk to the pupils about "God's poor escaping from the prison house of slavery." To help "God's poor" was the central purpose of his life, and had been so since his early youth when he joined the Anti-Slavery Society in his native Pennsylvania. When a young man of twenty-four he rescued a free woman of color who had been kidnaped from his father's house and from that time he considered it his life's mission to assist fugitive slaves.

The most outspoken Abolitionist in Delaware, Garrett was also the most dangerous threat to slaveowners in that part of the country. His home in Wilmington had been a refuge for runaway slaves since he settled there in 1822 and was one of the most efficient "stations" on the Underground Railroad system. Utterly fearless, he carried on his work right under the noses of the authorities. Wilmington was the route most traveled by slaves escaping from the eastern shore of Maryland and making their way along the swamps and waterways as they moved northward toward Pennsylvania. Both Harriet Tubman and Frederick Douglass had come through this town when they escaped. A fugitive's hope was never greater than when he reached this point in his journey because he was then only eight miles from free soil.

Wilmington's very nearness to free Pennsylvania made it the most hazardous of stops and required superlative skill on the part of Underground agents to get runaways safely over the line. Sheriffs' and slaveowners' representatives combed the Wilmington streets and closely watched all roads leading north from the town. Father Thomas was admirably fitted for his mission. Blessed with boundless resourcefulness and vitality and the knack of making friends, he developed a network of anonymous helpers of both races ready to do his bidding at all times. They kept him informed of danger, guided slaves to his house and were part of a chain of communication between innumerable links of the Underground Railroad in and around Wilmington.

Quakerlike, Garrett had never encouraged slaves to flee, knowing the perils involved and the heavy penalties which awaited them if they were caught. Runaways were dangerous examples and were often marked by a brand "S" on the cheek, an eye gouged out, an ear torn off or missing fingers. Once a slave's urge for liberty overcame his fear of being "sold down the river," mutilation or death, and he embarked on his perilous journey, he knew through the unfailing grapevine that if he could reach Father Thomas' house in Wilmington, he was safe. Garrett was never known to surrender a fugitive. Utterly fearless, he'd calmly wave off the pistols and bowie knives pursuing slaveowners thrust into his face and say, "On with thee. Anyone who stoops to such low methods is a coward and I will have no dealings with him." He used every remedy in the lawbooks to prevent a fugitive's return and when he exhausted legal channels he had no hesitancy in assisting a slave in his own self-help toward liberty.

Several times a week, and later almost every night, an exhausted fugitive slipped out of the shadows and tapped lightly on the window of the hardware shop on Shipley Street. A few seconds later the slave was swallowed up in the darkness inside, and it was as if the slave had vanished from the face of the earth. The most rigorous search by the authorities who kept close watch on his house proved fruitless. Sometimes members of a whole family arrived singly during the course of a night.

He'd hide the slaves until they were fed and rested from their long ordeal and it was safe to send them onward. He'd then direct them to his wife Rachel's kinsfolk, Isaac and Dinah Mendenhall, who lived ten miles away near Kennett Square, Pennsylvania. If word came that the Mendenhall house was being watched, he'd reroute them to the home of John and Hannah Cox, another Quaker couple near Longwood, or he might send them to Chandler and Hannah Darlington, whose home was just over the line. Then he'd post a letter to William Still, energetic Negro secretary of the Pennsylvania Anti-Slavery Society's vigilance committee, informing him of a "shipment of black Bibles" or "bales of black wool." The Pennsylvania "conductors" forwarded the fugitives by various routes to Philadelphia where William Still received them, documented their escape and dug up money to send them on to New England or Canada.

In his highly dangerous operations, Garrett used bold methods to escape detection. He'd think nothing of dressing a slave in Rachel Garrett's clothes, complete with shawl and heavy veil. He'd leave the house with his "wife" hanging onto his arm, graciously assist "her" into his carriage, drive leisurely through the streets of town until he came to the outskirts. Here "Rachel" was suddenly converted into a Negro man, hurried into a waiting carriage and carried on to the Mendenhalls' as fast as the horses could gallop. Garrett might even send a slave on his way walking slowly through the heart of Wilmington with a hoe or rake over his shoulder—or, if a woman, a basket of clothes on her head—knowing none would suspect the fugitive of being other than a Negro servant going to work.

Everybody in Wilmington knew of Garrett's activities, since he made no secret of them. The people of color almost worshiped him, and referred to him as "Our Moses." He had earned their devotion through his willingness to pay whatever it cost to uphold his ideal. In 1848, Elizabeth Turner and C. T. Glanding, Maryland slaveowners, sued Garrett and another Quaker, John Hunn, claiming the two men had harbored a family of eight fugitives and helped them escape. From the evidence, it appeared that Garrett had scrupulously followed the law and had the fugitives discharged from prison where they were being held, there being no evidence they were slaves. Nevertheless, the slaveowners were determined to press the case and ruin Garrett, and it was said that the jury was packed to ensure his defeat.

The suit was brought in the federal circuit court at New Castle under an old federal law of 1793 allowing slaveowners to recover penalties from any person who harbored a runaway slave. Two of Delaware's ablest lawyers argued the case and Chief Justice Roger B. Taney of the United States Supreme Court sat with U.S. District Judge Willard Hall to hear the trials. When the jury brought in verdicts for the slaveowners, Mr. Justice Taney held that under the law they were entitled to two penalties for each slave harbored. The ruling and the verdict were staggering blows for Abolitionism as well as Garrett, but when the marshal of the court turned to Garrett after the verdict was in and remarked that he hoped Mr. Garrett would mind his business from now on and stop meddling with slaves, Garrett rose and addressed the court and crowd of spectators. Said he:

"I have assisted fourteen hundred slaves in the past twenty-five years on their way to the North. I now consider this penalty imposed upon me as a license for the remainder of my life. I am now past sixty and have not a dollar to my name, but be that as it may, if anyone knows of a poor slave who needs shelter and a breakfast, send him to me, as I now publicly pledge myself to double my diligence and never neglect an opportunity to assist a slave to obtain freedom, so help me God!"

He spoke for more than an hour through hisses and cheers, but when he finished one of the jurors leaped across the benches and grasped his hands. There were tears in his eyes.

"I beg your forgiveness, Mr. Garrett," he said.

The fines amounted to $5,400 and wiped out Garrett's life's earnings. Even his household furniture was struck off at auction to help pay the fines. He cheerfully started all over again at sixty, borrowed money to rebuild his business, eventually repaid his loans and prospered even more than before the trials. Above all he kept his courtroom pledge of 1848. By 1863, his records showed that 2,700 fugitive slaves had passed through his hands in their flight to freedom, not counting the hundreds he had helped before he began keeping records. He was so successful, particularly after he joined forces with Harriet Tubman after her escape in 1849, that Maryland offered a reward of $10,000 for his arrest in that state. Father Thomas laughed and said he knew he was an old man but he was worth more than that; if Maryland would raise the reward to $20,000, he'd come over and collect it himself.

Through nearly fifty years of exceedingly dangerous work, Garrett never lost his sense of humor. One downstate slaveowner threatened to shoot him on sight if he ever showed his face in those parts. Garrett replied, "I think of going that way before long and I will call upon thee." Some time later the slaveowner who made the threat was flabbergasted to find Thomas Garrett standing at his door.

"How does thee do, friend?" Garrett asked cheerfully. "Here I am, thee can shoot me if thee likes."

And, of course, there was no shooting.

Garrett's influence on serious-minded little Robert Fitzgerald was tremendous. While others who supported slavery stressed the unfitness of the black man, he pictured the slave as brave and enduring and eager to help his own cause. He told of the men and women who risked everything in their desperate break for liberty; how they became hunted creatures lying out in the swamps for days without food or water; how they hid in potato holes and haystacks, waded through deep marshes, swam rivers, shivered through snowstorms and walked barefoot for hundreds of miles to reach free territory. When Father Thomas talked about "God's poor," the magnificence of their efforts shone through their poverty of circumstance. As a small boy listening to these eloquent pleas, Grandfather knew without knowing how or why that some-day he would be a part of the great effort Garrett described.

7

WHEN Grandfather was fourteen, his family moved to
Chester County, Pennsylvania. One Saturday morning in
early 1855, Great-Grandmother Sarah Ann drove with Great-
Grandfather Thomas over to Upper Oxford township to buy a
farm. Her secret pocket bulged with their savings of over twenty
years—$2,000 tied up in a cloth. When they finished their business
that day they owned a twenty-five-acre farm free from encum-
brances for which they had paid $1,632 in cash. Back in Delaware
a short time later the Fitzgeralds loaded their household goods
into the Dearborn, tied the cattle behind and journeyed through
the country to their new home in time for spring planting.

It was an excellent piece of property, uplands on high ground
where one could stand and look in all directions over the neatly
fenced fields and rolling blue-green hills of Chester County. The
farm was in the little village of Hinsonville on the edge of Upper
Oxford township on the main turnpike between Philadelphia and
Baltimore and eight miles north of the Maryland line. The five-
room log house, which sat close to the road behind a row of tall
maples, was not a large one but it was ample for their needs. There
were three bedrooms upstairs under the eaves and downstairs were
the kitchen and parlor. What they liked most about it was the
great stone fireplace in the parlor which Grandfather said was so
wide that a child could sit on each end of a big log blazing in the

center without being burned. Outside near the house was a deep limestone well and beyond the house was an apple and peach orchard. A good-sized barn stood in the front field near the road. The house and barn have long since disappeared but if you visited the spot today you would find a wide depression in the empty field where the cellar used to be.

What was most important to my great-grandparents, who now had a son who was a serious scholar and wanted to go on with his education, was that their farm was a few hundred yards down the road from the site where a new school was to be built. Several months earlier the Pennsylvania legislature had chartered Ashmun Institute to be located near Hinsonville as an "institution of learning for the scientific, classical and theological education of Negro youth of the male sex." The foundations of the school had not yet been dug, but the village was a prosperous one and there was a meetinghouse and burying ground adjoining the school site. It was a good place for the Fitzgerald family to settle.

By this move the Fitzgeralds anchored themselves more firmly to the aspirations and traditions of the Negro race. Such anchorage was not an automatic process for them; in fact, considering the later history of their close relatives, it was a deliberate choice. Anyone who has been part of a family of mixed bloods in the United States or West Indies has lived intimately with the unremitting search for whiteness. To deny that it is part of one's heritage would be like saying one had no parents. It did not matter how far back the mixture took place or whether the proportion of white blood was great or small. There needed only to be evidence of the mixture.

It was a primitive urge, born of ancient bitter knowledge in the jungle through nature's slow mutations over millions of years. Weaker animals survived when they escaped detection by losing themselves in the mass of their surroundings. The mink, brown in summer, turned ermine in winter and blended himself with the snow. The chameleon turned green in a thicket of leaves and brown when he crawled on the bark of a tree.

It was first a search for safety and then a quest for acceptance—a false god having many worshipers, a phantom and mirage—but the quest would continue as long as the flat surface of color remained the lone dimension of a human being. During two hundred or more years of American slavery and the century of its aftermath, one lesson was pounded into the brain day after day, generation after generation. Whatever notions one might have about the rights of man, one thing seemed certain: so long as white men enslaved and oppressed black men, so long as white men were the hunters and black men the hunted, whiteness—the ability to pass unnoticed in the crowd, the power to avoid humiliation and abuse —was one's most immediate and effective protection, beyond even the law. I daresay that if the country had been settled by black men who enslaved white men, we might have witnessed a relentless search for blackness instead of the other way round.

The Fitzgeralds lived in a border zone where two slave states touched upon free Pennsylvania. The growing traffic of runaways made every recognizable person of color suspect; the slightest taint of pigment was a double hazard. If you were not a potential victim of kidnapers, your color automatically raised the issue of your slave or free status when slave hunters were scouring the countryside in search of fugitives. A freedman's certificate of manumission was as precious to him as a passport now is in a foreign country and was recorded at the local county courthouse for his protection. After 1851, not even being born free made one safe, for the stringent Fugitive Slave Law prohibited a person of color from testifying as to his own status. He must find white witnesses in the community who knew the circumstances of his birth and were willing to take the stand in his behalf.

Since the chief argument for continued slavery in America was that the black man was by nature inferior to the white and fitted only for bondage, the issue was fought out in the blood as well as in legislatures and on battlefields. Color was the badge of inferiority which survived slave chain and auction block. Official recognition was given to gradations in color for nearly a half century after the Civil War ended. United States Census enumerators were directed to be particularly careful to distinguish "blacks" (defined as those having three-fourths or more of black blood) from "mulattoes" (three-eighths to five-eighths black blood), "quadroons" (one-fourth black blood) and "octoroons" (one-eighth or any trace of black blood). In the search for whiteness, mixed bloods reversed the definitions. An octoroon had seven-eighths or more white blood, a quadroon three-fourths white blood and a mulatto five-eighths to three-eighths white blood.

Consequently, an octoroon felt superior to a quadroon; a quadroon felt superior to a mulatto; a mulatto felt superior to all who were less than mulattoes, and so on down the line. Among mixed bloods, one never made the mistake of calling an octoroon a quadroon or a quadroon a mulatto, although all mixed bloods were loosely called mulattoes. When people had the same parents and the proportion of white blood was not a factor, gradations of color and features determined prestige within the family. Of these, complexion had the greatest single value. Seldom was there a greater struggle for supremacy than among sisters and brothers who knew all the subtleties of caste. The wider the variations among them the more bitter the struggle. Even when variations were so slight as to be scarcely discernible to an outsider, family discussions about them were like monastic arguments during the Middle Ages about the number of angels which could stand on a pinpoint. A mere feature which cast doubt—an off-shade coloring, bulge of nostril, fullness of lip or crinkle of hair, even the color of the gums or soles of the feet—could upset the precarious balance in a household and set off quarrels full of recriminations and stinging insults.

"They would have thought I was white if you hadn't been along," was the biting accusation made against a darker member of the family who bore responsibility for humiliations in public.

Being intensely human, the near whites of a family exploited and boasted of the advantages of a white skin. At home they were the family showpieces, the ones to whom most deference was given. Away from home they had easy access to a white world from which the others were shut out and faithfully reported back the details of their fine treatment. Having a power of choice, they could throw off the burden of color and walk anonymously as persons, being accepted literally upon face value. A white skin has been a cruel weapon in the world at large but infinitely more cruel in the intimacy of family relationships.

The sliding scale of color bedeviled everyone, irrespective of where one stood on the color chart. There was always somebody whiter who had an advantage over him and somebody darker whom he could look down upon. If there was nobody whiter, he still must admit he was not white. If white families split apart on the issue of slavery, many colored families separated on the issue of color. What began as a convenience often became a way of life. Near whites might associate with and marry only near whites or whites, taking the first step toward disappearance into the anonymous background. The first generation who made this fateful decision to move across the line lived in constant fear and shame. They carried the secret of their past; they feared embarassment or betrayal by their darker relatives; they were ashamed to mention race or racial justice and were terrified that the "black blood" they had deserted might reappear in one of their children. They were often more prejudiced than the most die-hard slave-owner.

Their darker sisters and brothers "married colored," of course, and sometimes there developed in the same locality the "white Does" and the "black Does." Often the white Does would not go all the way; they'd stay on the fringes of the colored community but kept to themselves and severed contact with their darker relatives. In time they became little pockets of lost tribes in rural sections, inbred through marriage of close cousins, sometimes crossed with Indians, and known as "We Sorts," "Moors," "Cajuns" or "Turks" depending upon the region in which they were found. They disclaimed all connection with colored people and were usually unacceptable to the local whites.

Against this background it would have been easy for the younger Fitzgeralds to gravitate toward the group they most closely resembled. It was hard not to be ashamed of one's color when slave-owners were screaming that free Negroes were "the most worthless and indolent of the citizens of the United States, the very drones and pests of society." That the slave-owning states had passed laws to guarantee this state of affairs was beside the point. As mulattoes, the Fitzgeralds occupied a no man's land between the whites and blacks, belonging wholly to neither yet irrevocably tied to both. They would always be at the vital nerve center of racial conflict, stretched taut between strong bonds of kinship and tides of rebellion.

Great-Grandmother Sarah Ann had already detected fissures in her family fortress in the heated discussions among her nieces and nephews who showed more white blood than their Fitzgerald cousins. They felt they had as much right to belong to the white race as to the colored. When any talk of this sort came up Great-Grandmother Sarah Ann had to consider Great-Grandfather Thomas. He was the darkest member of the entire clan. At huge family gatherings his copper skin and frizzy hair stood out in marked contrast to the white-skinned, blue-eyed, straight-haired Burtons and Valentines. She had long ago decided that what was good enough for her Thomas was good enough for her and the children. It was she who encouraged Great-Grandfather Thomas to buy and settle in Hinsonville.

Hinsonville was no ordinary village. It was a thriving settlement of Negro farmers who owned their own land and had built their own church in 1843. At the time the Fitzgeralds moved there one tenth of the township's property owners were colored farmers. Their holdings were small—most of them owned less than fifteen acres—but they were hard-working folk who managed to earn a fair living. Their children attended the Harmony Grove District School and most of them could read and write. It was because of the industrious locality that Ashmun Institute was being built near Hinsonville.

The colored folk shared the traditions of liberty which were strong in eastern Pennsylvania. Some of them had been free since before the American Revolution and had grandfathers who fought in it. Wherever one went in Chester County one was reminded of the struggle of the newborn nation for independence. When the Fitzgeralds drove to the county seat at West Chester, they passed Chadd's Ford and Brandywine Creek some twenty miles northeast of their farm, scenes of desperate battles of the Revolution when George Washington's army vainly tried to halt the British troops in their march against Philadelphia in 1777. A little north of there was historic Valley Forge. There was hardly a blacksmith or miller in the county who did not tell you proudly it was on this very spot that his grandfather shod horses or ground meal for Washington's army.

Other colored families had gained their freedom through Pennsylvania's act of gradual emancipation in 1780 and still others had come from Delaware and Maryland where they had purchased their liberty, been manumitted or had escaped from slavery. But whether they were old settlers or recent arrivals over the Underground Railroad, a fierce determination to maintain their freedom at all costs pervaded their lives.

Ask any Negro family around Hinsonville about the Christiana Riot and they'd talk of it as if they had personally been part of it. The little town of Christiana, fourteen miles west of there beyond the Octoraro Hills in neighboring Lancaster County, burst into national prominence one foggy September morning in 1851. During the early hours around dawn a band of resolute Negroes armed with corn cutters, scythes, clubs and revolvers barricaded themselves in William Parker's stone tenant house near Christiana and fought off a party of slave catchers accompanied by a posse and headed by a U.S. Marshal's deputy. When the battle was over and the posse had fled, a Maryland slaveowner, who had come to Lancaster County looking for four ex-slaves missing from his farm, was lying dead in the path and his son was desperately wounded from eighty shots drilled into his body. Thirty-eight men and women were arrested, along with two white Quakers who had refused to join the posse, and charged with treason against the United States. Feeling ran so high against slaveowners, however, that not a single conviction resulted.

The local residents later called the riot "the first battle of the great Civil War," and Pennsylvania made "Riot House" a historic shrine, although there is nothing left of it but a pile of stones in the field where Parker's tenant house stood. But if you mention Christiana to some of the older Negro residents of Chester County today, they will beam with pride, get out a worn clipping, point to the picture of a white-bearded old man and tell you of a grandfather who was one of the last survivors of the Christiana rioters.

It was a natural environment for the Fitzgeralds. Chester County was heavily populated with mulatto families like themselves. In some townships the mixed bloods outnumbered the blacks, which accounted for the fact that Pennsylvania's colored population was one-third mulatto at the time of the Civil War. It meant that Great-Grandfather Thomas could assume his right-

ful place as head of his family and travel about with his wife with
less restraint and less chance of an incident. He took great pride
that first year in riding up to the county seat to list his property—
twenty-four acres more or less, a house and barn, one horse, three
head of cattle, $530 at interest and a dog. His acreage compared
favorably with that of most small farmers in the county. His
children could now attend the local schools and Robbie could go
to Ashmun Institute someday. He was a free citizen in a free
state.

The Fitzgeralds were one of the first two families to move to
Hinsonville to be near the new school, but more followed. Great-
Grandfather Thomas took advantage of the business opportunities
created by the building operations at Ashmun Institute. He hired
farm hands to help with his crops and harvest. He invested some
of his money in a near-by brickyard, bought another horse and
wagon and joined the crews of Negro farmers and laborers who
hauled dirt and stones, dug foundations, made and laid bricks for
the first buildings. In their spare time the three Fitzgerald boys
worked on the brickyard and learned the brickmaking trade.

On Sundays the Fitzgeralds attended little Hosanna Meeting
House across the road and two of the Fitzgerald babies who were
born and died in Pennsylvania were buried there in tiny unmarked
graves. The colored folk were exceedingly proud of their church,
which, though it could scarcely hold a hundred people, was
dedicated to the "elevation of the colored people." The church
elders maintained strict discipline over the decorum of those who
attended the church. There is a record of one who was hauled
before the justice of the peace for having "performed worldly
business" on Sunday by "vending and selling cakes, beer, ice cream
etc. at Hosanna Meeting House." In spite of his confession,
thirteen witnessess were brought to testify against him and make
sure of his conviction. He was fined four dollars or six days at
hard labor on bread and water.

All was not well at the little church when the Fitzgeralds arrived
in the village. Some years earlier it had been used for anti-slavery
meetings, and Frederick Douglass and Harriet Tubman had spoken
there. The meetings were held on Saturday evenings and, according to some of the local residents, the church had been used as a

transfer point for fugitive slaves going west to Christiana in Lancaster County. Week ends provided the best opportunities for escape since slaves were off duty from Saturday noon until Monday morning. If they were successful in reaching Hosanna Meeting House while the meetings were in progress they mingled with the congregation and would drive away in a wagonload of free Negroes who hustled them on to the next Underground station. This legend seems quite probable, since the church faced a crossroad which ran past the end of Great-Grandfather Thomas' field and connected with the New London road going west. Great-Grandfather's later experiences with his barn tended to confirm the story.

At any rate, a new minister came to Hosanna in the early 1850's and after the enactment of the Fugitive Slave Law he objected to the anti-slavery meetings. A faction developed within the congregation and the conflict became so violent the church doors were closed for a while. When the split developed those who supported the minister's stand were branded by the others as informers who worked with kidnapers and slave catchers. The stigma attached to one leading family in particular and remains a strong legend around Oxford today.

As newcomers, the Fitzgeralds remained aloof from the warring factions but they soon discovered that no one could remain apart from the anti-slavery struggle. Their farm was on a public artery of travel, placing them in the center of both fugitive slave traffic and border strife which increased in intensity as the Civil War approached.

Hinsonville was one of the numerous little Negro settlements which sprang up and clustered along the southeastern border of Pennsylvania during the 1840's and 1850's. The lower counties of Pennsylvania had long been sanctuaries for fugitives from Virginia, Delaware and Maryland. The Underground Railroad originated in the eastern part of that state and this section had more routes than any other area in the northern states. At least eighty families in Chester County alone operated "stations" or signal posts. The Negro residents ably assisted the regular Underground agents, although Abraham D. Shadd was the only Negro on record in the county as having operated a station himself.

Slaves disappeared from Maryland in droves and poured across the line in hay wagons, oxcarts, broken-down buggies or on mule-back. Harriet Tubman was credited with having personally led three hundred to freedom. Some started out alone on foot with nothing to guide them but the North Star, but every slave knew that if he once crossed the line into Pennsylvania he would find friends and protection. Many a hard-pressed fugitive who avoided the public roads and lost his direction in the woods on a stormy night when the North Star was invisible thrashed about searching for the boundary stone between the two states. The stones were placed five miles apart and lucky indeed was the fugitive crawling on his hands and knees whose fingers suddenly came in contact with the stone. Running his hands quickly over the surface, he could locate the engraved *M* on one side, then find the *P* on the opposite side which told him which way to go and that he was on free territory at last.

Many fugitives continued their headlong flight until they reached the safety of Canada. Others were content to settle a few miles north of the line wherever they could find shelter and work and where they could make plans for the rescue of relatives they had left behind. They took up residence among the free Negroes, intermarried with them and hired themselves out as farm hands or house servants. Some of the more industrious bought an acre or two of land and farmed for themselves. Whether they stayed or hurried on farther north, every little Negro village was a temporary haven for a fugitive slave.

This had been going on for years, but after 1850 the exposed little Negro settlements north of the Maryland border were constant targets of disruptions and raids given impetus by the Fugitive Slave Law. Slaveowners and their agents now charged into free states at will with their cumbersome legal papers, accompanied by a United States Marshal and a *posse comitatus*, and demanded the return of Negroes who had established themselves in a community and lived there for many years as free persons. Under cover of the law, bands of marauders with faked warrants also came over the line.

Treachery was part of this lawless business. On the surface life went on placidly enough but underneath the village seethed with rumors and counter rumors and every household was on the alert. Great-Grandmother Sarah Ann learned never to trust a peddler going from door to door selling wares. Too often a hired man had disappeared after one of those peddlers came through the village. The Fitzgeralds never went to bed without barring the door heavily and setting a loaded musket within reach. Great-Grandfather Thomas taught each of his sons to shoot straight, for they never knew when they might have to fight for their lives.

White and colored informers in Chester County who worked with slave catchers and kidnapers in Maryland cared little whether their victim was a fugitive, a freedman or a free-born person. They got their share of a reward or cut of the profits in either case. In fact, they made more money when they put the finger on a free Negro since the sale price was higher than a reward.

Negroes of lower Chester County were still haunted by memories of the notorious Parker kidnaping which followed on the heels of the Christiana Riot in December, 1851. Thomas McCreary, a mail carrier from Elkton, Maryland, had long been suspected of being a kidnaper. He once stood trial in Baltimore for Negro stealing but was acquitted. Brought up in Chester County, he had relatives there and was familiar with many households in the area. He knew as well as did everybody else that Elizabeth and Rachel Parker were free born.

In mid-December McCreary snatched sixteen-year-old Elizabeth Parker from the home of Matthew M. Donnely in East Nottingham just over the Pennsylvania line, placed a stick in her mouth and tied a cloth over it to prevent her outcry, carried her off to Maryland and sold her south to New Orleans for $1,900 before her abduction was discovered. People said Donnely was a member of McCreary's gang and had hired Elizabeth to make her kidnaping easier. Two weeks later, McCreary knocked on the door of Joseph C. Miller's farmhouse in West Nottingham where Elizabeth Parker's younger sister, Rachel, had lived and worked for six years. Under the pretext of asking directions of Mrs. Miller, he seized Rachel, dragged her out of the door and into a waiting carriage. Miller heard her screams and ran to her rescue, but McCreary fought him off with a bowie knife while his companion whipped up the horses and knocked Miller to the ground as he reached for the bridle. They raced down the road toward the Maryland line a mile and a half away.

Miller and a rescue party followed the kidnapers to Baltimore, arriving in time to have Rachel transferred from the slave pen to a prison and to arrange for filing a petition for freedom. On the way home he suddenly disappeared from the train and a few hours later his body was found hanging from a tree at Stemmer's Run, a short distance from Baltimore. He had been poisoned with arsenic and hung up to look like a suicide.

The aroused citizens of Chester County, headed by Dr. John Miller Dickey, who later founded Ashmun Institute, raised funds to help the Parker girls establish their freedom. Elizabeth was found and brought back from Louisiana and the girls were finally returned to Pennsylvania in 1853 after a trial in which forty-nine white witnesses came down from Pennsylvania and testified as to the girls' parentage, birth and early life. The trial cost Pennsylvania $3,000, and another $1,000 was raised and spent by Dr. Miller's committee of distinguished citizens. McCreary was never seen in Maryland again but, according to local legend, his work was carried on by Matthew M. Donnely and there were strong rumors that one of the leading Negro farmers in Upper Oxford township and a pillar of Hosanna Meeting House worked with Donnely as an informer.

Farmer X lived near the west branch of Big Elk Creek a mile south of the Fitzgerald farm. On moonlit nights he would follow the creek bank until he reached the woods on top of a hill near Donnely's house where he met with Donnely and a gang of Maryland kidnapers. He supplied them with information on any colored folks around the locality whose descriptions corresponded with those of wanted fugitives or who would have difficulty proving their free status if kidnaped. After a seizure was made and a Negro victim disappeared below the Maryland line, Farmer X would again slip down to the woods, look under a stone for the money Donnely left for him and make his way home along the creek bank. It was said his activities bothered his conscience so that he stayed drunk most of the time.

When Farmer X died his son continued the informer's trade. The son was a farmer and grazier, and while the Fitzgeralds were not ones to deal in gossip like everybody else they were suspicious of his suddenly increased wealth. It quadrupled in the first three years after their arrival in Chester County. No one knew how he got his money and most of the villagers said it was "blood money." They claimed he posed as a friend to runaways, herded them into his big white canvas-topped wagon and, instead of driving them forward to the next Underground Railroad station, carried them back over the Maryland line and delivered them to slave catchers for a reward.

Great-Grandfather Thomas listened to the rumors and kept his own counsel. In Delaware he and Great-Grandmother Sarah Ann had learned to attend strictly to their business of making a living. They were not "joiners" of reform movements but they were stubborn in what they believed to be right. They did not pass judgment upon Farmer X's son but they dealt with him at arm's length and Great-Grandfather Thomas made sure that whenever he had to do business with him it was in writing. Without fanfare they met the issue squarely when it confronted them.

In time Great-Grandfather Thomas noticed that his barn began to attract a lot of strangers. Three well-traveled Underground Railroad routes fanned out within a few miles of his farm and one went right past his place about a mile to a lane which led into Hambleton's farm, an active Underground station. Hambleton's place was so close the Fitzgeralds could see the double chimneys of the big two-and-a-half-story stone house rising out of a hollow beyond two ridges to the northeast. The house is still there today.

On the road to it, little Hosanna Meeting House on the right and Great-Grandfather Thomas' barn on the left were easily recognizable landmarks. When a shabby stranger slipped out of the woods at the end of his field one evening around dusk and asked Great-Grandfather Thomas if he could sleep in his barn, he thought little of it. He sent him up to the loft and told him to stop by the house next morning for breakfast, but the stranger was gone before dawn and Great-Grandfather Thomas thought one of his cows gave a quart less milk than usual.

Before long strangers came along pretty often asking to sleep in the barn. Great-Grandfather Thomas never turned anyone away; he merely relieved him of his pipe or smoking tobacco or

matches if he had any before sending him up to the loft. He was
very careful never to ask a stranger's name or where he came from
or where he was bound. He discouraged all confidences; the less
he knew about strangers the better.

"Don't tell me anything about yourself," he'd say. "Just mind
yourself and don't set my barn afire. If you're here in the morning
you'll get breakfast. If you leave before day, you'll find your
tobacco and pipe on the ledge by the barn door as you go out."

If Great-Grandfather Thomas found the traveler in the loft
next morning and he was not in too big a hurry to be off, he'd
send him down to the house to cut firewood for Great-Grandmother Sarah Ann, who fed him a huge breakfast before he went
on his way. My grandfather said the Fitzgerald children were
taught never to ask questions about who slept in the barn the
night before or show surprise if they saw an extra place set at the
table.

Not all the strangers who slept in the barn were nameless, in a
hurry or without money, but it was a point of honor with Great-
Grandfather Thomas never to accept pay from his "guests" for
their night's lodging and breakfast.

"Bread cast upon the waters will return after many a day," he'd
tell them. "Who knows? Maybe somebody will do a good turn
for one of my great-grandchildren some day."

There were the heroic words and deeds which kept hope alive
among people of color during the riptide of those years and which
brought emancipation nearer. Then there were the small, persistent, unheroic acts of obstinate folk like my Fitzgerald great-
grandparents and their neighbors who never dreamed of making
history. One of these was Great-Grandfather Thomas' reaction
when he went to the polling place to vote and was turned down
flat. Negroes had voted in Pennsylvania twenty years earlier but
the Supreme Court held in 1838 that a Negro was not a freeman
within the meaning of Pennsylvania's constitution and thus was
not entitled to vote. The constitution was amended at the next
election to limit the franchise to white freemen.

Great-Grandfather Thomas knew far more about the habits of
farm animals than he did about those of politicians and was unable
to fathom the legal acrobatics which defined a free person of color

as not a freeman, but he understood the meaning of taxation without representation. So he protested in the only way he knew how and, curiously enough, his protest found its way into the record. He refused to pay his dog tax.

Each year property owners were required to list the number of horses, oxen and cattle they owned and whether they had a carriage, a watch or a dog. The township collector gathered an annual dog tax of one dollar from all dog owners although no tags were issued. It was called Dog, Poor and Military Tax and was pretty steep at that, considering Great-grandfather Thomas paid less than three dollars combined state and county taxes on all his other property.

Every year some fifteen or twenty people in the township failed to pay the tax and the collector, in order not to be charged personally with the unpaid assessments, sent a list of the delinquents to the County Commissioners for exoneration. To justify his exoneration, he wrote in an explanation after each name, such as "poor," "no good," "dog died," "has no dog," "left the county" and so on. Now, right in the middle of the list for 1860 appeared two names without explanation—Thomas Fitzgerald and Wesley Jay, both free men of color.

I can almost see Great-Grandfather Thomas now, the twinkle gone from his brown eyes, his square jaw thrust out, counting out his state and county taxes (which came to $2.97 that year) and laying the money on the counter at the county courthouse. When the collector reminded him that he was a dollar short he looked that gentleman straight in the eye.

"I know it. I'm not going to pay the dog tax, sir. I wouldn't pay these others but you'd foreclose my property if I didn't. If I can't vote I don't see why I have to pay taxes."

The flabbergasted collector, who had found Tom Fitzgerald an amiable man, couldn't think of a single reason to write after his name to explain his nonpayment. Great-Grandfather Thomas never got to vote in Pennsylvania, although he lived there more than fifteen years. By the time the state removed the color restriction in 1873, the Fitzgeralds had pulled up stakes and gone south.

8

GRANDFATHER grew up with a passion for knowledge.
Unlike his brothers, who cared more for the bustling activity of the brickyard than they did the discipline of a classroom, he was a bookworm. He'd drive his father's oxen along a furrow with a book in one hand. When he was not studying he was drawing sketches in a small notebook he always carried about with him. Of coarser texture themselves, Billy and Richie Fitzgerald held their scholarly brother in awe and generally followed his leadership in crucial family decisions.

When Grandfather was sixteen he persuaded his parents to let him go to Philadelphia to enter the Institute for Colored Youth. For many years it was the only secondary school in the country for young people of color. They were generally excluded from the private seminaries and academies where most high-school instruction was given in those days. Under Quaker supervision, it was widely known for its excellent training and high standards of scholarship. Because of its work, the emancipated Negroes were not without a few of their own capable guides in the steep climb out of slavery. The Institute turned out a majority of the ablest colored teachers and leaders among the freedmen after the war and furnished most of the Negro candidates for professional schools. Chartered in 1842, it continues today as Cheyney State Teachers College near West Chester, Pennsylvania.

His two years spent at the Institute for Colored Youth nurtured the missionary spirit which was awakened in Grandfather as a little boy in the African School of Wilmington. He absorbed the radical thinking of his time, attended anti-slavery meetings and listened to Negro abolitionists such as William Still, Henry Highland Garnet, Harriet Tubman and Frederick Douglass. He said he was once privileged to sit on the same platform with Susan B. Anthony, the great woman suffragist who got her early political experience in the anti-slavery crusade. From fellow students whose slave-owning fathers had freed them and sent them north for an education he heard firsthand accounts of the woeful conditions among the colored people under slavery and their longing to be free. His interest in political issues was aroused by the bitterly fought campaign of 1856. The newly organized Republican party entered the Presidential contest and the furor in Pennsylvania was heightened by the fact that in a normally anti-slavery state, James Buchanan, standard bearer of the pro-slavery Democrats, was a native son.

What made the deepest impact upon this thoughtful youth, however, was the fateful Dred Scott decision of 1857 which had grave consequences for all free people of color. Before that decision it was widely assumed that free colored persons were citizens of the United States. Now Chief Justice Roger B. Taney, who wrote the opinion for the Supreme Court, held that the descendants of African slaves, whether emancipated or born of free parents, were not included in the word "citizens" used in the Constitution nor were they intended to be included among the people who framed and adopted the Declaration of Independence. He observed that they were regarded "as beings of an inferior order" and "had no rights which a white man was bound to respect." Ironically enough, Mr. Justice Taney nearly forty years earlier had won fame as a practicing attorney by his passionate defense of the Declaration of Independence in securing acquittal for an anti-slavery* minister in Maryland charged with inciting slaves to riot. Now history flowed backward and his opinion had stripped every vestige of citizenship from free persons of color and left them almost indistinguishable from slaves.

It was a grave but determined young man who returned home

in 1858 to further his education at Ashmun Institute, so proudly referred to as "the nation's first pledge to emancipation." In later years it was hard to say which fact loomed higher in our esteem—Grandfather Fitzgerald's war service or his enrollment as one of the first few students of the college which trained Negro leaders before Emancipation. Both facts grew in significance to our family as postwar historians either ignored or passed over lightly the Negro's contribution to his own cause. Grandfather was our personal statistic, our invisible footnote which we added mentally to textbooks where reference to the Negro was at best bleak or disparaging. The story of the beginnings of the school which played so important a role in his development was always an inspiring one to his five daughters although they could not attend it themselves.

That a tiny outpost of higher education for Negro men should be set up seven years before the Civil War, within a few miles of slave territory and in quiet defiance of threatened border raids and stubborn local opposition, was one of those remarkable flashes of idealism which light up the pages of history. Ashmun Institute might never have been established had not the Parker kidnaping aroused such influential citizens as Dr. John Miller Dickey, pastor of the Oxford Presbyterian Church. Dr. Dickey was a scholarly man of Great-Grandfather Thomas' age, who towered six feet four inches in his stockinged feet, was broad shouldered and commanding in appearance, had kindly eyes and the strong yet sensitive face of an ascetic. Not only was he beloved by his own congregation but it was said hardly anybody around Oxford got married or bought a piece of property without coming to him for advice. The Negro residents looked upon him as a trusted friend.

A graduate of Princeton, he had founded the Oxford Female Seminary and held a chair there as professor of history and philosophy. Like his minister father before him, Dr. Dickey was an ardent worker in the Colonization Society and devoted much of his energy to that movement. His sympathy for the slaves had been aroused when he worked as a young probationer in Florida and came in contact with slavery, but like many conservative men of his time whose deep humanitarian instincts made them foes of the institution, he believed the most practical solution was gradual emancipation coupled with resettlement of the freed Negroes in Liberia.

In line with his conviction, Dr. Dickey had for some years considered the possibility of training Negro missionaries for work in Africa, but the idea did not crystallize until his experiences with the Parker case. One day in 1852 while he was busily engaged in writing letters on behalf of the Parker sisters, there appeared in his study a young Negro Methodist minister named James R. Amos, son of a farmer who lived a good distance north of Oxford. Young Amos preached occasionally at Hosanna Meeting House and had some education but felt he needed far more for effective leadership of his flock, so he had come to get Dr. Dickey's advice and assistance in gaining admission to some academy.

Young Amos' faith was as challenging as it was naïve. He had just about asked for the impossible. Higher education for Negroes was almost unheard of. Oberlin College in Ohio was the only northern institution which welcomed them as students but Dr. Dickey was apparently unaware of Oberlin's reputation. In any event, after much effort he succeeded in having Amos enrolled in a Philadelphia school connected with the Presbyterian Synod, only to discover the white students objected so violently to his presence that he was shortly reduced to the position of porter. Amos tried to continue his studies there, but the opposition of the other students remained so fierce that he was compelled to withdraw altogether.

Back he came to Dr. Dickey with his troubles and the Presbyterian pastor found himself not only writing appeals for the Parker case but sending off dozens of letters on Amos' behalf to northern colleges which sent either negative replies or ignored his inquiries. He tried to tutor Amos himself but the pressure of his other work made it impossible to give the young man the continuous instruction he needed. He was now more than ever convinced of the futility of Negroes' efforts to establish themselves as free people in the United States.

Amos, however, refused to be disheartened by his dilemma. The young man cheerfully walked the long distance from his home to Oxford and waited about patiently for whatever hurried instruction

Dr. Dickey could give him. He confided to the older man that on the way to and from Oxford he always stopped to pray at a certain stone. He felt sure that God would answer his prayers and the way would be opened for him to realize his ambition for further training.

As he brooded over Amos' problem, the idea of an academy for young Negro men began to grow in Dr. Dickey's mind. Its primary purpose would be to train missionary leaders for Liberia. The school would be named Ashmun Institute in honor of Jehudi Ashmun, agent of the Colonization Society and Administrator of Liberia from 1822 to 1828, under whose leadership the tiny colony of American Negroes on the west coast of Africa had become an independent self-governing community.

Dr. Dickey went to work on his idea as soon as the Parker trials ended in January, 1853. Difficulties confronted him at every step of the venture. The white residents of Oxford would hire Negro servants and farm hands and risk their own safety helping fugitive slaves but they were strongly opposed to a Negro college in their midst. Even an institution in aid of colonization *outside* the United States was not welcome in the Oxford community. Even among people opposed to slavery the view was widely held that Negroes were a degraded race destined always to occupy the lowest position in society. Thus it was better to leave them in abject ignorance than educate them to become dissatisfied with a lot they could never hope to improve.

Even Dr. Dickey's doting congregation gave him no support in his unpopular effort. His Presbyterian colleagues were at first only lukewarm toward the idea. He met stiff resistance from landowners in trying to locate a site for the proposed school. His wife, of Quaker parentage who shared his concern for the welfare of colored people, actually found the site. She pointed it out one day as they were driving along the Jennersville Road on one of their many excursions about the countryside in search of a place. It was a thirty-acre farm high on a hilltop near Hinsonville, over-looking the cultivated fields and valleys of lower Chester County and surrounded by the tiny farms of industrious Negro families—a perfect site for the school.

Dr. Dickey's plan was finally approved by the Presbyterian

General Assembly in the fall of 1853 and a committee was appointed to carry it out. Since the committee had no funds for the purpose, Dr. Dickey bought the farm site on April 1, 1854. Four weeks later the Pennsylvania legislature granted a charter for the school and Dr. Dickey promptly mortgaged his own home to raise money for construction of the first two buildings.

If the white folk displayed only hostility or indifference to the new school rising on the hilltop, the colored folk supplied more than their share of enthusiasm. The very idea of a college for Negro youth was the most hopeful thing which had happened to them. No group of people had hungered more for education and nowhere had it been more stubbornly withheld or more grudgingly bestowed. The school was a community project, involving the labor and skills of most of the men in the immediate neighborhood and attracting laborers for miles around. Their descendants around Oxford will tell you that each brick was laid on with prayerfulness and rejoicing. A traveler along the Jennersville Road from Oxford in those days might hear the whole hillside reverberating with song as the structures went up.

Here was a school literally built upon prayer. The stones for the early foundations were quarried from near by and there is a legend that once during the construction young Amos came down to view the building operations. He stopped at his customary place of prayer close to the site to offer thanks for the realization of his dream and found his prayer stone was missing! He was overjoyed later to discover it among the foundations of the building. Perhaps the most symbolic feature of the Institute was its cornerstone, which was part of a broken tombstone. On the back was carved a hand pointing toward heaven. On the front was engraved the name of the school, the date and motto, "The night is far spent, the day is at hand." The new buildings faced due east toward the rising sun.

Ashmun Hall was completed and the Institute was ready for dedication on December 31, 1856, with Rev. John Pym Carter, A.M., of Baltimore, installed as principal and faculty of one. Next day the school opened with only two students—James R. and Thomas Amos. Two years later Mr. Carter reported to the Board of Trustees headed by Dr. Dickey, "There have been connected with the Inst. to this date Robt. Fitzgerald, Rev. W. H. Hunter, Clem Robinson, Mahlon Van Horn, Sam'l. Hall and Richard Maywood." Earlier that school year the two Amos brothers and Armistead Miller, a young student from Liberia, were licensed as ministers and sent to Africa.

Grandfather now divided his time between his farm chores and going to school on the hill. His parents had come to lean upon him more and more since Lizzie and Billy had both married and were living down in Oxford. Great-Grandmother Sarah Ann had given up going to market to stay at home and care for five-year-old Mary Jane and baby Agnes, born in 1859, but she sold her butter and cream among the folks in the neighborhood and boarded one or two of the students of the Institute.

My grandfather used to tell a story about one of the boarders who had a voracious appetite, particularly for sweets. It was during harvest time and Great-Grandmother Sarah Ann had made a huge pan of bread pudding to feed their family and the hired men and had set it on a side table to cool. The young man couldn't keep his eyes off that pudding and finally he asked Great-Grandfather Thomas if he could just have a taste. It was just before dinner and very irregular, but Great-Grandfather Thomas indulgently told him to help himself. He gobbled up a saucerful and said it was so good he'd like another little taste. When he finished the second helping and eyed the pan for more, Great-Grandfather made him sit there and eat the whole pudding. He groaned and protested halfway through, but Great-Grandfather solemnly pointed to the pan each time he emptied his saucer. By the time he got through, the gluttonous young man not only didn't want his di..ner but was permanently cured of eating sweets.

These were the happy times before the war when the younger Fitzgeralds had corn huskings, gathered nuts and went duck shooting in the fall, went riding in sleighs over the snow in winter, and dragged in a Yule log from the forests to burn at Christmastide. Young Robert Fitzgerald would sit around the fire with his schoolmates, roasting raw coffee beans over the coals and talking of the future. These young men were bound together by a common purpose, that of proving themselves. A Negro was forever on trial, carrying always a heavy burden of proof that he was not by nature degraded or inferior, for he stood against the accumulated weight of words, laws, customs and the sanctity of judicial precedent. Slavery robbed him of the right to speak only for himself or be judged by individual merit. In every act or utterance, he must plead for millions of others. In a country where individual freedom was most idealized, he was charged not only with his own performance but with that of every other person of color of whatever character, ability or station.

Each learned that since he could never escape the burden of race, he must dedicate himself to it—to the cause of "my people," that diverse, unpredictable mass of humanity compounded of many nations, tongues and customs, uprooted, dispersed and hammered into a new race of men by common oppression and indestructible faith. As every dedicated spirit has done, Robert Fitzgerald and his classmates would agonize over each unseemly act of the black man with the shame of personal guilt and exult over each triumph with the pride of personal achievement. And their descendants would do the same for many generations.

Dedication was the hallmark of Ashmun Institute. It closely resembled a monastery with its atmosphere of piety and stern discipline, the daily prayer sessions and Bible lessons, the constant emphasis upon temperance and devotion to duty. The students were solemn young men, conscious of their great opportunity and the heavy responsibilities which awaited them as ministers of God and leaders of their people. Most of them had taken the temperance pledge as had Grandfather, and many of them were committed to leaving for Africa upon the completion of their studies. Liberia, "the glorification of God in Africa," was held before them constantly as the land of promise for colored youth. Always in the background were indefatigable Dr. Dickey and the American Colonization Society, which viewed the Institute as a recruiting center for enterprising immigrants to the African colony.

It was this latter aspect of the Institute which gave young Robert Fitzgerald greatest difficulty. Shortly after his enrollment he professed the Presbyterian faith, although he had not formally joined the church. He faithfully attended the prayer sessions, diligently studied his Bible and catechism, listened intently to his fellow students in their practice sermons to Hosanna's congregation and struggled with his own sense of unworthiness as a Christian. There was a great deal of pressure upon him to become a minister and leader in Africa. He had qualities of leadership, was a good student, came from a good family and had taken the pledge of temperance. Nothing more was needed except his commitment.

Here he was like a repentant sinner at the mourner's bench who finds conversion too great a leap of faith, or perhaps his own faith collided with that of his tutors, for he could never bring himself to sign up to go to Africa. He could not deny the harsh judgment of Dr. C. Van Renssalaer of the Presbyterian Board of Education at the time of the school's dedication. In his keynote address Dr. Van Renssalaer declared: "The gloomy future of the colored population is impenetrable on the proposition that the population is to remain permanently in the United States. . . . Will the race rise to social equality and partake of the political privileges with other classes in the same community? This is . . . improbable. . . . Far better for our coloured population to retire from an unequal contest against inveterate prejudice, than stand disheartened and dismayed before the discipline of its stern emergency. God will repair their losses in a better way and in a better land. . . . Ashmun Institute wisely looks to Africa as the seat of its principal influence."

Nor could he deny the crushing severity of the Dred Scott decision. Indeed free Negroes were stranded at a halfway station between slaves and citizens. Philadelphia was a haven for fugitives and platform for Abolitionists but it turned a chilly shoulder upon equality-minded colored folk. They were excluded from theaters, restaurants, inns and hotels. They were compelled to ride on the outside platform on streetcars and when they took the matter to court their exclusion from the inside of the cars was upheld. They were generally unwelcome in the churches and meeting houses and while their children were not barred from the district schools their presence was treated with indifference.

Yet there was the miracle of knowledge through which he could leap over barriers and elevate himself above the miserable anthill of color. There was the fact of his nativity, his roots struck deep in native soil. Did not his parents own a tiny portion of American earth? What had he, born in the United States, seven thousand miles away from Africa, in common with that continent or its people beyond some remote ancestor he had never known? For that matter, what had he in common with Sweden, Ireland or France, the origins of other remote ancestors?

Was it not the *promise* of America rather than its *fulfillment* which had lured the men and women of so many nations to her shores? Did not the common love of liberty create a new nation and hold it together in the hour of its greatest need? Should he leave his native land because the promise had not yet been fulfilled in his case? If the Scripture which he was required to study so assiduously supported slavery, as some believed, it also sustained faith. "Faith is the substance of things hoped for, the evidence of things unseen," he read. Faith was stronger than words, stronger than chains or the lash, stronger than hatred and prejudice, stronger even than life or death.

The Civil War cut short his schooling in 1861; but it corroborated his faith.

9

THE Civil War was the only war of importance in our family. We had no menfolk enlisted in the Spanish-American War and World War I to relate personal memories and make them real to us, but the Civil War was as close to us as if it had been fought yesterday. Grandfather's memories and modest trophies kept the Yankee cause shining brightly in our home.

If the Rebels had their monuments and symbols, we had ours. Under Grandfather's bed lay his musket and rusty saber, his bayonet and cavalry pistol, an 1856 Springfield model. The saber's blade was as dull as its back and the firearms had not been loaded for years, but their lack of utility made them no less significant in our eyes. They were symbols of courage and of a tradition which made us stand tall. When other children boasted, "My father is a preacher," or "My father has an automobile," I'd counter with, "My grandfather was a soldier for the Union and fought for freedom." Few of my playmates could match that!

There were other symbols too, which miraculously survived three quarters of a century, not as impressive to me in those years as the musket and saber, but which were to serve as windows through which I later glimpsed Grandfather's youth. Like many young men of his time, he kept a diary during and after the Civil War, closely scribbled in tiny notebooks and meaningless to me in childhood. For years Aunt Pauline kept them carefully buried underneath old letters and papers in her top desk drawer. She claimed that in a spell of being helpful while she was away from home one day, I cleaned house and dumped some of Grandfather's letters and diaries down the well along with old shoes, tin cans and bottles to help fill it up. I could not deny it, for only two small volumes of the diaries are left, but fortunately the Fitzgeralds had remarkably long and accurate memories.

Grandfather never got over his soldiering. You could always get him to talk about the Civil War, and while he was not a boastful man he'd say with considerable emphasis, "Your Uncle Richard drove mules for the Union, but I was a sailor and a soldier." When I'd lead him about the town, he'd press hard on my shoulder when he wanted me to get in step, and, having shorter legs than his, I'd have to skip now and then to keep the rhythm. His Presbyterian soul frowned upon such frivolities as dancing, but marching was an honorable activity of which he approved.

I remember how once when I was sweeping the parlor, to make the work go faster, I had put a record of one of Sousa's marches on the little victrola with a morning-glory horn. I was whirling about the room using the broom as a dancing partner when Grandfather stormed inside from the porch, flailing the air with his cane.

"What're you doing in here? There'll be no dancing in this house while I'm head of it," he scolded.

Up went the broom on my shoulder like a musket and I paraded noisily back and forth, thumping the broom on the floor and clicking my bare feet on the rug as hard as I could.

"I'm not dancing, Granpa, I'm marching!"

"Well, see to it that you do march!" he said doubtfully. I'm sure I never fooled him one bit.

As a child I heard the names of mysterious places where Grandfather had been and fought—Harpers Ferry, Antietam, Culpeper, Fredericksburg, Petersburg, Appomattox River, Boston, New Orleans—magic names which stuck in my memory.

I accepted his military service as the natural consequence of being a Yankee. I did not know then that being a soldier at all was for him a personal triumph. He was almost twenty-one and not quite ready for college when the Civil War began. The clash of arms which disrupted the nation also threatened the very existence of Ashmun Institute and scattered its student body. Half of the students had to drop out during the first year of the war for lack of tuition and scarcity of scholarships. During the next four years the school came near closing its doors more than once because of threatened raids from Maryland. Conspiracies of official silence would envelop the fate of the Negro race for many weary, uncertain months and higher education for colored men had to await the outcome of the struggle.

By 1861, however, the school had developed a tiny driving force which would emerge as a spearhead of leadership after the war. Six of the young men who pioneered before disunion would be heard from again. Dapper Christian A. Fleetwood, who looked like a dandy and wore heavy sideburns, a long mustache and small tuft of beard, would distinguish himself on the battlefield as sergeant major of the 4th U.S. Colored Troops and become one of the fourteen Negroes in the Civil War to receive the Congressional Medal of Honor. Scholarly Reading B. Johns, who wore glasses and whose heavy curls fell in ringlets about his ears, would press on to a degree from Princeton Theological Seminary and one day would stand before the Connecticut legislature as its chaplain. Brilliant Mahlon Van Horn, from New Jersey, would return after the war to take his degree, go south and be elected to the Mississippi legislature. Later he would serve as United States Consul to the then Danish-held Virgin Islands. William H. Hunter, a preacher from Virginia who had made his way to Pennsylvania to attend the school, would return to his native state after the war and help build the first schools and churches among the freedmen. Peter Plato Hedges would do the same thing in North Carolina. Robert Fitzgerald would work in both states, and the reports sent back from these young men to their school would inspire a steady stream of missionaries to men and women fresh from slavery and eager to learn.

From the very beginning of the war, Robert Fitzgerald was determined to get into the fight. He knew that the blue uniform of the United States was the greatest of all prizes to be won, since those who wore it with honor in defense of their country could no longer be denied the right of citizenship. In this desire my grandfather reflected the universal feeling among the free Negroes of the North. There were no more fervent supporters of the Union cause than they, and they were among the first to rush to the colors when Lincoln called for 75,000 volunteers of three-months' men to subdue the rebellion.

Robert Fitzgerald could not wait to finish school. In company with his brothers, several of his fellow students and some other young men of Hinsonville, he went to the nearest recruiting office to sign up. It was a stinging blow to them when they were told to go home again, the army was not taking colored boys. Never was patriotic enthusiasm crushed by more heavy-handed political expediency. It was the same everywhere in the North. Word had been passed down from Washington not to accept Negroes in the volunteer regiments. Those who had mustered in were quickly mustered out again. The colored people were to have no part in the "white man's war." The free Negro of the North was to be measured by the Negro slave in the South.

Four more slave states left the Union after Lincoln's call for volunteers and he dared not risk the four remaining loyal slave states by putting Negroes into uniform. Most Union officers—some Abolitionists excepted—doubted they'd make good soldiers. Some Yankee troops threatened to lay down their arms and go home and their officers to resign if colored recruits were taken into their ranks. The uniform of the United States might be worn by immigrants just off the boats who could speak no word of English, but not by native-born colored men.

When patriotism collided with prejudice, prejudice was victor. One doughty ex-slave named Nicholas Biddle, who peddled wares around Pottsville, Pennsylvania, had managed to attach himself to a body of troops. Four days after the fall of Fort Sumter he marched with his regiment in full military dress through the streets of Baltimore as the troops changed trains for Washington. Biddle got no farther. White rioters rushed the ranks with clubs and rocks, shouting, "kill the nigger in uniform!" and felled him with a stone that split his head open.

That summer of 1861 was an unbearable one for the Fitzgerald boys. It was cruel for them to have to sit on the side lines while feverish war preparations went on. Banners waved in every township. The villages were suddenly swept clean of their young men.

Every able-bodied youth, it seemed, itched to get into the fight
to lick the Rebels and teach them a lesson. Meanwhile, invading
Union generals were permitting local slaveowners to enter federal
lines and reclaim their fugitives while the more realistic Confederates were using their Negro slaves to build the breastworks
at Bull Run.

It was galling enough to know that one's country considered
one unfit to wear the uniform; it was worse to explain to unin-
formed local patriots one's presence at home when other young
fellows were marching away to the war. There were those intolerable moments when a group of fresh recruits passed the Fitzgerald
boys on the road and, not knowing they were colored, yelled out,
"Hey, Yank, whyn't you join the colors?" If they gave no answer,
the next remark was apt to be, "You must be a damned doughface
or a secesh!"

Great-Grandfather Thomas urged his sons to be patient, that
the Lord would work it out in His own time and His own way,
but patience has never been a virtue of youth. Great-Grandmother
Sarah Ann chewed her lips in silence; she could tell them nothing
more than to listen to their father. Billy Fitzgerald declared he
didn't care much; with a wife and baby to take care of he didn't
see any sense in going off to shoot Rebs when there were so many
Negro haters right in Pennsylvania; but his brothers knew he was
just talking to hear himself talk and to hide his disappointment.
Hotheaded eighteen-year-old Richie said he'd break the next man's
jaw who asked why he didn't go to fight the secesh, and he got
his chance a short while later. Robbie said little; he consoled himself by reading every scrap of war news, following every skirmish
and campaign, analyzing every political speech in the newspapers
and keeping himself informed.

Then they began to hear of boys they knew joining up with the
white regiments and keeping their mouths shut about their race.
Sixteen-year-old Edwin Belcher from Philadelphia slipped off and
joined the 73rd Pennsylvania Volunteers that August. He was to
serve with his regiment throughout the war, rising from private to
captain and becoming a hero in the battle of Lookout Mountain,
Tennessee, in October, 1863. When he was discharged with honor
nobody in his company was the wiser.

Well, that was one way of getting around all the humbug about not letting colored men fight as soldiers. Pennsylvania, with her twenty thousand mulattoes, was a natural breeding ground for this sort of thing. Before the war was many weeks old thousands of mixed bloods were entering white regiments. Some never recrossed the line and others were not known in the official records as Negroes until many years later when they applied for their pensions. An incredible number of patriotic "Indians," curly-haired "Mexicans," swarthy "Italians" and dingy "Irish" began showing up at the recruiting places. Local officers weren't too particular how they filled their quotas as long as no fuss was made, and a man who could pass for anything but colored was readily accepted.

The Fitzgerald boys considered this course, but it would have been an act of disloyalty to their father, whom they revered, to have gone off somewhere and joined up as white men. He'd always taught them, "Never be ashamed of what you are. Just be the best you can be and show what colored men can do when they have the chance." To join a white regiment would be taking all the credit from the black side of the ledger which needed desperately to prove that colored men were brave and giving it to the white side which needed no boosts. One's courage only built the white race higher without proving a thing about the colored man.

A Negro who "passed" was like a spy, watchful of every move, fearful of being exposed by a chance meeting with an old acquaintance. If his fellows found out about his race, they were likely to drum him out of camp as they would a traitor or thief. Ashamed of the low jokes they'd told about "niggers," "darkies" and "baboons" in his presence—jeers they wouldn't dare repeat before any self-respecting colored man—they'd feel betrayed and in their guilt they'd turn upon him as the coward and sneak. Such a man nearly always found himself enduring the coarse jokes and insults in silence or joining in the vulgar laughter to show that he was part of the crowd. Pretty soon he would grow to hate himself, for having denied part of himself he would not be able to accept the other part and wound up hating both.

It would take more than official rebuffs to keep a Fitzgerald out of the fight altogether. That summer a big Union supply depot opened at Perryville, Maryland, on the banks of the Susquehanna

River, to receive mules and animals for the Bull Run campaign and to move supplies southward for the troops. To transport its supplies from the North to the southern fighting fronts, the Union needed a large force of teamsters, wagon masters, mule drivers and hostlers for the long wagon trains. It also needed wheelwrights and blacksmiths, road and bridge builders. The Quartermasters of the Civil War had no troops; they hired civilians to perform these tasks. They took on men as they needed them and let them go again when a big campaign was over. Laborers' pay was $20 a month; a teamster got $25, a wagonmaster $35, and the pay increased with the various skills.

Word passed around that the Quartermaster's Department had a recruiting office at Fifth and Walnut streets in Philadelphia and was hiring every able-bodied man it could find who was not under arms. The Fitzgerald boys and other young colored men from Chester County answered the call. They could handle horses and mules, the pay was good and they'd be in the war at last. Robert Fitzgerald packed his books and put them away, stuffed a small Bible and a tiny sketchbook in his shirt pocket and followed his brothers to Philadelphia, where they all signed up and were sent down to Perryville along with some of their Burton and Valentine cousins.

Great-Grandfather Thomas joined his sons and hired out as teamster and assistant wagonmaster for several months that winter but returned to his crops when spring planting time came around. In early 1862, the Fitzgerald brothers were transferred to the Washington supply base and scattered throughout Virginia as the Peninsular Campaign got under way. Richard spent most of that year driving mules around Harrison's Landing and Fortress Monroe, swearing and fuming each time he lost a bucket from underneath his wagon and had two dollars docked from his pay. Billy wound up driving a one-horse cart on detail at Acquia Creek, while Robbie landed in a construction corps with Banks' army building corduroy roads and pontoon bridges.

For one of delicate health he chalked up an amazing record during the next two years. When he was not chopping down trees and building roads and bridges, he was driving a team in the wagon train or filling in as a company cook in a regiment. He proved a reliable worker and sometimes he was detached from his outfit and sent hurriedly from place to place delivering cavalry horses. He said these lonely pilgrimages were the most terrifying because death to him was better than being captured by the Rebels. He was at Harpers Ferry building pontoon bridges in late summer, 1862, and got out just before the federal garrison with its eleven thousand men and large stores of equipment fell to Stonewall Jackson. He delivered horses to Antietam, to Culpeper and to Warrenton, Virginia. He hauled pontoons from Acquia Creek and helped to lay them across the Rappahannock River under murderous Rebel fire just before the Union troops gallantly but vainly stormed the heights of Fredericksburg.

It was a mean life which offered neither the prestige of a uniform nor the protection of a musket. Of all the branches of the service, the Quartermasters' men were the least trained, least educated, least organized, least protected in battle and most maligned of the Civil War. The teamster and laborer crews were the motliest assortment of men ever collected for a mass operation. The great war machine had gathered up "contrabands"—ragged slaves who escaped to the Union lines and offered themselves as cooks, scouts, guides or pick-and-shovel men. It recruited tatterdemalions and drunks; desperadoes and thieves; stragglers and bummers who sought refuge in the rear; hard-bitten farmers who fought the war between crops; seedy, decrepit old fellows who had been rejected for service under arms; Indians and immigrants, "free issues" and "we sorts"; mysterious men who came out of the shadows lured by the Quartermasters' pay and vanished again when the war ended; and eager young colored men from the northern and middle states patiently waiting to prove themselves.

They were there because the Quartermasters asked no questions about background or race and wanted only to get the job done. The Quartermasters were having a hard time at that and took what they could get. They had no regulation clothing or equipment for their men; their raggamuffin corps looked like an army of scarecrows. They wore what they could buy, beg, borrow or steal, odds and ends which gave them a dilapidated appearance but usually some cast-off insignia which stamped them unmistakably as Union men.

There was nothing to make a man stick to this disreputable-looking army except the pay, sheer love of excitement, or an idealism stronger than the abuse heaped upon its members. Yet Grandfather Fitzgerald and many others like him stuck, endured the jeers and humiliations, the curses and abominations which offended his pride and aroused his resentment. He drove his body to limits his mother would not have believed possible, clamped restraints upon his indignation, ignored the taunts and kept going. When there was a halt or a rest, he'd take out his Bible and read a chapter or sketch in his notebook a bridge, a river bank or a general riding past. Day by day through menial tasks he was earning his citizenship.

The most that could be said for his ignominious drudgery was that he was in the thick of things, sharing the dangers and hardships with the rest. The teamster and laborer crews were the fighting man's lifeline. He relied upon the Quartermasters' civilian army to set up supply bases, field hospitals and army headquarters; to provide transportation for the wounded and prisoners of war, replacements of horses and mules lost in battle; to lay telegraph lines and railroad tracks; to keep a continuous flow of food, guns, ammunition, medical equipment, forage for animals and luggage for field and staff officers moving from Washington down to men on the battlefronts.

Wherever the armies went, the wagon trains followed or sometimes even plowed ahead to build and stock supply bases, drop off crews to lay down plank roads or corduroy roads for the troops or throw up bridges over rivers and creeks. Day and night Washington residents heard the unbroken thunder of heavy wheels and hoofs on the cobblestone streets as the wagon trains rumbled southward across Long Bridge or straggled back again bringing wounded and dying men from the front lines. When a whole army was on the march, at its rear wound the long, snaking line of canvas-topped wagons, five hundred strong and miles in length, weaving and bobbing up and down the ridges like a giant white caterpillar, throwing up great columns of dust over the countryside.

Grandfather usually drove a four-horse or six-mule team but there was every conceivable type of team in the line when it

started out—regimental wagons carrying medical supplies, regimental papers, luggage, small-arms ammunition and field artillery;
two-horse ambulances; forage wagons bulging with hay for the
animals; kitchen wagons loaded with bags of coffee, barrels of
beef and pork, boxes of bread, kettles, pots and pans, and company
cooks armed with nothing more defensive than a butcher's knife
or iron skillet. The endless white line was broken here and there
by the black-topped sutlers' carts which followed the armies and
peddled tobacco, newspapers, sweetmeats and other wares to the
soldiers. Up and down the line rode wagon masters, urging teams
forward to fill long gaps, untangling snarls and pulling crippled
wagons out of the way. The wagon masters were sometimes accompanied by volunteer corps and a guard usually escorted the
trains behind and in front to protect them from Rebel skirmishers'
fire.

Moving men under orders on a forced march with rifles and
bayonets for protection was one thing; moving untrained civilian
drivers and mules over the dust-choked or mud-clogged roads in
all kinds of weather was another. Wagons broke down or sank
to their axles in mire. Men beat and cursed their mules and the
mules balked. Delay upon delay piled up the teams, jammed the
roads, snarled the traffic and held up vital supplies. Crossing small
streams, drivers often ignored the water buckets under their
wagons and let their animals stop midstream to drink, obstructing
passage and causing more delays. Dust strangled and blinded the
men; animals dropped dead from exhaustion and bad treatment;
supply lines crawled, stopped, crawled again; battles were lost
because ammunition never arrived in time; wounded men died
because they did not reach hospitals quickly enough. Trains could
seldom move more than fourteen to seventeen miles a day in the
best of summer weather; in winter, a day's march slowed down to
twelve miles.

Mix-ups along the road were bad enough, but encampments
were sheer bedlam. When marching troops halted and bivouacked
for the night, the men usually fell out and camped off the roadside in the nearest grove or clearing. Miles behind, their regimental
wagons seldom caught up with them until several hours later.
Teams could not jump ditches or maneuver about in gulches as

could men on foot, and drivers had to jog along the road looking for a convenient turnoff, jamming traffic again and milling about in confusion until regimental guides rescued them and led them to their regiments. Often it was nearly midnight when kitchen teams showed up, and the fighting men who had run out of rations and couldn't borrow any had to go to bed without supper, roundly cursing the drivers in particular and the entire Quartermasters' Corps in general. Before dawn the unwieldy, fragmentized caterpillar which had scattered into hundreds of pieces during the night had to reassemble, but it was hours before the ungainly caravan was bobbling down the road again. Miles behind its marching men it was often cut off by flank movements of the enemy and left to disintegrate in pandemonium.

Sometimes the teams had hardly unhitched for the night when orders arrived that a segment of the train be detached and follow a body of troops elsewhere. Drivers set out, traveling without lights, their sole guide a dingy white pocket handkerchief pinned to the back of the wagon master at the head of the line. They drove as hard and fast as they could over roads that oozed black mud from steady rains and the churnings of thousands of horses and men, often without guard and in plain sight of Rebel campfires, raked by skirmishers' fire.

Soldiers in the front columns usually sensed the pull and tug of the battle lines and were often more aware of impending victory or defeat than their generals. Not so with the unarmed teamsters in the rear, who lived in a fog of rumors and tangled movements. They were the last to know what was going on and the first to be slaughtered when lines caved in suddenly and there was a bloody rout. Chaos prevailed when a fighting line collapsed and men streamed to the rear. Trains lost their wagon masters and regiments, drivers went mad with fear, cut loose their animals and fled into the woods, or were shot and sabered by Confederate cavalrymen. Driverless horses and mules stampeded, wagons overturned scattering supplies and equipment in all directions and barring roads to retreat. When the panic subsided and some semblance of order was restored, the laborers' corps were sent out on the battlefields to bring in the wounded, bury corpses and rescue what equipment they could.

Throughout the war, enlisted men swore at the teamsters and the teamsters swore at their animals and the holy crusade to save the Union mired in muck and blood and the fields of Virginia stank with unburied corpses. The Quartermasters appealed for uniforms, guns and training for their men but their pleas were ignored. It was not the glory in battle Robert Fitzgerald dreamed of, and yet, however much the boys in blue sneered at the teamsters and contrabands, the Quartermasters' reports gave mounting evidence of the thankless toil of these men in the long nightmare of advances and retreats.

The black men were good workers, steady under fire, eager to follow orders and help the Union; they bore more fatigue and exposure than many of the white soldiers and laborers, and their assistance was of immense value to the Union army. In fact, at the end of 1862, Quartermaster-General M. C. Meigs reported that the large numbers of Negroes employed for the necessary labor of the army posts had freed the white soldier to perform his purely military duties, "and enabled him to preserve his health and acquire that proficiency in drill and the use of arms which has made the troops in the Department of the South so efficient in every field."

Fine, thought young men like Robert Fitzgerald, but not enough. If they must bear the risks of war, let them at least have recognition as soldiers and the dignity of uniforms. What Grandfather did not realize then was that he and his father, brothers, cousins and thousands of other colored men were building a record which slowly wore down the resistance to the idea of Negroes in Yankee uniforms.

10

GRANDFATHER FITZGERALD was delivering horses somewhere in Maryland in late September, 1862, when news of Lincoln's preliminary Emancipation Proclamation reached the battlefields. A few days earlier one of the bloodiest battles of the war had ended with an inconclusive victory for the Union at Antietam. Mr. Lincoln had been waiting for a Union success to issue the momentous declaration that on January 1, 1863, "*all persons held as slaves within any State . . . the people whereof shall then be in rebellion against the United States, shall be then, thenceforward and forever free.*"

Behind Lincoln's pronouncement, viewed by him as a purely military measure at the time, stretched eighteen long months of staggering Union losses in Virginia. The Peninsular Campaign against Richmond had fizzled; the Union army was now on the defensive. Lee had turned the tables and invaded Union territory. He was now threatening to take Washington and many Yanks were beginning to believe him invincible. Union generals came and went; Lincoln was berated as a blundering fool. Some Yanks said disgustedly that the war to save the Union was turning into "a nigger's war" and they were going home again. Enlistments fell off. Desertions multiplied. Fever and dysentery were killing off more Yanks than battlefield casualties. Northern states could no longer fill their volunteer quotas and Congress was turning to conscription.

Grandfather's brothers, too, had grown tired of a war which seemed to have no end. Billy had gone home to his family and Richard had given up mule driving and gone to sea. He had clung on, partly out of deep conviction and partly because he was caught up in a swelling movement which swept him along although he did not fully comprehend its magnitude or direction.

In his wanderings about Maryland and Virginia with the teamsters, he saw that there were not two but three armies in the field. The Union had chosen to fight in southern territory among four million slaves intensely interested in the outcome of the contest. One out of every three persons in the South was a slave; these people knew their fate hung in the balance. A sprawling army of blacks materialized when Union and Confederate lines made contact. Official Washington clung to its political aims—to suppress the rebellion and bring the erring slave states back into the Union fold—but enmeshed in every political argument and military event was the insistent question: *What was to be done with the Negroes?*

While Washington was silent or fumbled with piecemeal answers, the Negro slaves were trying to answer the question themselves. It came slowly at first; it was wholly spontaneous, but it moved with inexorable logic toward the only possible result. Notwithstanding official denials or rebuffs, to the Negro slaves the Union armies meant freedom!

Grandfather had seen them appear wherever the federal armies encamped. They came singly, by twos and threes, and sometimes with their families, little children in their arms and small bundles of rags on their backs. They came in rickety wagons, on spavined horses and half-starved mules. They came driving steers and oxen or carrying chickens and turkeys for the Yankee soldiers. Shadowy figures slipped from the swamps; exhausted swimmers crawled up river banks; desperate horsemen galloped through Rebel picket lines in a dash for Union outposts. They swarmed into the camps with small gifts of food and valuable information.

Some brought maps of the Rebel lines and movements and a remarkable knowledge of the enemy's strength and plans. Some were excellent guides who knew every stream, rivulet and forest path in the locality. Some brought Union soldiers who had been trapped behind the Confederate lines and whom they had nursed back to health and guided to safety. They were driven away only to come back again. Nothing stopped or dismayed them. Convinced that liberation lay with the Union, when they could not seek refuge within the Union lines they worked their way around them and flocked northward, homeless and wandering but always confident that freedom lay just ahead.

Working side by side with contrabands, Grandfather was often amazed to discover they were well informed, understood the issues of the war although they could not read and write, and were eager to perform any task to help the Union lines go forward. Men whose masters described them as shiftless and lazy threw themselves into work with a song of joy, and no matter how the battles went they had an unshakable faith that the Union cause would triumph.

From property to contraband of war to freedom and citizenship was a long and grueling march. In the early days of the conflict many Union generals favored returning fugitives to their masters. Officers who refused were threatened with court-martial. Five months after the war began, Congress passed a law confiscating all slaves whose masters had used them in the military service of the Confederacy, but when General Frémont began emancipating the confiscated slaves in Missouri, Lincoln repudiated his order. Lincoln also dismissed the action of General David Hunter in the spring of 1862 which declared all slaves free in Georgia, South Carolina and Florida. Moreover, when that hard-pressed general failed to get reinforcements from Washington and organized Negro soldiers into the 1st South Carolina Volunteer Regiment, Washington ordered the troops disbanded and the crestfallen Negroes were sent home again without pay.

By the summer of 1862, however, it seemed clear that slaveowners in the rebellious states had no intention of accepting the Congressional plan for gradual compensated emancipation of slaves. Firm action was necessary to keep the Union from falling apart. Slavery had already been abolished in the District of Columbia. In June, Lincoln approved a law abolishing slavery in the territories. A month later the Enlistment Act was passed including a provision for the use of Negroes in military service; a second Confiscation Act freed all slaves of disloyal masters coming into Union-held territory. And now within one hundred days all slaves in Confederate territory would be "forever free."

Grandfather received this news with mixed feelings. The proclamation did not go far enough. It did not free more than eight hundred thousand slaves in the loyal border states. Mr. Lincoln believed that the colored people could not live among the whites as free citizens and had prefaced his proclamation with the statement that he would continue his efforts to colonize Negroes elsewhere. He gave no recognition to the efforts of loyal free Negroes and was silent on their use as soldiers. Yet it was a beginning. If the proclamation went into effect, it would be impossible to control slaves anywhere.

A few weeks later, Grandfather paid the major installment on his citizenship. He was transferring horses from Harpers Ferry to Washington and was at a little place called Wenner, just east of Knoxville on the northern bank of the Potomac near Point of Rocks. The hamlet was so tiny that it appeared on none of the war maps. No battles were fought there, but it was a place of destiny for Robert Fitzgerald.

He was traveling at night when suddenly he heard the crack of musketry from Rebel skirmishers. He remembered scrambling down an embankment with his horses, then the shock of bullet against bone. A shot struck the rim of his left eye, shattering a piece of the bone and embedding itself behind the eyeball. He remembered very little after that until he found himself in a hospital temporarily blinded. He spent two weeks in darkness, but since he was one of the lesser casualties and the hospital was jammed with wounded and dying from Antietam, he was discharged without an operation as soon as his sight cleared. By December he was back on duty in Washington.

All through that winter of 1862-63 the gunshot wound plagued him more than he dared admit to anyone. There were periods of fading vision when his movements were reduced to guesswork and he groped along, sensing rather than seeing what happened about him. He could feel the bullet with his fingers, but army surgeons warned him that its removal might cause the loss of his sight altogether, so he took his chances, endured the recurring headaches and plodded about in a blurred world, desperately clinging to his job.

If he stayed close to the battles and kept himself in readiness, the time would come when he could enlist. Anybody could see that the war was going badly for the Union. Sixty thousand men a day were coming down with fever, ague, dysentery and pneumonia. Something would have to be done to infuse new fighting spirit into the demoralized Union lines and buttress the lagging reinforcements. That *something* embraced the hopes of colored men to defend their nation. Frederick Douglass had predicted from the outset of the war that the Negro would join the fight before it was over. He wisely observed that once a black man got into the uniform of the United States with a loaded musket on his shoulder, no power on earth could deny that he had earned the right to citizenship.

Public opinion was shifting slowly from horror at the thought of Negro troops to the realization that Negroes were needed to help win the war. The Attorney General's office had issued an opinion that a free person of color, if born in the United States, was a citizen. Congress had authorized Mr. Lincoln to use persons of African descent in whatever military capacity he saw fit. Northern newspapers were beginning to look favorably upon the idea, but the Confederate South screamed that turning Negro slaves with guns in their hands against their masters would be an act of barbarism calculated to bring about the annihilation of the Negro race. Some southern newspapers considered the whole idea of Negro troops a grim joke typical of the "Gorilla" in the White House who probably had Negro blood in his own veins. In the face of these attacks and ambivalent northern opinion, Mr. Lincoln was reluctant to put Negroes in uniform during the hundred-day waiting period granted to southern slaveowners in which they could lay down their arms and accept a plan of gradual compensated emancipation of their slaves.

While official Washington temporized, some practical-minded Union generals proceeded to organize Negro troops on their own authority. By October, 1862, General Jim Lane had raised the 1st

and 2nd Kansas Colored Volunteers, who saw action against a
Rebel force at the Osage River in Missouri without having been
officially mustered in. Around the same time, General Butler
organized the free Negroes of New Orleans into the 1st Regiment
of Louisiana Native Guards and set them to guarding railroads
and bridges. Official Washington chose to ignore these moves, but
word was filtering back north that the blacks were dependable and
brave.

Finally the War Department gave General Rufus Saxton permission to reorganize the disbanded 1st South Carolina Volunteers.
The regiment was mustered in on November 7, 1862, as the first
Negro regiment with official military status, under the command
of Colonel Thomas Wentworth Higginson, a Massachusetts
Abolitionist. Six days later, 240 of the men were assigned to a
foraging expedition on one of the small Rebel-held sea islands of
the Doboy River, a few miles east of Darien, Georgia. Five out
of every six had never before handled a gun and one fourth of
them had been under arms less than two weeks, but the men
threw themselves into their mission with fervor and the "grim
joke" became a terrible reality to the Rebels in the skirmish which
followed. The Rebels hastily withdrew and the Negro troops
completed their foraging mission. Jubilance over their success
spread from the Sea Islands to the North and even Mr. Lincoln
was convinced. When his final Emancipation Proclamation was
issued on January 1, 1863, it contained a clause guaranteeing that
former slaves would be received in all branches of the military
service.

Well, thought Robert Fitzgerald, if former slaves could fight
as soldiers, surely free men of color would be accepted. He waited
hopefully for his own state to act, but there was no immediate
response from Pennsylvania. Massachusetts took the lead instead.
Governor John A. Andrew raised the famous 54th Massachusetts
Volunteers and was recruiting the 55th within two months after
the issuance of the Emancipation Proclamation. Massachusetts
had a very small colored population but the energetic governor
put recruiting agents in the field and men came from many states
to join up. He declared, "I rejoice in having been instrumental in
giving them a chance to vindicate their manhood, and to strike

a telling blow for their own race and the freedom of all their posterity. . . . No one can ever deny the rights of citizenship in a country to those who have helped to create it or save it."

Frederick Douglass approached Governor Curtin of Pennsylvania to request that he raise a Negro regiment. The governor flatly rejected the idea and held out against recruiting Negro troops until Pennsylvania itself faced invasion and the state went on an emergency basis. In June, 1863, Lee's advance columns marched toward Chambersburg on their way to Gettysburg. Only then did Camp William Penn near Philadelphia receive its first Negro recruits. Robert Fitzgerald was not among them. Two weeks earlier he and his cousin, Joe Valentine, had gone to Philadelphia and joined the crew of the steamer *Continental*.

Grandfather's decision to move toward the navy at this time was motivated by his resentment over the pay of Negro soldiers who had already enlisted. A few weeks earlier Secretary of War Stanton had ruled that Negro soldiers would receive only ten dollars a month, of which three dollars might be given in clothing. White soldiers received thirteen dollars monthly pay exclusive of clothing. Governor Andrew had promised the first northern Negro regiments which he had recruited in Massachusetts that they would receive equality in every respect with the white regiments from that state. His promise had attracted men from many states. The ruling was announced after the Massachusetts Volunteers had departed for the South.

The War Department had chosen to treat Negro soldiers on the same level as contraband laborers. Grudgingly they were given the uniforms but they would not have the pay of free men. Governor Andrew appealed to Secretary Stanton to rescind his ruling but Stanton replied that the duty of the Negro soldier to defend his country in the same manner as the white soldier did not depend upon what the country paid and added, "the true way to secure her rewards and win her confidence is not to stipulate for them, but to deserve them." True, thought the Negroes, but it was an odd justice which required the same sacrifices from the black soldier that it did from the white with little more than half the pay. It was not the *amount* which galled, but the *difference!*

Since the Union navy made no such differences and paid each

man according to his rank, Robert Fitzgerald and Joe Valentine shipped to New York and, on July 29, 1863, enlisted for one year. The navy had avoided the bungling errors of the War Department through a simple common-sense plan. At the outset of the war, Negro fugitives escaped by waterways and made their way to Union vessels in whatever craft was handy. They found both a haven from slave catchers and a place to serve. Secretary of Navy Welles advised ships' officers that the contrabands could be neither expelled from the ships nor forced to work without pay. His directive concluded, "You are therefore authorized, when their services can be made useful, to enlist them for the naval service, under the same forms and regulations as apply to other enlistments." Thus escaped fugitives and free Negroes served on board the United States vessels without segregation or difference in pay. Farmers and laborers were converted into powder boys and gunners, and before the war ended nearly thirty thousand black men wore navy middies and supplied one-fourth of all enlistments.

Robert Fitzgerald and Joe Valentine, having had no previous nautical experience, were rated as landsmen drawing sixteen dollars a month and assigned to the receiving ship U.S.S. *North Carolina* in Brooklyn Navy Yard for a two weeks' training period. As soon as he got into his navy togs, Grandfather rushed out and had a picture taken of himself to send home to his folks. It was a daguerreotype of a round-faced beardless young man of twenty-two, a wisp of mustache carefully trimmed on his upper lip, dressed in a short open navy jacket and middies, his round sailor's cap tipped jauntily toward the right eyebrow, his neckerchief loosely tied in front and a metal identification tag hanging from a cord about his neck.

He had achieved his dream; he was officially in the war; but he was to learn that each step forward against unreasoning prejudice was made at high cost. He arrived aboard the *North Carolina* to find the crew still buzzing with excitement over the draft riots in New York two weeks earlier where draft headquarters and a Negro orphanage were stoned and burned by men who resented being drafted into a "nigger's war." The atmosphere was still tense and the men told tales of horror from firsthand observation. A squad of marines had been dispatched from the *North Carolina* to assist in quelling the disorders, but of the three eighteen-man howitzer crews that went ashore, seven men had deserted in the confusion, taking with them seven army pistols and eight swords. The riots had spread to Boston and other cities and hundreds of terrified Negroes were left homeless and without food and shelter.

Robert Fitzgerald had no time to brood over the violence against colored people. He was rushed through the essentials of deck drill, steering, rowing, knotting and splicing ropes, climbing riggings, bending and reefing sails, manning and firing nine-inch and twelve-pound guns aboard the training ship. Then he was transferred to the sloop of war *Ossipee* and shipped to New Orleans with 335 men to join the Western Gulf Blockading Squadron then under Commander Bell.

The voyage south was a rough one; men were jammed on top of one another on the narrow decks, sleeping in piles against boxes and lifeboats or wherever they could squeeze themselves. From New Orleans they sailed to Galveston, where Robert and Joe were among the thirty-three recruits picked up by the U.S.S. *Bienville* for transfer to the U.S. bark *William G. Anderson* in which they patrolled the Gulf of Mexico from the Rio Grande to New Orleans and sailed up and down the lower Mississippi.

Grandfather's naval service was dogged by misfortune. There were little military action, much drudgery, unbearable heat and dampness, bad food and illness among the men. He spent his time pumping out leaks in the engine room, transferring heavy bags of coal from a near-by schooner through choppy waters or clinging to the ship's side painting its hull. He soon contracted bone fever and malaria.

The men on board the *William G. Anderson* were dissatisfied, and deserted whenever they got a chance. The ship's commander, Acting Volunteer Lieutenant F. S. Hill, had been engaged in some questionable operations and was under fire. Shortly before the new recruits came on board, the ship had captured the Rebel schooner *America* trying to run the blockade from Corpus Christi with fifty-one bales of cotton on deck. A prize crew was placed on board to guard the *America*, but that midnight she capsized and the prize cotton was dumped into the sea. The crew spent all night rowing about in small boats rescuing the "drift cotton" and managed to haul in some forty-odd bales. Instead of sending the cotton to New Orleans for military adjudication, Commander Hill had it placed aboard the bark *Sol Wilder* and shipped to a brokerage firm in Boston where it was sold and the profit divided among the officers and crew.

Wind of this black-market transaction got to higher authorities and an investigation followed. In October, Hill was relieved of his command and transferred to another vessel. He was later court-martialed and tried in Philadelphia, convicted of "scandalous conduct tending to the destruction of good morale," fined $900, and reprimanded by the Secretary of Navy. Under these circumstances the ship's crew was apprehensive and its officers short-tempered.

Young Fitzgerald had not been on board two weeks before he ran into trouble. The ship's log of September 29, 1863, contained the cryptic entry: "*At 5:30 Robert Fitzgerald put into double irons on bread & water 5 days for insolence.*" What constituted my grandfather's "insolence" will never be known. He never revealed the incident and must have felt it a disgrace which was better forgotten. Other men were placed in irons from time to time for fighting, deserting ship or stealing provisions from the kitchen quarters, but his offense involved some show of spirit. The discovery of this log entry ninety years later delighted some of his grandchildren, who were rebels themselves and prone to get into difficulties with their superiors over matters of principle.

To Robert Fitzgerald it was anything but delightful. While he lay in the brig, the ship pitched and tossed in heavy rain squalls. His confinement must have ended in illness, for he was released without explanation three days later. Within three weeks he was invalided, and the blindness that followed the gunshot wound of the previous year returned. By Thanksgiving, without ever having gotten into action, he was sent north for discharge on the supply ship U.S.S. *Circassian*. The hospital ticket from his ship attached to his transfer papers stated that he "is affected with Amaurosis. The loss of vision is so great as to render him unfit for service. There is no evidence that the disease originated in the line of duty, although the patient attributes it to a gunshot wound while serving in the army." The ticket was signed by three ship's surgeons who had examined him.

Grandfather's brief, inglorious career in the navy ended after four months with the verdict of blindness from a battle wound that was not regarded as official. The *Circassian* proceeded northward slowly, picking up sick officers and men on the way, supplying the Mobile Bay fleet with meat and provisions and battling heavy gales, with a leak that drew ten inches of water. Robert Fitzgerald sat out the trip in a frenzy of frustration, unable to see the one bit of action which enlivened the voyage when the *Circassian* chased a British vessel, *Minna*, bound for a Rebel port, and seized her as a lawful prize worth $30,000. He could only hear the scurrying sounds, the guns going off and fragments of the story from other men.

Eight days before Christmas they reached Massachusetts and Robert Fitzgerald was sent to Chelsea Naval Hospital. The bone fever subsided after several weeks and his vision partially returned, but doctors could offer him no hope for permanent recovery and told him his days of active service were over. He might have accepted their judgment and gone home when he was discharged had he not heard tales of the Negro troops on the battlefields which circulated wherever colored soldiers and sailors gathered.

The Louisiana Native Guards had fought splendidly at Port Hudson and Milliken's Bend, but the 54th Massachusetts Volunteers in South Carolina had covered themselves with glory. The regiment had left Boston that May bound for Hilton Head. Six weeks later it stood before the almost impregnable breastworks of Fort Wagner on Morris Island awaiting orders to assault. Led by their commander, Colonel Robert Gould Shaw of Boston, they were to lead the brigade, and everything depended upon their gaining the parapet of the fort. At the signal the black regiment started forward over the half mile of sandy marshes which lay between them and the foot of the breastworks. Not a sound came from the fort until they were within two hundred feet of the parapet; then the Confederates let loose volley after volley of musketry and artillery. The men in the front ranks were mowed down, but the black men kept advancing and did not pull back until they were ordered to do so. When the grisly encounter was over three hundred black corpses lay outside the fort. Colonel Shaw was killed with his men. The attack was a costly failure which proved that Fort Wagner was impregnable, but one other important fact was clearly established that night. Never again would the white soldiers and officers who witnessed that ghastly engagement doubt the courage of black men.

The most moving part of the story was that the men of the 54th had given their noblest sacrifice *without a cent of pay!* When the regiment learned it would receive less pay than white soldiers, the men voted to serve without pay until the inequality was removed. Governor Andrew, having failed to move the War Department, hastened back to Massachusetts and laid the matter before the state legislature, which promptly voted to make up the deficiency so that the Negro soldiers of the Massachusetts regiments would receive the same pay as white soldiers. When Governor Andrew notified the regiment in South Carolina of this action, the men politely declined Massachusetts' generous offer. Three times the regiment mustered in for pay and three times it refused the money. The men declared they would give their soldiering to the government free of charge until it saw fit to treat them as free men. Their action in serving without pay for eighteen months stirred the nation and moved Congress to rectify the matter.

Listening to these tales of heroism, Robert Fitzgerald carefully made his plans. He learned that Governor Andrew, encouraged by the success of the first two Negro regiments, was recruiting a third —the 5th Massachusetts Cavalry. On January 14, 1864, he was discharged from the navy as totally unfit for service. The navy was through with him, but this stubborn young man was by no means through with the war. The very next day he volunteered as a private in the 5th Massachusetts Cavalry, was assigned to Company F and sent to Camp Meigs, Readville, Massachusetts.

The man who had refused to lie about his race to get into the army now filled out his enlistment papers, giving Boston as his address and swearing upon oath that he had never been discharged from service as a result of disability. He was among the first to enlist in the new regiment, and that he was accepted at all was possible only because of the notoriously lax methods of medical examination given to Civil War recruits. In those final desperate

months of the conflict any man who could stand up was sent to
the front. The examining surgeon blandly swore that Robert G.
Fitzgerald, the enlistee, was in good physical condition. With a
flourish, Grandfather proudly signed his name to the oath of
allegiance to the United States at the bottom of his enlistment
papers. That same day he began to keep a diary.

11

June 15, 1864. Aroused this morning at 2 o'clock by the harsh command 'to arms!' 'fall in!' 10 a.m. Engaging the foe with infantry and artillery. Driving him slowly from a line 4 deep the woods so thick no mortal can see more than 15 or 20 yards. Grape, canister & shell whizzing in every direction. Emerged from the woods in the face of a terrific fire and in front of the Rebel breastwork, a falter, our noble colonel wounded but mounts his horse & a charge upon the fort. It is ours; but few prisoners are taken. Have sent a brass 12 lb. Howitzer down to City Point drawn by 50 of the boys.

FROM ROBERT G. FITZGERALD'S DIARY

A PARAGRAPH hastily scribbled in a private soldier's note-book on the battlefield described accurately the first skirmish in the Battle of Petersburg, 1864. This record by an obscure man about other obscure men whose courage was far greater than their military skill that day was more authentic and loomed larger in the eyes of Robert Fitzgerald's descendants than all the brilliant voluminous accounts of Civil War battles.

Grandfather's one obsession when he mustered in with the 5th Massachusetts Cavalry at Readville on Washington's birthday, 1864, was to prove his manhood in battle. It was the dominant theme of his diary and was shared by the men in his regiment. It exceeded the normal standards of loyalty. From the moment he put on a uniform he was driven by a compulsion to excel which made no allowances for inexperience, fear, frailty of body or individual capacities.

Every Negro soldier who mustered in knew that he was up against the stubborn belief that Negroes lacked both the intelligence and bravery of white men. The Yanks interpreted the absence of widespread revolts among the slaves during the war as cowardice rather than caution or restraint. They were deeply skeptical about Negro troops. Their experience with the blacks had been confined largely to contrabands and laborers; they had yet to accept them as equals and fighting comrades. Generals, plagued with battle inefficiency and increasing desertions among white troops, were even more dubious about the fighting qualities of colored soldiers. If a white man defaulted, it was an individual defection; if a colored man failed, the whole race was at fault.

Fortunately for Grandfather and his mates, the regiment had good officers who were sympathetic and knew what was at stake. Their commander, Colonel Henry S. Russell, was a man of intelligence, conviction and battle experience. Two members of the famous Bowditch family of Boston, distinguished in the sciences and known for their Abolitionist views, were also among the 5th's officers. Only men of high moral stamina or ambition for promotion would accept commands in Negro regiments. They risked their reputations and their lives to a much greater degree than officers in white regiments. The butt of jeers and criticism from their own ranks, they also faced terrible threats from the Confederates, who hated and feared the Negro troops more than any other sector of the Union army. No greater humiliation could befall the Rebels than to retreat before or be captured by units containing former slaves. They had issued orders that all white officers of black regiments, if captured, be denied treatment as prisoners of war and be put to death as outlaws and insurrectionists.

When Captain Charles P. Bowditch, commander of Company F, discovered that Private Fitzgerald had some education, he immediately appointed him company clerk for three months and Grandfather gladly assumed the task. Record keeping had been part of his Quaker training and he was meticulous in his work.

His eyesight was none too reliable but he bent close to the pages to keep the lines straight. He was soon familiar with the name and background of every man in his company, brooded over each casualty or mishap as he entered it into the record, noted sadly that four men had died of illness in the hospital before the regiment left camp and was relieved that only one man had deserted—a member of the company's band.

Company F's muster roll, which he recorded, was typical of the Union's nearly 200,000 Negro soldiers. Its 83 enlisted men came from seventeen states, Canada, the West Indies and France. In other companies some even came from Africa. Over half of the enlistees were born in slave states and had come to Massachusetts in order to enlist. Most of them were boys in their teens and young men in their early twenties, but a number were over forty. About one-third were married and had children, and they represented eighteen different occupations. The largest group included farmers, but there were cooks, waiters, blacksmiths, saddlers, teamsters, plasterers, painters, masons, carpenters and seamen in the ranks—all equally determined to make good cavalrymen. Grandfather listed himself as a seaman with a mother and two sisters as dependents.

At the time the 5th Massachusetts Cavalry went into camp, Lieutenant General U. S. Grant was made commander of all the Union armies and was determined to produce decisive results. Training of any sort was nominal at that time, but the normal two-year period required to train both horse and rider for an experienced cavalryman was, of necessity, cut to two months. What the men of the 5th got by way of training was good for dress parade but practically worthless on a battlefield; they were hurried through the essentials of quick bridling and saddling, drilled briefly in Cooke's Cavalry Tactics—single-rank formation—instructed in drawing, swinging, parrying and thrusting sabers while in saddle, but given almost no instruction in infantry fighting in the event they were dismounted. By early May, after only two months in camp, they were ordered to report to Washington for active duty.

Governor John A. Andrew visited the camp the Sunday before the regiment left for the field. Grandfather's diary reported the regiment's enthusiastic reception of the man responsible for putting them into uniform :

May 1. This morning rainy and very disagreeable. I feel very unwell, the bone fever is getting worse. I begin to feel homesick as I have not received a letter from home since the 26th of March, they used to write 2 a week. Today I have finished my diary of the quarter, dating January 14th to May 1st. This morning we had a fine sabbath school. 6 P.M. Today we had the extreme pleasure of hearing from Gov. Andrew's own lips the facts relating to the Bounty and monthly pay of colored soldiers. We all feel perfectly satisfied now. The regt. gave him nine rousing cheers and he walked down the line with hat in hand notwithstanding the rain. A true patriotic man.

The Massachusetts governor's visit was a significant moment in the life of the 5th Massachusetts Cavalry. It was the only colored cavalry raised in that state and the men felt a certain distinction in belonging to an elite corps of the Union army. They sat astride their horses in complete battle equipment behind the color guards who bore the Union flag and their regimental banner—a dark blue, gold-fringed insignia in the center of which was the golden embroidered United States shield and eagle and the simple inscription FIFTH CAVALRY REGIMENT in a circle of thirty-four gold stars. It hangs today in the circular Hall of Flags in Boston's State House with the massed banners of other Massachusetts Volunteer regiments of the Civil War.

For many of these men their uniforms measured their leap almost overnight from chattel property to manhood. So precious was this battle gear to them that unlike many soldiers at the front who threw away their equipment in actual combat, they held on to it grimly under all circumstances. One wounded Negro soldier after a battle was seen crawling painfully toward the rear dragging his entire regalia. When offered to be relieved of it, he shook his head and said he wanted to keep his equipment so that all could see he was a soldier and not mistake him for a contraband.

Robert Fitzgerald's company pulled out of Readville with the 5th's Second Battalion on May 6, bound for Washington. His regiment was heading for the Virginia front at the beginning of the final big campaign of the war. Two days earlier General Grant and the Army of the Potomac with General Meade in command had left winter quarters at Culpeper with more than 100,000 men and 50,000 horses, and was now engaging Lee's forces in the first great battle of the Wilderness Campaign. Around the same time, in the West General William T. Sherman's army was pulling away from Chattanooga to begin its march through Georgia. South of Richmond, Major General Ben Butler had begun a movement from Fortress Monroe up the south bank of the James River to harass Lee from the rear, or take Petersburg and cut Lee's railroad contact with the South and West. This was the Union's first co-ordinated effort to engage the Confederate armies as heavily as possible on all fronts simultaneously and prevent the shift of Rebel forces from one area to another as had happened in the past. Grant was looking for a decisive victory to conclude the war before the November elections if possible. The 5th Massachusetts was being shipped out to join the Virginia sector of this campaign.

Grandfather Fitzgerald was anxious to get to the front, but he left Massachusetts with some regret. He had found friends in Boston and the kindly atmosphere had left a deep impression. He had also met a young lady formerly from the South named Miss Annie Thompson, "who is just in the bloom," he wrote, but added that "many of the men long for a change of place, to go to the front where we can prove our love of liberty and that we be men." As the troops boarded a transport at East Greenwich, Rhode Island, he wrote in his diary:

May 6. . . . 2 P.M. As I look upon the scenery of the Eastern Gates and perhaps for the last time, I can but thank God for raising up such friends for the colored man. . . . Born in a border state as I was, I can fully appreciate the difference between the frank open manly principle of these people and the would-be Lords of the South. We are cheered in every town we pass through. When leaving Readville I was surprised to see a great many white people weeping as the train moved South. And I have formed a firm conclusion that these people are our only true friends.

He was even more surprised at the continued excitement and interest which his regiment evoked as it traveled south. The idea of Negro troops, which had been unthinkable in 1861, was now accepted as commonplace by many, with wide-eyed curiosity by some and wild enthusiasm by a few. A year earlier the 54th Massachusetts had by-passed New York City to avoid threatened insults; now the 5th landed on the East River, marched across town and took the ferry for New Jersey without incident. The atmosphere of Philadelphia, too, had greatly changed. Early in 1863, recruiting agents for the Massachusetts Volunteers had to sneak their recruits onto the cars one by one to prevent mob violence. Now the Negro troops ate supper at the famous Cooper's Shop, a volunteer way station for transient Union soldiers, without commotion. Young Fitzgerald noted, "A gentleman there expressed himself much pleased with the appearance of the regiment, and hoped we as men of color would win a name that will stand in our favour upon the record of our country."

His train passed through Wilmington at two o'clock Sunday morning, May 8. Like most young men, he wanted his folks to see him in his bright new uniform. Richard had dropped in on him at camp just before he left Massachusetts when the S.S. *Norman* was in port at Boston, and he had been glad "to see a dear brother so far from home." Since he had not found time to have a photograph taken in his cavalry outfit, he had hoped somehow the home folks would be in Wilmington when his train came through. "I could only drop a few lines to Aunt Lizzie on the track. I am sad to leave Wilmington, my native town without seeing a relative, or even a friend," he wrote.

That evening his battalion reached Washington after a derailment some twenty miles from the city. "There was a terrible smash up in the train," he recorded. "A bundle belonging to our company fell on the track and threw the wheels off and caused a dreadful smash from which we escaped only by a miracle. I was thrown from the car down an embankment and into a gutter and was taken out by one of our kindhearted fellows. Some had their faces smashed up, but none were killed; three cars were smashed all up and pushed from the track."

Washington seethed with feverish operations and war rumors. The 5th was quartered on Arlington Heights with two other Negro regiments to await orders. When the orders came the regiment received its first bitter disappointment; the men were told to turn in their sabers. They were to be transferred to the infantry for thirty to sixty days. Robert Fitzgerald commented caustically on May 10, "The government is about transferring the regiment into infantry, but if they do they will lose some men." Then he trudged off gloomily to Washington to express $270 of his bounty pay to his father and to take "a long farewell of my dear friend Annie E. Thompson," who had apparently come on to Washington as a volunteer worker in the Sanitary Commission.

The new orders, the dismal downpour of rain which seeped through the small tents and soaked the men's belongings combined with disheartening news from the battlefront to make Private Fitzgerald's stay in Washington a melancholy one. Next day the dismounted and disarmed 5th Massachusetts Cavalry was ordered to report to Major General Butler at Fortress Monroe. The men were somewhat consoled when they heard that several white cavalry outfits waiting at Washington for new mounts had also been ordered to turn in their sabers and join the infantry. What General Grant needed most right now was a marching army that would hammer away at the Army of Northern Virginia, front and rear, until one or the other of the two forces was destroyed.

Most of General Butler's men were bottled up in a narrow neck of land on the south side of the James River called Bermuda Hundred, but on his way up the James he had dropped off General Hinks' division of Negro troops at a little steamboat landing called City Point where the Appomattox River emptied into the James. Robert Fitzgerald's regiment was put on a transport, sent down the Potomac and up the James to City Point where they were attached to Brigadier General E. W. Hinks' 3rd Division, XVIII Corps, and became part of the famous Black Phalanx on the Petersburg front.

The regiment went into camp in the middle of a wheat field, received muskets and other infantry equipment and began musketry drill and picket duty. For the next four weeks, young Fitzgerald lived in maddening proximity to battles which never came close enough to involve the 5th, and fretted away on picket duty and long reconnaissance marches which never found the enemy. His camp was about twenty miles from Richmond and he could hear the heavy guns and the fighting around Fort Darling between Petersburg and the Rebel capital.

He circulated among the other Negro regiments quartered near by and found old friends. Two of his old classmates from Ashmun Institute were there—William H. Hunter and Christian A. Fleetwood, the latter now a sergeant major in the 4th U.S. Colored Troops. He also found his uncle-in-law, Abe J. Valentine, the doughty teamster of fifty-five who had joined up with the 6th U.S. Colored Troops.

He learned that none of the colored troops in this area had seen action, and, like his own regiment, they were restive for combat yet uncertain as to how they would be received by the white regiments on the Virginia front. The stories they had heard were not at all reassuring. Only a few weeks earlier, up at Alexandria, a Michigan trooper from Kilpatrick's cavalry outfit had run his saber through a Negro guard when ordered to halt.

There was no uncertainty as to what Negro soldiers might expect from the Rebels. By now news of the Fort Pillow massacre in April had reached the troops in Virginia. That Union-held garrison about forty miles above Memphis had attempted to hold out against a Confederate cavalry corps under the Rebel Forrest who later became head of the Ku-Klux Klan after the war. More than half of its slim force of defenders were Negro soldiers of the 6th U.S. Heavy Artillery under the command of Major L. F. Booth and a section of the 2nd U.S. Light Artillery. Major Booth refused General Forrest's demand for unconditional surrender, and in the ensuing battle Booth was killed and the fort overrun. Hopelessly outnumbered, the garrison finally surrendered, but with cries of "No quarter!" and "Black flag!"—contemptuous reference to the Union flag when defended by black soldiers—the Confederates set upon the wounded soldiers and unarmed civilians inside the fort. Women and children were slaughtered indiscriminately. Men were bayoneted and sabered, shot down from behind and clubbed to death as they lay helpless on the ground. Some were nailed to the walls and set on fire to burn to death. When details of the massacre reached the nation a Congressional investigation was made, but the Richmond *Enquirer* openly demanded that the Fort Pillow example be followed in Virginia and suggested that no Confederate soldier should soil his hands by taking a black man prisoner.

Robert Fitzgerald learned what every other Negro soldier had to learn: that he had only two courses of action—victory or death. Time and again in this strangest of wars among kinsmen, the enlisted men of both armies made little private truces in the lull of battle. When the dug-in lines faced one another, firing on both sides of the entrenchments ceased by tacit consent to allow men to answer the calls of nature or fill their canteens at a common stream. Between fights the blue and gray troopers fraternized unashamedly. These truces, however, never extended to the Negro sector of the Union lines. There the Rebel musketry was hottest and unceasing. The black soldiers were not even permitted to come on the field after a battle under a flag of truce to gather up their dead and wounded as the white Yanks were allowed to do.

A few days after his arrival, Grandfather saw the fruits of Rebel hatred. Pickets returning from the outposts reported that a heavy Rebel force lay at their rear and brought in the body of a picket killed that afternoon. He wrote, "He was first shot in the calf of the leg, which disabled him, then they came up to him and broke his skull with the butt of their muskets. His brains were scattered over his face and head. Can such men eventually triumph? God forbid!"

Several nights later the 5th Massachusetts pickets had their chance to retaliate against a Confederate soldier. Fitzgerald's diary reported that they captured him about a mile and a half from their entrenchments. He was armed with a knife and revolver and his pockets were loaded with Rebel scrip, greenbacks, gold and silver.

"Saved him!" was Fitzgerald's brief comment.

Reading this record, one could only marvel at their restraint. White officers who served with Negro regiments were struck by this curious humanity in their men and wrote of it often during and after the war. Considering the many indignities they had suffered at the hands of white men, the Negroes were surprisingly lacking in personal bitterness. There was little of the impassioned hatred the Rebels might have expected. In fact, there were numerous instances of deep compassion for their enemies. After the assault on Petersburg, General Hinks was amazed to see two wounded colored soldiers crawling toward the rear and helping along a Confederate prisoner more disabled than they.

And perhaps, in the long run, this trait hammered into them by hard necessity would be their greatest contribution to their country. They were the conservators and peacemakers rather than the warriors and pioneers. They had learned to withstand and to endure rather than to conquer and destroy. Their precarious position had taught them to weigh and to deliberate, and the sorrows of their enslavement had filled them with mercy instead of vengeance. Theirs was more often a wisdom of the spirit than of books, and their natural instinct was to share rather than to withhold.

This trait of humility cropped up constantly in my grandfather's diary. It had deep spiritual roots. He wrote, "I cannot but acknowledge here the kind and protecting hand of Providence to me an unworthy and undutiful child. And I trust that the season of refreshing will soon come." On June 10, the anniversary of his leaving home to join the navy, he wrote, "Oh, what sorrow I have experienced through the past 12 months, but it is for the welfare of good government and to establish a noble principle. How good the Heavenly Father has been to me a very unworthy and reckless boy during my wanderings from 1861 till now. I have thought I could [not] have gone through what I have, but I trust that I may return home safe. . . ."

He went on picket duty in late May. The sun shone with dazzling brilliance and the sky was deep blue. At home in Pennsylvania the roses would be in bloom and the young corn a foot high. Here in Virginia the trees were scorched and broken, the fields were rutted and crisscrossed by entrenchments or grown up in weeds, the birds were hushed and the only sound was the continuous roar of distant artillery. Between duties he found time to sketch a lovely view of the bend of James River above City Point, to read his daily Bible lessons and copy a favorite verse from the New Testament in his diary. Off duty he and his tentmate, Corporal Joseph Henry, a young teamster from Bucks County, Pennsylvania, took baths in the James and swam out around the government transports anchored midstream.

General Butler visited the camp and inspected the regiment on

May 24, congratulating the men on their high morale and promising them they would soon be mounted. Grandfather made a pencil sketch of the general in the flyleaf of his diary and wrote, "He is a fine old fellow. . . . I feel very well satisfied with this kind of service."

That same afternoon the Negro troops at City Point were electrified by news of the splendid fighting of the 1st and 2nd cavalry regiments under General Wild at Wilson's Wharf across the river. Confederate General Fitzhugh Lee had ridden down to Wilson's Wharf with a large cavalry force supported by artillery to dislodge the Negro troops, demanding unconditional surrender and promising to treat the black regiments as prisoners of war. General Wild and his men refused to surrender, whereupon Lee's cavalry dismounted and fought as infantry. The inexperienced black soldiers were driven into their entrenchments, but while Lee charged the works repeatedly with heavy assaults, the black lines held. Lee had to abandon the attack and withdraw. Northern newspapers hooted at the dashing Confederate general for his humiliation at the hands of raw colored troops while it had nothing but high praise for the Negro cavalry.

Robert Fitzgerald could hardly contain himself when he saw General William F. Smith's divisions passing through to take transport for the Battle of Cold Harbor. His impatience increased when the 5th Massachusetts was left behind for more picket duty while other colored regiments advanced on a Confederate fort several miles away. He wrote: "May 31st. This morning everything is lovely. We can see the fight at Fort Duncan quite plainly, it is distant only 3 miles, and one can see the flash and the course of the shell as it makes its horrid circuit through the air. The 4th, 5th, 6th and 22nd Col. troops are participating in it. I almost begrudge them the honour, though it is a solemn fight."

He didn't have to wait long after that for action. On the 9th he noted, "All bustle this morning. Butler's troops engaged near Petersburgh and 500 of our Regt. sent to assist. . . . 4 P.M. Wounded coming in by the dozens." There were now unmistakable signs of a major campaign in the making. Federal gunboats kept up a continual shelling of Rebel positions on the north side of the James while the shelling on land grew more intense. The 5th was put to marching all day on reconnaissance. On June 14 Private Fitzgerald reported, "Fell in with the boys for reconnoitre at about ten this morning. Marched to line of pickets furthest out on the road leading to the river. Fell back and was reinforced by the 4th Mass. Cavalry and advanced on the road to the left. Marched through woods over large plantation and through slave quarters up narrow glens and halted in a shady nook under a hill as a reserve, the main body going on, but found no enemy save two rebel officers belonging to the signal corps. Returned safe."

Night after night for two weeks he and his company mates were called from their blankets to stand under arms nervously fingering their muskets until daylight, every minute expecting a Rebel attack or orders they were to march on Richmond. But when the big moment finally came, the 5th Massachusets was not headed toward Richmond. It marched southwest toward the city of Petersburg.

In five weeks of marching and fighting that ended at Cold Harbor on June 3, Grant had lost sixty thousand men to Lee's less than half that number. Though badly hit, the Army of Northern Virginia was still intact and now deeply entrenched between Grant and the Confederate capital. It was useless to storm those Rebel entrenchments, so Grant decided to slip away from Lee, camouflage his movements, bring his entire army south of Richmond and move on Petersburg in a surprise attack before Lee could get there.

Petersburg lay on the south bank of the Appomattox River twenty-two miles south of Richmond and about eight miles from City Point. The nearest railroad center to the Rebel capital, it had four rail connections to the South and West and was the supply line for the Army of Northern Virginia. If Grant could take Petersburg and cut off Lee's supplies, he could force Lee's army to fight or starve. Once Petersburg was in Union hands, Grant supported by Butler could attack Lee from the rear and end the war in Virginia quickly.

At the moment Robert Fitzgerald stood in line waiting to march in the early hours of morning on Wednesday, June 15, neither he nor his commanders knew that there were fewer than three thousand defenders in the Rebel trenches before Petersburg, according to the later account of Confederate General Beauregard in command of Petersburg's defenses. Petersburg could be had for the asking. Grant suspected this to be the case but somehow his estimate failed to percolate down through the chain of command. A week earlier an order to take the town had ended in a fiasco. Now another attempt was being made by Butler with the help of "Baldy" Smith's XVIII Corps and General Hinks' division of Negro troops.

The Union army was standing on the threshold of its greatest opportunity since the war began. As the minutes dropped slowly into the void of that night, Robert Fitzgerald stood waiting in darkness, seeing indistinctly the blurred shapes of men around him and straining his ears to catch details his eyes refused to yield. He learned finally that they were waiting for Kautz' cavalry column to pass before the march advanced.

The men murmured softly, like birds at dusk. Here and there a song rose briefly and guttered out; once or twice a nervous laugh broke the silence, but for the most part the men stood quietly, tense, waiting. And while he could not see their lips moving, he knew they were praying as he was praying. Earlier, he had scribbled hastily in pencil in the front of his diary above his name and post office address: "In case I should be shot please send this to my home." He was about as ready as any man can ever be to face death.

At dawn he fell in with the marching men behind Kautz' cavalry. It had not rained for two weeks and the fine soft dust, ankle deep, swirled about under the horses' feet and settled down upon the foot soldiers, filling their throats with choking silt. Fitzgerald plodded along, panting heavily, coughing and spitting, his eyelids reddening from the grit, his battle gear growing heavier with each step, the old sickness of chills and fevers creeping along the marrow of his bones, his legs feeling rubbery and weak.

The wide ranks spilled out on both sides of the Broadway road. Baldy Smith's two white divisions were on the right; Martindale's men were advancing by the river and Brooks' men were in the center; Hinks' soldiers were on the left near the City Point railroad. They had gone about two and a half miles and reached the railroad track when the column halted suddenly. Shouts up ahead were followed by a burst of musketry and artillery. The firing came from the left of the road just ahead of the Negro troops. It took a little while to find out what had happened. General Hinks rode forward to investigate and found that the Rebel brigade had thrown up a strong position on Baylor's farm about five miles out from the city to halt the invaders.

To take the Rebel outpost, the advancing troops would have to move off the road and come out of a thick woods through which ran a creek and a swamp, clear a field of four hundred yards over open, rising ground in the face of scathing enemy fire. Hinks reported the situation to Baldy Smith, who ordered him to deploy his Negro troops and clear out the Rebel fortification. Hinks marched his two brigades off the road and toward the woods and formed two battle lines with skirmishers in front.

Duncan's brigade formed the first line, while Holman's brigade, with a wing of the 5th Massachusetts Cavalry including Robert Fitzgerald's company, formed the second line. And here came the first hitch. The men of the 5th were willing enough, but neither they nor their officers knew anything about infantry formation, having been trained only in single-rank cavalry tactics. They were so awkward in maneuvering that it took three quarters of an hour to get the lines formed.

It was seven o'clock before they started through the woods. Up ahead at the edge of the forest, Robert Fitzgerald could hear Captain Angell's battery popping away, returning the Rebel fire and in position to cover Hinks' men as they advanced into the clearing. He went forward with the rest, but the next thing he knew he went down into swamp mud, stumbled about over tangled roots and underbrush, splashed through the creek and clambered to the other side to find the lines had disintegrated. Companies and regiments were mixed up and men had scattered into ragged little knots and were milling about without direction. The woods were so dark that he could see only a few yards ahead of him, and his vision was so poor that he found himself bumping into trees as he tried to run forward. Shells whizzed past, snapping off trees and setting the dry brush on fire all about him. Men were yelling and screaming and the battlesmoke and burning woods were so blinding he could tell only by the sound of the batteries which way to go. He groped toward the sound and a few seconds later stood at the edge of the woods where the first jumbled line blinked in the glaring sunlight and stared across the wide field and up the hill.

At the same moment the Confederates on top of the crest poured a volley of canister, spherical shell and musketry down the slope. Captain Angell's battery stoutly answered back and the first lines staggered from the trees, open targets for the Confederate guns which swept the field from end to end. Robert Fitzgerald began to run. Across the field, men dropped in their tracks, but their comrades scrambled over them and kept going. On the far left Fitzgerald could see some of his regiment falling back in confusion but the oncoming waves behind them swept them forward again. It was useless to fire their muskets at that distance; they had to fix bayonets and plow doggedly up the slope. They could see the Stars and Bars of the Confederacy—hated symbol of enslavement and oppression—fluttering on top of the Rebel fort.

The 5th Massachusetts was coming in at an odd angle and catching some of the enemy's cross fire. Halfway up the hill the regiment's commander, Colonel Russell, who was leading their charge, went down with a wound in his left shoulder. For several terrifying moments the regiment swirled about like an armed mob without a head, but when the men saw their wounded commander remount his horse and charge up the hill, they broke into cheers and surged forward once more.

Now the Confederates could see clearly the solid lines of black soldiers, stabilized after the first shock of gunfire, rolling out of the wood and across the field in a dark tidal wave. Fitzgerald was hurled forward by a cheering, yelling, screaming ground swell of men gone mad with the first taste of victory. Skirmishers cleared the piled-up brush and leaped into the rifle pits, but the Rebels had not waited to be taken prisoner. They fled toward Petersburg in panic, leaving behind one twelve-pound howitzer.

Hordes of black soldiers swept over the breastworks, and some of them turned the piece of artillery around toward the fleeing Confederates, but nobody knew how to handle it and the Rebels were already out of musket range and well on their way toward the main Petersburg entrenchments. Grandfather tumbled into a rifle pit gasping for breath and the next moment he was being thumped, pounded, smacked and almost smothered by his frenzied comrades. A pandemonium of joy broke out. The men danced and capered about the captured field piece, patted it, kissed it, hugged and kissed one another, threw their caps in the air. Tears streamed down their faces and many sobbed unashamedly.

One would have thought they had just captured Robert E. Lee himself, the way they behaved over the howitzer. Reverently they placed it on a cart and fifty of them acted as a guard of honor to carry it down to City Point. For the rest of their lives they would be telling their children and grandchildren how the blacks swept up that hillside and how the Rebs turned tail and skedaddled back toward Petersburg at the very sight of them. They had stood the test of fire without flinching and they had a twelve-pound howitzer to prove it. Their story would be an armor of pride for their descendants, for there were those in later years who would have these descendants believe that freedom was a gift bestowed upon them by the magnanimous North to whom they owed an eternal debt of gratitude.

It was one of the bitter ironies of war which prevented Robert Fitzgerald and his mates from marching triumphantly into Petersburg on the night of June 15, 1864. Most accounts agree that General William F. Smith's costly error in timing that night threw away a golden opportunity for the Union and lengthened the war by nine months. The black troops had done their part well. They had opened the road to Petersburg early that morning for Baldy Smith's divisions to pass. Around ten o'clock they met up with other Rebel pickets on Bailey's Creek near Bryant's house, close to the main Confederate defenses, and drove them beyond a heavy woods into their breastworks. By noon the entire Union force of ten thousand men was standing before the Petersburg fortifications.

After many elaborate surveys of the situation and much dilly-dallying, General Smith finally ordered an attack on these breastworks at sunset. General Hinks' colored troops rolled forward carrying the brunt of the fighting. They swarmed into the rifle pits, took two-thirds of the three hundred Confederate prisoners and captured nine of the fifteen guns which fell into Union hands that evening. That they had not faltered under deadly fire was clear from the six hundred corpses scattered in front of the Rebel works. Most of them came from the ranks of the colored soldiers.

By nine o'clock that evening, every Confederate defense outside Petersburg was held by the Union, and there was nothing to prevent General Smith from taking the city. General Hinks was beside himself with joy. His men, flushed with their earlier successes, were eager to finish the job. Nothing lay between them and Petersburg except empty trenches and silent guns. It was a clear, warm evening, the moon was shining brightly, and General Hinks recommended to General Smith that they march on Petersburg without delay and occupy the town by midnight.

For some unaccountable reason, not clear even to Grant, who pondered it in later months, General Smith seemed content to wait until morning to renew the attack. Not even the arrival of the advance columns of General Grant's Army of the Potomac moved him. Hancock's II Corps, coming up and sensing victory in the air, wanted to push right into Petersburg, but Smith merely asked Hancock to relieve the Negro troops in the captured trenches. He sent the colored troops to the rear and made a personal appearance before them to commend them on the splendid fighting they had done that day. Then he retired to his tent to write a glowing report to Grant advising that he now held the key to Petersburg.

The key never turned in the lock. Robert Fitzgerald rolled up in his blanket that night confident he would be in Petersburg shortly after daybreak, but during those silent hours Lee's best veterans had been rushed into the town to dig new entrenchments and mount additional guns. By morning General Smith faced a formidable and determined Confederate army and the black troops' shining hour had passed. Petersburg had now become an impregnable fortress. In the next three days of terrific fighting, the Union lost more than eleven thousand men to Lee's five thousand without gaining an inch, and the city withstood a siege which lasted into early 1865.

Yet it was not a total loss, for the black troops had established that day the value of even poorly trained Negro soldiers. Their assault on the Petersburg defenses coincided with Lincoln's ap-

proval of an act of Congress equalizing their pay as of January 1,
1864. They had not let the Union down, and in the months to
come their record of courage under fire would be the greatest
single argument in favor of giving the Negro soldier the vote.

If Grandfather Fitzgerald knew the Union had made a terrible
blunder that day, his diary gave no hint of it. He was too immersed
in the fragmentary duties of an ordinary foot soldier to see the
whole or be critical of the outcome. He recorded with satisfaction
the six Negro regiments which fought together in the battle of the
15th and added, "I hope the colored troops may always be kept
together."

He was detailed as surgeon's orderly for a few days and sent
down to City Point, which had become Grant's headquarters.
"Thousands of wounded and dying here. . . . There is wonderful
work being done by the Christian Commission. . . . poor wounded
or sick soldiers who are not able to buy are given such little things
as they want. . . . City Point is one immense hospital. Dear
ladies are here all the way from Boston belonging to the Sanitary
Commission as nurses . . . . aroused at 2 A.M. & ordered with the
Surgeon to report to brigade headquarters at Point of Rocks where
we arrived about daylight after a tiresome march, the other orderly
having to carry my baggage, for I could not see and the march was
too hard. . . . Joined the regt. & marched in the scorching sun
about 14 miles, now in front."

For several days his regiment was on picket duty "under the
Rebel breastworks. . . . Can see the Rebel signal flag in motion.
. . . 7 P.M After wading and splashing in the river mud, I am now
sitting cramped up on what I call an island with water on every
side and stooped down so as not to be seen by the Rebel soldiers.
I am in the very face of their fort and in reach of their rifles, but
hid. . . . Mud up to the thighs. . . . Very much surprised that
our line was not attacked last night. About 12 I distinctly heard
swimming which approached my post but I suppose I was seen as
it quietly moved back. It was so dark I could not see as my sight
is so bad. . . . it was but 2 hundred yds across to them & this
morning we can hear as well as see them. Can hear what they say."

Grandfather's army career came to an abrupt end shortly after
he came off picket duty in the mud of the Appomattox River. The

regiment was sent to Point Lookout, Maryland, to get horses and better training in cavalry tactics and to guard prisoners. On July 8, he was ordered from the ranks by Captain Bowditch and into the hospital. He had typhoid fever. His regiment lost twenty-five men during the next few weeks, many of them from typhoid. He clung to life, recording his illness in one-line entries: "Very sick with fever. . . . still high fever. . . . weak in all my joints. . . . Mother arrived here this morning. Oh, what a relief to me. . . . Dear Mother is still here. She has not succeeded in getting a furlough yet. . . . I am afraid mother will have to leave without me."

Great-Grandmother Sarah Ann stayed with him ten days, making the rounds from surgeon to surgeon to arrange a furlough without success. The night she sailed for home a terrible tornado came up "such as I never before saw which blew my window out and I thought was going to blow the building down. The bed and room floor was covered with sand. I feel alarmed for Mother's safety."

It was September before Grandfather was out of the hospital but the old blindness returned and someone had to lead him about the post. He was honorably discharged on October 4, 1864, by reason of poor eyesight, and this time the discharge was final. His regiment remained at Point Lookout until March, 1865, when it was ordered to field duty near Richmond. He later learned that the 5th Massachusetts had the honor to be among the first troops to march into fallen Richmond in April of that year and raise the Union flag. When the regiment mustered out of service several months later, it had lost 7 enlisted men killed in battle and 116 killed by disease. It had been cavalry in name only and what little fighting it did occurred on that June morning on foot at Baylor's farm near Petersburg. But while it achieved very little in the way of military distinction, its brief though confused show of courage that morning was enough to give Robert Fitzgerald a pride which would be felt throughout his family for the next century.

12

AT TIMES in our house Grandfather's role as a Yankee
soldier was sapped of some of its nobility by the guilty
reminder of Rebel ancestors whom Grandmother never let us
forget. My Fitzgerald grandparents looked at the Civil War as
people viewing opposite sides of a coin. Both had suffered much
hardship in it and both rejoiced that slavery was ended. But where
Grandfather's memories evoked a youth fired with a great humanitarian ideal which had triumphed, Grandmother remembered slow
starvation, invasion and disaster. He had the pride of the victorious; hers was the defiance of one whose cause has perished.
She was the last tragic symbol of aristocracy defeated on the
battlefield but determined never to surrender the vestiges of its
arrogant past.

This dual heritage had its complications. One never knew when
there would be a flare-up of the old conflict at home to match the
edginess of almost daily experiences outside. There were days
when Aunt Pauline arrived from school, flushed beyond her
normal ruddiness and unusually short tempered, a sign that she
had suffered one of those periodic visits to her classroom by a
white supervisor accompanied by a needless humiliation.

"Contemptible old Rebs!" she exploded. "They've never
stopped fighting the Civil War. They go out of their way to insult
me. Calling me by my first name in front of my class. It just

makes my blood boil. I feel like walking right out of that school and never going back. I spend a lifetime trying to teach my children respect for themselves and respect for authority, and those dirty Rebs come right behind me and tear down everything I've built up."

I'd heard these protests many times before. My aunts hated the visits of school officials because, while they had found some measure of dignity in the teaching profession, they could not wholly avoid the belittlement of white superiors which made them feel ashamed and degraded. The children, sensing their humiliation, often became insolent and rebellious and it sometimes took several days to get the class back to normal after one of these visits. I heard the same angry comments at the end of each month when my aunts received their salary envelopes addressed to them by their first names without the courtesy titles used for white teachers.

Such conversations often led back to the Civil War, and for my benefit my aunts would talk of Grandfather's military service as if in retelling the story of an honorable past they somehow gathered strength to combat an almost intolerable present. Grandfather's triumph with the Union was an incontrovertible fact of history which helped offset what now appeared to be the reverse of a Union victory.

Grandmother seldom joined in these discussions. There had been little glory in the war for her; in fact, it had represented a come-down for her Smiths and all the old aristocratic families which peopled her childhood world. In deference to Grandfather, she was usually neutral on the subject, but once in a while she rose to the defense of her forebears and reminded us of an ancestry we preferred to forget.

"Always talking about Rebs, Rebs, Rebs," she said. "My daddy was a Rebel, and I'm a Rebel, too. Pauline Dame, you're the last one to get on your high horse about Rebs. There's not one of those white folks in the school system that's any whiter and haughtier than you. You look and act just like a Rebbish Smith, and you can't help yourself. You're one of them."

Aunt Pauline could find no answer, for she bore a more striking resemblance to the Smiths than any other of my grandparents' children. While there were many who thought her looks and haughty bearing constituted her greatest asset, she alone knew how truly they were her greatest cross. She and Aunt Maria were so inordinately fair of skin that their appearance caused no end of confusion and embarrassment in the small town of Durham where they had grown up, lived for most of their lives and knew almost everybody. They'd get on a streetcar and Negro men who had known them for years suddenly ignored their presence as if they did not exist. Later they'd be told,

"I thought you were a white Reb and I wasn't taking any chances on getting familiar."

On the other hand, white men jumped up with great ceremony to offer them a seat on the car, only to have them shake their heads silently and move toward the rear with smarting cheeks and mounting embarrassment. When they were downtown shopping, colored friends seldom exchanged greetings until they were close enough for unmistakable recognition. If they failed to see a friend at the next counter, they were accused of "passing" and the friend's feelings were hurt. If they made a point of greeting the friend, the white clerk who had just served them courteously instantly changed her manner to one of contempt.

Listening to their troubles, Grandmother was sometimes seized with a fit of melancholy and her eyes smoldered with prophetic fire.

"Children, it's like the Bible has said. God will visit the sins of the fathers upon the children unto the third and fourth generations." And while she didn't say so, one knew Grandmother was talking about the Smiths. Her prophecy was disquieting to Aunt Pauline and somewhat terrifying to me, for I was fourth generation and filled with imaginings of the fateful retributions in store for me. I could only hope that the breads of charity which Great-Grandfather Thomas Fitzgerald had cast upon the waters would redeem me from the dark, sinful acts of Sidney Smith.

Thus Grandmother sailed back and forth like a shuttlecock between the extremes of her own dual legacy as half slave and half slave-owning Smith. The Smiths were her roots and her kin; she saw them and herself as the essence of southern gentility. Whatever else went with the war, she clung to this and strove to maintain it through the denouement which followed. She talked more often of "before the war" than she did of the conflict itself; in some ways, I suppose, Appomattox represented a loss to her, for while it severed the legal ties which bound her to the Smiths it also thrust her into a life with which she would always be at odds.

The Smith plantation before the war was the only life she knew, the boundary of her universe and the standard for most of her values. It represented prosperity, gracious living and social prominence. Like most plantations it was almost entirely self-sufficient. The Smiths had their own mill, blacksmith shop and carpentry shed. They produced most of their food and clothing on the premises. The menservants learned trades and the women were taught to weave and to sew. Grandmother talked constantly of their bountiful supply: the great smokehouses in which hung hams, sides of bacon, cured beef and salted pork; the cribs piled high with corn, wheat and rye; the granaries bulging with bins of meal, flour, sugar cane, potatoes, nuts, dried fruits; tubs of lard and butter. She talked of everything in great quantities: hundreds of chickens, turkeys and geese, dozens of hogs and cattle which fed in the orchards, the cider mill and creamery, the huge flower gardens and vegetable plots.

Her strategic position in the Smith household, reinforced by her father's acknowledgment and affection, had permitted her to come in contact with leaders in public affairs, to overhear discussions on a high cultural level and to consider good living her natural birthright. As Miss Mary's chief assistant, her duties included inspecting the hams and meats in the smokehouse, the state of the grain bins, the number of new chickens hatched, the eggs laid and production of milk, the cows which came in fresh and the sows which had litters. She thus identified herself with lavishness and endless supply.

There was also her Christian training which she prized so highly and which was the foundation of her later strength. As a child she had memorized the Lord's Prayer, Creed, Ten Commandments and Cathechism found in the Book of Common Prayer and she taught them to her children without the aid of a book. Of course, there were always slavery and the awful things she saw and heard about which she could do nothing. When old Aunt Delia, the cook who had been in the family for years and completely bossed the kitchen, came right out and said, "How many times I spit in the buscuits and peed in the coffee just to get back at them mean white folks," she knew what slaves really thought of their masters. And when she heard her father discuss the slave laws of North Carolina—how a servant convicted of rape could be castrated, or if he gave false testimony each ear was nailed to a pillory for an hour in succession and then cut off—she knew what masters would do to control their slaves.

She'd often heard Mary Ruffin Smith complain to her women friends that slavery was the greatest evil on earth and that the true slave was the Southern woman. The men occupied themselves with their professions, hunting and riding, or politics, while the woman of the plantation had to carry the main load. She had to regulate the lives of many human beings in detail and do their thinking for them in addition to caring for her own family. It was unthinkable under slavery to let them do their thinking for themselves.

When you came right down to it, she said, if you weren't in the business of buying and selling slaves for profit, they cluttered up the place and cost more than they were worth. In 1860, three of the thirty Smith servants were in their seventies and no longer able to do much work. Seventeen others were less than twenty-one, and nine of these were under fourteen years of age, hardly able to earn their own living. Sooner or later, everything which happened in the slave quarters had to be resolved by "Miss Mary." She had to look after the old folks, give medicine to the sick, bandage the sores and cuts of slave children, run down to the cabins when a mother was in childbirth. She must order food and clothing and parcel it out among them, find clothes and refreshments for slave marriages, approve husbands for the women and wives for the men, arbitrate in their family squabbles, supervise the training of growing girls, be present at all their prayer meetings, bury them when they died and keep the whole kit and caboodle in smooth working order. She seldom had a minute to herself day or night, since she was "on call" at all times for any emergency in the cabins. It was a thankless job at best, and anybody with an ounce of horse sense knew slavery didn't pay.

Of course, when Miss Mary bemoaned her lot she generally

added that you couldn't turn loose on the public a parcel of ignorant Negroes who couldn't take care of themselves. Echoing the dominant retort of her class to northern criticism, she said the North needn't be so high and mighty condemning the South for slavery when it had dumped shiploads of Negroes into the South through its slave trade and piled up big fortunes on the cotton southern slaves had produced. In the same breath with her complaints about the evils of slavery she remarked that if the Yankees ever came to Chapel Hill and freed the slaves, for the Smiths it would be like dumping $45,000 into Price's Creek. For Miss Mary was a shrewd business woman and good administrator and she valued the Smith slaves as a large part of their wealth.

Miss Mary was stingy with her purse, her patience and her affections, but always in the background was a gentler influence at work. Northern-born, thoroughly anti-slavery Miss Maria Spear preached a silent gospel by example. Where Miss Mary was adamant and harsh, Miss Maria came behind her with a kind word. She taught slave children that God knew no differences between white and black, masters and servants. When growing disunion made her views unwelcome in the Smith household she left, and 1860 found her living in Chapel Hill with two free mulatto women as house servants and companions.

This was Grandmother's world which the Civil War disrupted. What had seemed so solid and secure to her at seventeen before North Carolina left the Union in 1861 was all but shattered four years later. She reached her twenty-first birthday in February, 1865, two months before General Johnston surrendered the last of his ragged Confederate armies to General Sherman on April 26, some fifteen miles from the Smith place near Durham Station, Orange County. Those four years were more than difficult for Grandmother. Her job as intermediary between the Smith house and the slave quarters made her role one of duplicity. She watched the smokehouses grow emptier and emptier, the corn and meal disappear from the bins, the hogs and chickens vanish and the crops go to seed. Miss Mary held her responsible for finding out what happened to their dwindling supplies and the slaves depended upon her not to inform on them.

They couldn't get salt for their food or oil for their lamps; their shoes wore out and their clothes wore thin. Miss Mary complained that she was head over heels in debt trying to support a lot of trifling folks who'd leave her tomorrow if the Yankees came. She tried to hold things together, but she could no longer afford big dinners, and her own dresses grew threadbare, faded and patched. She took to ripping up the bed sheets and the curtains to make bandages for the Confederate soldiers. And she insisted that two of the Smith daughters sleep outside her door for fear she would be murdered in her bed.

Having been virtually free all her life, Grandmother could not fully appreciate what emancipation meant when it came. For weeks that spring of 1865, the Chapel Hill folks had been in a panic as Sherman marched north from Columbia into North Carolina driving Johnston's men before him. Everybody knew about his march through Georgia and those who had seen that country and fled into North Carolina said, "If a crow flew down that valley behind Sherman, he'd sure have to take his breakfast with him." By Maundy Thursday in Easter week, Sherman had reached Raleigh, less than forty miles away, and Johnston had retreated to Hillsboro.

On Good Friday the straggling supply trains from Johnston's battered army began moving through Orange County, and Wheeler's cavalry rode into Chapel Hill. The tattered soldiers vowed they'd never surrender to Sherman and they went through the countryside like a swarm of locusts, stripping everything bare so the Yankees couldn't feed off the land. They took every horse and mule they could find. They went from house to house begging for a meal or some bread. Grandmother said that when the Rebels left Easter Sunday afternoon, the whole county was clean as a whistle. There was nothing left for the Yankees to plunder.

Next morning at eight o'clock, General Smith B. Atkins, commander of the 9th Michigan Cavalry, rode into Chapel Hill at the head of four thousand blue-clad troops. The white people stayed indoors and watched the columns of soldiers ride past behind drawn shades, but the colored folk of the town met their liberators with wild cheers and Union flags miraculously retrieved from places of discard where their masters had tossed them. Grandmother didn't go to the welcoming! She was too busy helping Miss

Mary dig holes and bury the silver and other family valuables. Then they dragged brush over the places they had dug and built bonfires to hide their work.

Grandmother's youngest sister, thirteen-year-old Laura, was sent out to the road to meet a squadron of Yankees who rode up to the Smith place later that day. If Petersburg was Grandfather's most vivid memory of the war, the sight of little Laura, "pretty as a picture in a spick-and-span washed frock" speeding down the lane with her long curls flying in the wind and a Union flag and white cloth of surrender held high above her head, was Grandmother's. She told it as if it somehow placed her on the side of the Union although she was southern born and bred.

The Smith slaves had been told the Yankees would kill them all and most of them hid in the woods, but Miss Mary kept the Smith girls close to the house and assigned Grandmother, the oldest, to stand by the bonfires and talk the Yankees out of poking beneath them. Grandmother remembered how young Laura reached the soldiers and how the captain got down from his horse and took her flags. Then he lifted her onto his saddle and she rode back to the Smith house at the head of a column of soldiers in grand style, looking very delighted and not in the least like one who had just surrendered the Smith pride.

What Grandmother learned that day, all of Chapel Hill was soon to learn. She had on her best company manners and the Yankee captain returned them in kind. He was courteous, sent his men to find the slaves and tell them they were all free, told Grandmother not to worry, that she and her folks were safe enough as long as they gave no resistance, looked about the grounds for a bit and then rode away with his soldiers.

And so the war came to an end in Chapel Hill. The University buildings and books were neither sacked nor burned as the terrified townsfolk had expected. In fact, General Atkins proved to be both a soldier and a gentleman. His men conducted themselves with restraint and were extremely well behaved. So engaging was the Yankee commander that in less than two months after marching into Chapel Hill, he had conquered the daughter of the University's president and won her for a bride. They married in August, 1865. The town was shocked. The wedding caused almost as much of a furor as had Secession. People argued about it for months. Some said Miss Eleanor Swain was a turncoat, that a true southern girl would rather die than marry one of the conquerors. Others said from what they had seen maybe the Yankees were not as bad as they'd been painted. Grandmother Cornelia felt that if the ex-governor's daughter thought enough of a Yankee to marry him they must be mighty fine people after all.

Nothing was quite the same again. During the war, Miss Mary had come more and more to rely upon the four girls who were the only daughters she had ever known. Now she was almost alone with only an eccentric brother, who withdrew into himself, and one or two friends.* Aged beyond her fifty years and burdened with debts and worthless Rebel bonds, she made a proposition to her former slaves. If any of them wanted to stay on and work the crops for her, she'd stake them to food and clothes and let them live in their cabins rent free. Most of them accepted her proposal and life continued much in the same way on the surface, but tentatively and with odd formalities on both sides. The Smith girls remained with her in the Big House and Great-Grandmother Harriet, who was at last free to shut the door of her cabin, stayed on as Miss Mary's maid.

The plantation was turned in upon itself. After a year the University was closed and there was little outside stimulation. Miss Mary seemed to have an obsession about her girls. She was no longer their mistress, but the bond of blood could not be severed by Yankee bayonets. She was determined not to cast them adrift in the wreckage of the war. She'd see them through until they had all found good husbands, were honorably married and settled down. It was little enough to do for them and the least she could do to preserve some semblance of the proud Smith past.

Daily she cautioned them, "Now, don't you go out there in the blackberry bushes and get a baby," for she knew pretty octoroons were highly prized by Rebels and Yankees alike.

She needn't have worried about Grandmother Cornelia. She was the most high-minded of all the girls. She carried the image of her lawyer-father in her heart, of what he might have been if he had not drunk his life away, of what she might have been had he been possessed of more courage and less heart.

*Sidney died in April 1867, Francis 10 years later.

Annette soon married Ned Kirby, a young preacher of sorts from Chatham County with a devilish sense of humor and a knack for pleasing all ladies. Emma picked Henry Morphis of Chapel Hill, the son of Judge William H. Battle's slave girl and Sam Morphis, a colorful figure around the University. Laura finally married Grey Toole, a prosperous young barber from Charlotte who served only white patrons.

Grandmother waited and sewed for the old families of Chapel Hill and Hillsboro. It took her four years to find Grandfather Fitzgerald and the minute she laid eyes on him her search was ended.

13

AT TWENTY-FIVE, Robert Fitzgerald set out to join the "Yankee schoolmarms" in the South. He carried with him only his Bible, his faith and a few books and charts. Behind him lay a winter of teaching in Delaware and a year of training at Ashmun Institute—now Lincoln University—to become a missionary. Lincoln University students were granted commissions from the Presbyterian General Assembly's Committee on Freedmen to spend their summer vacations among the freedmen as teachers, catechists and licentiates. They assisted ministers in the field and in turn recruited promising young men for enrollment in their school. Among the many changes the war had brought was a reorientation of Ashmun Institute toward missionary work among the freed Negroes in the United States. Symbolic of its new approach was the school's change of name to Lincoln University in 1866. Young Fitzgerald was among the first of its ardent emissaries to carry on this important work.

He had known since his army days that he would return to the South. Emancipation was born in the violent chaos of war; a whole people had been jarred loose, cast up from unspeakable depths of poverty and ignorance and were trying to take the first terrifying step toward becoming free men. He had felt the turbulent force of this event, a force which needed direction. Educating the freedmen was the most urgent task at hand.

Few in those times could fully appreciate the vast release of pent-up emotions among four million people when they realized that at last they were their own masters. They had not owned their bodies and at times doubted that they owned their souls. The accumulated restlessness of a lifetime of unnatural restraints now propelled them in all directions at once. It was a time for casting off every obligation, for turning one's back on the sorrows of the old life and reveling in this new-found thing they had prayed for and which was now more compelling to experience than food or water. It was a time for walking off the plantation with all their belongings in a little bundle slung over the shoulder, for testing the ultimate limits of their freedom. As one former slave told his former master, he had to leave, to go away just to see if he could mind himself and stand on his own two feet.

To those who had borne the worst of slavery, freedom was the end of being nobodies, of being at the beck and call of the tiniest white child. It meant no more work, no curbs of any kind—work and restraints were the earmarks of slavery. It meant the right to roam at will, free as a bird, without carrying the hated "passes" or having to answer to patrols on the roads. Little wonder that in those first luxurious moments of liberty, millions were in motion following the Union armies. Nor was it strange that those who had watched their masters thought freedom meant that you could loaf all day and be high-toned like rich white folks, that you could pick up your heels and take off wherever the spirit led you, or drink as much corn liquor as you could hold and stay drunk as long as you chose.

In this restless movement were those for whom freedom meant an unending quest for loved ones. Years before, they had been parted; wives sold one way and husbands another, children separated from their parents and aged separated from their children. When the parting came, each had carried with him an image of his loved one and the place where he had left him. All his remaining years he would be inquiring of people if they had heard of a slave called "Black Cato" or "Yellow Sam" or "Sally," and trying to get to that place where they had been separated. He would describe the loved one in the intimate way he had remembered him—a charm worn about the neck, a dimple in the cheek, a certain manner of walking or smiling. It did not matter that children had grown up and lost childish features or that parents had grown old and white haired. The description remained the same.

There were the old and sickly who shrank from freedom. They had prayed for it longest but now that it had come they were terrified of it. They wanted only what they knew, the security of a cabin where they could spend their last days in peace and the kindness of a master or a mistress who would feed them and nurse them when they were laid up. There were the children who had no memories of slavery and could not understand what freedom meant. On the other hand there were those lean, hungry, bitter men to whom freedom had meant so much they had taken to the swamps and backlands, living on roots and herbs; desperate bands of hunted men who used to leave the swamps only at night to rob or kill for their needs without passion. Some doubted the freedom word when it came and stayed on in the swamps, preferring death or starvation to being re-enslaved.

There had been those first glorious months after Appomattox when the colored people had seen the coming of the Lord, had left the crops untended, the kitchens and nurseries deserted, had clogged the roads and flocked into the cities. Then hunger and homelessness pressed down upon them and they began to doubt the reality of their triumph. Freedom was not something you could hold in your hands and look at. It was something inside you which refused to die, a feeling, an urge, an impelling force; but it was other things, too, things you did not have and you had to have tools to get them. Few freedmen had tools in 1865; only the feeling, the urge.

Whatever else the freedmen lacked, there was in them a fierce hunger for knowledge. They believed, as perhaps no other people had believed so fervently, that knowledge would make them truly free, for had not their masters taken great pains to withhold it from them? Before freedom, "stealing learning" was a crime for which they could be whipped; now it held the magic of the rainbow after a violent storm. This hunger made itself felt wherever the Union forces appeared in the South. When the soldiers halted for a spell, slaves poured into the camps and pretty soon little schools sprouted among the Yankee regiments. The northern men had never seen anything quite like it—ragamuffins coming out of the fields and swarming to whatever place had a teacher. They brought with them old scraps of newspaper, a page from the Bible, a leaf torn from a young master's spelling book, a ragged almanac, a piece of broken slate—anything they thought would help them to learn. They wept tears of joy when they could recite the alphabet or read a line from the Bible or write their names.

Army chaplains who witnessed it were humbled by their hunger and their gratitude. They took these moving tales back to their churches in the North and soon a stream of missionaries flowed into the South in the wake of the armies to begin the redemptive work from slavery. The response was enough to fire anyone's soul. As Booker T. Washington said later, "It was a whole race trying to go to school. Few were too young and none were too old to make the attempt to learn." This almost universal desire for education among the freedmen was the most inspiring thing to emerge from the bitterness and misery of war. It struck deep chords in human memory, like the first elemental urge of man to lift himself from all fours and stand face to face with his God.

Grandfather Fitzgerald was on his way to answer this urge in 1866. He had just left the commencement exercises at Lincoln University in which the guest speaker was General O. O. Howard, chief of the newly created Freedmen's Bureau. General Howard had been commander of Pennsylvania troops throughout the war, at Bull Run, Antietam, Malvern, Gettysburg and as leader of Sherman's right wing in the march to the sea. His empty sleeve showing where an arm had been torn off by a Rebel shell gave mute testimony to his contribution, and he had spoken with deep emotion urging the young men of Lincoln "onward and upward" in the advancement of their race, "in this country and in Africa, but particularly in this country." When he finished, the men of Lincoln, many of whom had fought in the war, burst into resounding cheers. Next day Grandfather Fitzgerald resolutely turned toward his summer's work.

Had anyone told him his mission was one of the most revolutionary of his time, he would have been amazed. Yet he now presented a greater threat to the future of the South, as some were

determined to shape it, than he had when he stood in battle line
before Petersburg with a musket in his hand. He was now on his
way to arm the minds of the freedmen with bits of knowledge,
with disturbing notions of dignity and human rights and with a
gospel of thrift and independence.

Here was the rub. Liberty had come at the point of the sword,
but to maintain it a whole region must be redeemed. New bridges
of communication must be built between the whites and blacks,
too big a job to be done with hate, yet the war had left little
among the defeated Rebels but piled-up hate. White men were
determined that black men give them the same unquestioned
obedience they had exacted before the war; black men were
equally determined to be "treated just like white men." Until one
of these urges gave way, undeclared war would continue. What
Grandfather did not fully realize then was that only the guns were
silenced at Appomattox. Two powerful beliefs, more impregnable
than fortresses, battled on in the dark treacherous recesses of the
mind. One was the belief in the equality of man; the other, that
a black man had no rights which a white man was bound to
respect.

Back home among the peaceful rolling hills, the flourishing
fields and friendly neighbors of Pennsylvania, Grandfather had
almost forgotten the terrible cruelty of war. Now as he traveled
south through Virginia from Washington, the enormity of his
task began to dawn upon him. The merciless destruction seemed
even more stark in the desolation of peace. Hardly more than two
hundred miles from his home, it seemed like an alien country. He
traveled for miles without seeing a single farm animal. He rode
through a stricken countryside stripped of human cultivation
although the war had been over for more than a year. His farmer's
eye took in the abandoned plantations and weed-strangled fields,
the rusted plows left in their furrows, the blackened trees, charred
skeletons of barns and farmhouses, the broken fences, washed-out
bridges, torn-up railroads and ghostlike villages.

The people seemed more ravished than the land. Their clothing
was threadbare, their faces drawn and set, their eyes infinitely old
and listless and full of suffering. They moved as if under some
strange hypnotic power, doing things mechanically without

thought or feeling. Everywhere were gaunt, bearded young men, often with an empty sleeve or hobbling on a stump, still wearing their tattered Confederate uniforms held together over their wasted bodies with pieces of string because they were forbidden to wear "C.S.A." buttons. Here and there upon a farm which had been a battlefield, a solitary figure might be seen raking up the skeletons of men and horses to use for fertilizer. It was not uncommon to see a white woman, widowed by the war and bent over from misery and hunger, harnessed with her children to a heavy plow and dragging it slowly over a neglected field. Down near Petersburg haggard old women still grubbed among the ruins of the Crater in search of bullets to sell for scrap.

Near the larger towns hovered the bands of war orphans, hardened by hunger into scavengers, veterans of garbage piles, recruits for guerrilla gangs of marauders who preyed upon black and white alike. Most pathetic of all, it seemed to Grandfather, were the straggling caravans of homeless Negroes still roaming the roads in search of shelter, food and work. But for their labored movements, they might have been seedy scarecrows stuck in the earth, so wretched was their appearance. They plodded along barefoot or with rags bound around their feet and ankles. They wore odds and ends of cast-off clothing, faded and patched beyond recognition. Some had on sewed-up gunny sacks tied about the waist with cord. On their heads were battered relics of old hats or dingy bandannas and each carried his worldly possessions wrapped in an old quilt or tied in a piece of cloth at the end of a stick. They were unkempt and unbelievably grimy, and many of their children wore only a ragged shirt.

This was the backwash of a mighty current. A half million slaves were freed in Virginia, which had suffered most the exhaustion of war. Many of these wanderers had taken to the roads because their masters turned them out without a penny. Others were left to shift for themselves when their masters did not return from the war. Some had tried to settle on deserted farms and start little patches of vegetables, only to have the owners return and drive them off again. Some were mothers with several small children and without husbands. Unable to work and care for their brood, they went from place to place begging bread. These nomads had taken to living in old stables, under sheds, in pigsties covered with boards, in shelters thrown together from pieces of waste lumber, in caves and gullies under bridges and trestles or along the banks of streams.

The wretchedness and waste were matched only by the bitterness of a proud people in defeat. Grandfather's well-dressed appearance and energetic movement marked him at once as a hated Yankee. He was the object of malignant stares and occasionally an oath. He learned that Confederate women were more bitter about the war than the men who had fought in it. Theirs had been a war of endurance, of bereavement, of slow starvation, of the many humiliations to which they were subjected by crude soldiers. In Richmond after the Yankees marched in, some women preferred to go to jail rather than walk underneath the United States flag. And one Rebel housewife down near Petersburg had trudged twenty miles to Richmond for fear she would have to give the oath of loyalty if she took the cars.

Grandfather had a natural sincerity and modesty of disposition which invited friendliness. He struck up conversations easily and there were those who were more curious than indignant about his mission. He knew from experience that many Virginians had remained loyal to the Union during the war, but he learned this loyalty did not extend to acceptance of the freedmen as citizens.

"The Rebs don't hate the Yankees half as much for ruining their country as they do for turning loose the niggers," he was told. "The darkies may be free but they'll never be equal."

From some of the things Grandfather saw and heard about, there was much to support this opinion. Only a few weeks earlier, in Norfolk, a group of Negroes celebrating the passage of the Civil Rights Act had run afoul of a group of whites and bloodshed followed. Several weeks later in Petersburg, four Negro churches were set on fire at the same time. Two were saved, one burned to the ground and another was partially destroyed. And people were beginning to talk of a new movement which started up in Pulaski, Tennessee, called the Ku-Klux Klan. Its members indulged in strange nocturnal rituals, rode about in hoods and white bed sheets claiming to be ghosts of Confederate dead seeking retribution for the wrongs against the South. And they were succeeding in frightening many freedmen into giving up their freedom before they had even tasted it.

These were sobering reports, but there was a tenacity in Grandfather, in part the outgrowth of his frequent bouts with illness and in part the natural endowment of a pioneering spirit and restless energy which rose to its best when faced with opposition. If he couldn't go through a stone wall, he'd find a way around it. When he reached Amelia Court House, Virginia, where he had been assigned, he plunged himself into the work with missionary zeal. It was two months before he had time to write back to his school. This letter to Dr. Rendall, the school president, recording his first impressions of the job, has miraculously survived the decades. It was found in 1952 when Dr. Horace Mann Bond, now president at Lincoln University, was going through some old dusty papers which he had rescued from a basement in one of the school buildings. Written eighty-seven years earlier on lined foolscap, it read:

> Freedman's Chapel, 6 miles West
> Amelia Court House, Va.
> Aug. 28th 1866

Mr. I. N. Rendall,
Dear Sir,

You must pardon my long delay in writing to you. I have attempted to write you several times since coming here, but this is the first time I have succeeded. I have endeavoured to make myself useful since I left the college. I received a small outfit of books & charts from Mr. Main 821 Chestnut St. Phil. on the 22nd of June. I started immediately and on the evening of the 23rd arrived in Richmond. I taught sabbath school on the 24th which was Sabbath, and on the 25th arrived at Amelia C.H.Va. one of the most dreary looking places you ever saw, and on steping off the cars I conceited I saw some of the very faces I had met in the battle of Petersburgh which is only 25 miles from here. They seemed still to have that savage unsettled appearance, and we were somewhat alarmed to hear some of them use oathes in Speaking of us, but they made no further demonstration. Mr. Murphy was absent and the officer of the post recommended that Mr. Chrestfield to go south to Danville, Mr. Brown to a plantation 6 miles south of the C.H. and myself to a building which the colored people had commenced for a church; it was near 6 miles west of the C.H.

and I arrived there in the evening of 25th and was discouraged to find it without roof, door, or windows, the workmen having quit it for the summer harvest. I went around among them and was successful in geting a few to go to work with me next morning. I worked 3 days with them in nailing on the roof, carrying lumber making the floor &c and on the 4th day I commenced school with only 8 pupils. My working with them had a very good effect, for in a few days pupils were coming 5 or 6 miles to school. The 1st Sabbath I was here I had near 200 Sabbath scholars. They walk 10 miles some of them to our Sab. School. Mr. Browned [sic] joined me on the 1st of July (not having succeeded in geting a schoolhouse on the plantation). We have been very successful in sab. and day school and have 230 sabbath and 145 day scholars. I have written to some friends in Brooklyn for some pamphlets, Sab. S. books & papers to distribute to them. I have already rec'd & distributed to them part of a package of tracts, papers & old books, sent by Mr. Shearer of the A.F. Society of Richmond & he also said if we could raise $5.00 he would secure a library for our S.S. worth $10.00. I have the amount nearly raised, and hope to leave them with a good library and a well drilled set of teachers.

These people learn more rapidly than any school I ever taught, and if you approve of it, I shall remain here till the 1st of Nov. they insist on our staying and Mr. M—— has made arrangements to teach our latin and Greek lessons twice a week, so I think by that time we could have these people reading, writing and ciphering for enough to keep their accounts.

Mr. Rendall, has father paid that bill yet? He told me just before I left that he would pay the 1st thing after his crop was off; in this or the first of next month. If it is not paid by that time, by him, I will have enough earned to send it myself, and I shall do so. We get only $25.00 a month and board & pay our own passage home, so you can see Mr. R—— that after buying our summer & winter clothing, paying our passage home &c, even 4 months pay will look very small.

Can I look to come as I did last winter? In another session I hope to be able to master arithmetic or at least the one we used last winter & then I would be able to do a great deal of good in this quarter.

Mr. Murphy, the Superintendent of F.S. in this co. has over 300 scholars under his charge and a number of Schools. He designs building a high school and offers to secure the charge for me when I shall have graduated, now if there could be any arrangement made by which I could remain at the college that long, I would be willing to refund the expense with a small interest as soon after as I could earn it.

There are thousands of children in this county that [are] not in the reach of schools and I suppose the next 5 years will not find enough teachers here south to reach all the freedmen, and I think from what I have seen if they are not educated they will become a dangerous element.

Please give my kind regards to Mr. Westcott & to young Mr. R—— and write soon.

With much Respect

> Robert G. Fitzgerald
> Freedman's Chapel
> Amelia C.H.
> Va.

On the bottom of the letter was penned a note in President Rendall's handwriting. It ran:

Rev. A. D. White, I have not been very well for a few days and must defer answering your letter. The enclosed is from one of our students and may be useful to show that we are in the field.
Yours truly,

> I. N. Rendall.

Amelia Court House, county seat of Amelia, lies in the Virginia hills about thirty-five miles southwest of Richmond on U.S. Route 360 to Danville. It hasn't changed much from the "dreary looking place" Grandfather Fitzgerald found in 1866. The village has a population of nine hundred, a few dozen houses, one or two filling stations and a cluster of stores facing two sides of the courthouse square in which rises the stone soldier memorializing the Confederate dead. Its chief historical significance seems to be that Edmund Ruffin, father of secession in Virginia and the man credited with firing the first shot on Fort Sumter, lived in this county during his last days and shot himself there in 1865 rather than take an oath of loyalty to the United States Government.

The village also lay in the path of Lee's retreating army and is some sixty miles east of Appomattox Court House, where he finally surrendered to Grant. For a while after the war it was a Union army garrison. If you passed through there today and found Thomas Grey or Willis Wilkerson still alive—both former slaves and well over the century mark—they might reach back in memory and tell you how, as small boys, they watched the Rebel soldiers fleeing along the Amelia roads so weary from marching and fighting that they threw away their knapsacks and blankets along the roadside. Willis Wilkerson, who does not remember exactly how old he is but knows he was large enough "to run with the big boys in 1865," might add that he and other little freedmen slipped off from the plantations and hid from their masters in the woods when they heard that freedom was on the way, and how they came out of hiding after the Rebels had passed to gather up the precious supplies they had left behind.

A lonely mission of grief combined with this accident of geography to make Amelia Court House one of the first active centers of Presbyterian missionary endeavor. Shortly before the close of the war, Mrs. Samantha J. Neil, a young war widow from Pennsylvania, came to Amelia Court House searching for the body of her husband, a Union army officer who had been killed near there. Her search ended in failure, but while she was there her sympathies went out to the Negro freedmen and she discovered an answer to her bereavement and her life's work.

Mrs. Neil opened an outdoor school a few miles from Amelia Court House underneath the branches of a big oak tree, which quickly became known as "Big Oak School." Before long she had almost three hundred scholars enrolled, more than a third of whom were over sixteen years of age. Everybody who could flocked to the clearing to learn the ABC's, from white-haired grandmothers and grandfathers crippled with rheumatism to toddlers hardly able to walk. When cold weather came, an old wheelwright shop near by was offered to Mrs. Neil as a classroom and place of worship for the colored people. It was a dilapidated shedlike building, an open room with a dirt floor and a clapboard roof full of holes. For windows there were two openings sawed through the logs with cloth stretched across them in place of glass. The teacher's table was a rough board nailed to sticks driven into the ground, and the pupils sat on logs dragged in from the woods.

Such primitive beginnings contained the stuff of miracles. Mrs. Neil's work was so successful that she was able to enlist the support of the Presbyterian General Assembly's Committee on Freedmen, which reported after a visit, "we found no more successful school and church among the Freedmen than this." Half of the scholars had learned to read and all of them were studying the "usual branches taught in common school." A few of the more advanced had even tackled grammar.

By March, 1866, the Committee on Freedmen had commissioned Rev. T. J. Murphy, a Union army chaplain who had just mustered out of service, to take charge of the work at Amelia Court House. When Rev. Murphy arrived he was so swamped with appeals for teachers he wrote back to the committee urgently requesting capable assistants. Three months later he was joined by "two coloured students from Lincoln University," one of whom was Robert G. Fitzgerald.

Grandfather did not get back to Lincoln that fall as he had planned. What was to have been a summer's project extended over a year. The summer of 1867 found him still teaching in Amelia County. He found that year of voluntary exile one of the most strenuous he had ever experienced. At times he felt like a tiny ant pushing a huge boulder of crumb up the perilous ascent of an anthill. The crumb was crushing in weight but he dared not let go for fear it would roll back the infinitesimal distance he had moved it by exhausting effort. His enrollment had increased from 8 to 160 scholars in that year, but against the woeful ignorance of tens of thousands whom he could not reach, it seemed like dipping teaspoons from the ocean.

One needed the strength of ten men to carry out his duties. He acted as both teacher and catechist. His work was never done. He taught school six hours a day, five days a week. Twice a week he held night school for two hours for those who worked all day. Once a week he visited among the people helping them "to order their households." He held prayer meetings during the week, taught Sabbath school on Sunday, assisted fellow missionaries in conducting church services and often led the singing.

His life was full of interruptions, emergencies which needed attention, requests for advice of all kinds from people who had no one else to turn to. He might be called out of bed to sit with a dying man in the early hours of the morning, or asked to turn over his class to an assistant and walk five or six miles to sketch a school building. Sometimes he got a ride on a mule to make his rounds, but more often he had to walk many miles through the countryside, stopping for shelter wherever he could when night closed down on him and he could no longer find his way.

He gave advice on planting methods, and where he could he tried to get some of the farmers to rotate their crops and use diversified planting as he was accustomed to in Pennsylvania. He ordered seeds and supplies from the North, sent urgent appeals to friends and acquaintances for books and clothing, interpreted labor contracts, wrote letters for the aged, visited the sick, loaned what money he had to the needy, collected the monthly fee of fifty cents for the schoolwork when the people had it and corresponded with his school on behalf of young men who wanted to go to Lincoln. And when he had a spare moment he tried to study his own books to keep in shape for returning to school the next year.

At times he was engulfed by indescribable loneliness and an almost overpowering urge to escape. The unrelieved poverty and squalor which he saw all about him and could not remove often made him ill. Many of the freedmen were migrants, compelled to move from place to place to find employment. He would have a class just reaching the place where it could almost read when it would disappear overnight under the pressing need to find bread. As someone said, it was like preaching to running waters.

And being driven to find work on farms wherever they could be hired, the people were unable to settle down and develop stable habits. The great majority of them lived in old slave cabins, ramshackle huts about twelve feet square. Many of these one-room cabins had only one door, no windows and chimneys made of sticks and mud. They were often unchinked and the spaces between the logs were crammed with anything to keep out the wind and rain—a corn shuck, old rags or pieces of cotton. Families of ten and twelve crowded together and slept in one room on the dirt floor. They seldom had furniture beyond a crudely built bed, or table or stool, and their utensils consisted of one or two old pots and battered gourds. They usually sat on the ground and ate their cornbread and greens out of a common pot, wiping their fingers on their greasy clothing. They wore the same clothes for weeks at a time.

Had this been all Grandfather could see, he might have

given up in despair and gone back north again. But the miracle of it was that the freedmen wanted desperately to learn and to improve themselves. When he walked along the roads, they'd see him coming and leave their work in the fields to run down and beg him for books. Books were the one thing he had so few of that he sometimes felt that he and his pupils were trying to make bricks without straw. He had to teach from the Bible and the *Farmer's Almanac*. But sometimes he carried religious tracts in his pockets and distributed them among the eager hands. Parents who could not come to school told him that often what their children learned from him in class they brought home and tried to teach to a dozen or more older folk.

He found out also that in spite of the disorganization and wretchedness of their lives, whenever the freedmen made the effort to build a school or house of worship they tended to settle around it and their habits showed immediate improvement. They felt it was something that they *owned* and to which they *belonged*. It made a vast difference in their lives. It would take some of them quite a little while to move the awkward distance from saying "Master" to saying "Mister," but it had taken them no time at all to respond with glowing faces to "ladies" and "gentlemen" and "scholars." It gave them a new image of themselves. Such images lifted them up and made them strive and helped them blot out the images they saw when they learned to read the newspapers— "negro city buck," "moon in eclipse," "flat-nosed, bullet-headed, asp-eyed little darkey," "brazen-faced lady of color," "kinky-headed culprit," "decrepit old negress" and the like.

What always renewed his hope, however, was that despite a combination of forces arrayed against them and repeated efforts to reduce this conglomerate mass of human beings to the lowest level of existence, there was within them a fermentation which defied repression or degradation.

Not all of them were penniless and homeless. Indeed, many were stable, owned land, had trades, were possessed of some education, were industrious and reliable. Some lived in neat cottages, had little gardens, owned chickens and a cow and a few hogs, were well dressed and conscientiously paid in money or in kind for their education. In fact, Amelia County presented one of the many paradoxes of the slave-owning South. In some ways Grandfather found it not unlike Chester County, Pennsylvania. It was called a "mulatto" county because of its high proportion of mixed bloods.

Grandfather learned to his great surprise that Virginia had more free people of color at the time of Secession than did free Pennsylvania, that many of these free persons of color were prosperous, owned considerable land and some had even owned slaves. Back in Pennsylvania, Great-Grandfather Thomas' twenty-five acres had placed him on an equal footing with the majority of small farmers in the county and made him the second largest colored landholder in several townships. Here in Amelia County, seven free persons of color alone owned more than one hundred acres apiece in 1860 and their combined acreage exceeded three thousand.

The Harrisons and Andersons who attended his school were as far removed from the one-room cabins as the white plantation owners were themselves. In fact, although people spoke of the "white Andersons" and "colored Andersons," or "white Harrisons" and "colored Harrisons," it was hard to tell from looking at them which was which. It was no secret to anybody in the county how Henry Anderson, a large landholder, had felt about his three mulatto sons. He made his will in 1848 and died shortly afterward, leaving from one to ten slaves apiece to Alfred, Francis and William Anderson together with large tracts totaling more than a thousand acres. In like manner another planter, Nathaniel Harrison, who died some years before the war, left to his concubine, Frankey Miles, his eleven-hundred-acre plantation with all of its equipment and nineteen slaves. It was said that Frankey Miles was a shrewd business woman who kept every one of those slaves until the Yankees freed them.

The colored Andersons and Harrisons intermarried and continued to be prosperous after the war. They were fearless and self-assured, were businessmen of standing respected by both races and kept in close contact with their white relatives. Grandfather was so impressed by Frank Anderson's home that he made a water-color drawing of it in his sketchbook. It was a charming white cottage with two brick chimneys, green shutters at the curtained windows and a tiny front porch set in a wide lawn, surrounded by tall shade trees, flower beds, shrubbery and whitewashed out-buildings.

Having had a head start, they were the natural leaders and provided leverage for the others. Many of these descendants of planter blood held on to their land and you will find them today still living on parcels of the original tract granted by their great-grand-fathers. One of these is Mrs. Marguerite Anderson Richardson, a retired schoolteacher in her seventies, whose mother was one of Robert Fitzgerald's pupils and who holds the original will under which Nathaniel Harrison followed his heart with his worldly possessions.

One Thursday afternoon in late June, 1867, Robert Fitzgerald began Volume 4 of his diary, which he also used as his personal record of accounts and enrollment. He wrote:

June 28. I have just dismissed my school of freedmen, and am engaged in making out my reports to the General Assembly's Committee on Freedmen and to the Freedmen's Bureau. It is beginning to be warm, very warm. Mr. J. Davis and Mr. Wm. K. Price, students from the Lincoln University are with me. They are sent south as missionaries to the Freedmen of this Co. and are to operate under Rev. T. G. Murphy.

June 29. . . . Mr. Davis was attacked at the C.H. [Court House] by a Rebel, but was rescued by the Col'd people. Cause, being a Northern man.

I came to Virginia one year ago on the 22nd of this month. Erected a school, organized and named the Freedman's Chapel School. Now (June 29th) have about 60 who have been for several months engaged in the study of arithmetic, writing, etc. etc. This morning sent in my report accompanied with compositions from about 12 of my advanced writers instructed from the Alphabet up to their [present] condition, their progress has been surprisingly rapid. . . .

I must here express the gratitude I feel to the Divine Being for his Providence in sparing my life yet another year and placing me in a position to benefit my fellow man. I trust that I may be always guided by his Spirit and be placed in [a] way where I may be kept a humble and useful Christian, above all I want to be kept a Christian.

Like a clucking mother hen, Grandfather complained to his diary when the people were slow in paying for their tuition and made triumphant notations when they paid up. While the Presbyterian mission schools did not bar a child because he had no money to pay, the missionaries made every effort to have the people make their schools self-sustaining and succeeded in some instances. One day Grandfather would grumble, "The people have done very poor in paying the tuition of their children, only about one tenth of them paying 50 cents a month." A few days later he'd note, "The people sent for tuition 5 eggs and a chicken," or "Received 5 eggs from P. Hughes for Book," or "McGee paid in chickens 50c," or "Mr. Harris received on board; from Rebecca Zander 5 eggs and 2 small chickens; from Mr. Towns 1 doz. eggs."

His entries made frequent references to his health: "Had a bilious attack"; "ate an onion and feel unwell"; "was taken very sick last night at the Lyceum. . . . Mr. Harris & Holman were kind in rendering all the assistance they could, Mr. Harris going to the C.H. for a dose of oil"; "I feel very unwell today. Feel like going home"; "Feel very weak, this climate does not agree with me. I have not had my health this season as I had last. Have not been so stout, but I feel thankful to Great Author of my being, that I have been so well, and permitted to be engaged in doing good."

Each day he jotted down the problems with which he struggled:

Was to go down to the "Big Oak" Chapel to Mr. T. G. Murphy's preaching, but the young man's mule ran away, who was to take me. Had Sabbath School at my chapel and then walked down to preaching at the "Tobacco Barn" 3 P.M. by Rev. T. J. M. Had to assist in the exercises.

A man came to borrow money to [go to] the mountains for his sick child which had been sold and taken out there about the close of the war, but now the master refuses to take [care] of it and sends for him to take it. These are the people that said "the Negro can't take care of himself." They can scarcely take care of themselves.

Went down to the C.H. to Russell Grove Chapel, at the site of Miss Russell's old school. There was a large attendance. Mr. J. B. Given was expected to preach at the C.H. this afternoon but did not get there. Mr. J. C. Davis our Missionary preached. Saw my friends the Miss P's, but my usual timidness prevented an interview. . . . I had to act as chorister at the request of Capt. Whissiger & Mr. Davis though a very unwelcome task before a crowded house. . . .

Went to see one of my little sick scholars who is an orphan and is afflicted with fever & chills though only 11 years old. Poor little fellow was very glad to see me, and had little store of presents laid up for me. Cannot get out to school for a week or fortnight if he improves. I was sorry to leave the little fellow, but he can and does read his Bible.

This evening at Mr. R. A. Anderson's. . . . I did not start for Mr. A's till late and was therefore caught in the night and had a very rough time getting along over the washed roads occasionally falling into gullies up to my neck. Was followed in the dark by something which I afterward found to be a cow with a long chain & ball attached to her neck. She had been placed there to graze.

When Grandfather made out his July report, he made the following summary:

Whole number of pupils enrolled since beginning of term 1867, 19th of February. 153. Average att: 100 over 16 years of age; 18 under 6; 20 in ABC, Spelling: 151; Reading: 151; Writing: 100: Mental Arithmetic: 153; Geography: 153. No. in S. School 150: No. in Church 140; No. in Lyceum 180. Rec'd in Money & Board $12 for asst.

Then he laboriously copied the names of his 153 scholars alphabetically in his diary. When he had finished this chore he made the following comment:

Who without experience in the matter, can imagine the anxiety and care, of a teacher for those consigned to his care and training? I can say thus far I have sown in tears; may I reap in joy. I have each eventide asked God to Bless the day's work and sanctify the spear'd of his kingdom, and how gratified I feel to see my efforts so successful; to see the community establishing Lyceums, Churches, Schools, and improving so much in their general deportment, industry, frugality, etc. etc.

They tell me before Mr. Lincoln made them free they had nothing to work for, to look up to, now they have everything, and will by God's help make the best of it. I feel that the harvest truly is great but the labourers are few, and my prayer to God is that he may send more laborers into his vineyard.

Before he left Virginia, Grandfather had a brief excursion into politics. On July 10 he recorded that he had received in his mail "a yearly report of General Ass. Com. on Freedmen and a request signed by 30 persons rec'd begging that I accept the nomination as delegate to the coming Constitutional Convention, commencing Thurs. Aug. 1st at Richmond." The petitioners declared "we believe you are the most reliable we can send to represent our interests in that important Body." Grandfather was so impressed that he copied the entire letter in his diary, but added: "A startling announcement to me, and I feel that it is almost unkind to request me to fill that very important post which will incur the utmost hatred of the whole white population and then too I am so unprepared for that post, but still how willingly would I serve were I qualified for so important a trust. I must insist on their selecting some other for candidate."

Not only did Grandfather fail to convince a delegation which waited upon him that he was not qualified for the task, but he ended up by sending out notices for a meeting at which to elect delegates to the convention, reporting the meeting to the Richmond *Whig,* which published his letter, attending the Republican convention and recording an accurate account of it in his diary. A number of political meetings followed the convention in preparation for the coming vote. It was the first time Negroes were being registered to vote in Virginia since the American Revolution and both interest and feeling ran high. Grandfather attended a huge mass meeting at Amelia Court House two weeks before his school closed and reported that the speakers "Advocated a unanimity of feeling between the races and a quiet acquiescence on the part of the white to the black holding office, etc., etc."

Great-Grandmother Sarah Ann came down to visit him and see the countryside before he left Virginia. She liked the area and the people so well that Grandfather took her about to look over tracts of land for sale. Grandfather wrote, "We expect to buy and settle in this Co. if we can get a suitable tract." They found nothing satisfactory, however, and the day for Grandfather's school closing arrived without any decision being made. It was preceded by an important business trip to Richmond about which he said, "We purchase the store goods today for Freedman's Store Association which I have been laboring to establish for the last 4 months, and which I want to see in practice before I leave."

Grandfather's last day in Virginia was a deeply moving experience for him. He could look back over the fourteen months of his labors and see solid achievement. He was leaving behind him a school valued at $250, an enrollment of 160 scholars and a freedman's store. He had helped in the growth of Big Oak and Russell Grove schools and churches in the county. Of this day he wrote:

Aug. 23. A beautiful clear day. Early at the Chapel. Mr. Price and myself are engaged in making out our programme of the duties of today. 9 A.M. a large no. of cook's team with provisions etc. on the ground. People coming in every direction to participate with us in the grand anniversary which will be the last in which I can be with them. I am all nervous in anxiety for the wellfare of the occasion.

At 11 had the children all form into line and march with singing from the Chapel down to the deep shade of the wood. Made a countermarch in good order and filed into Mt. Zion Church (obtained for the occasion); the examination was conducted with energy. . . .

At 1 P.M. called the audience together and commenced speaking of the children which was well done and some of the dialogues & pieces was loudly applauded. Singing good. There are before us the finiest audience I have ever seen in the State. The committee on arrangements insisted on me asking my friends to take dinner with me which I did, and we had a sumptious feast. My friends, then the children, then the parents. After dinner ice cream. . . . We returned to the stand and had an able and eloquent address from Mr. Cook of R [ichmond] who told the people of the duties devolving upon them as citizens lately placed upon the platform of political equality. His advice was very commendable & well received.

At 5 P.M. Commenced the sad parting, the shaking of hands and God Bless You and tears told, with unmistakable certainty how well the work has been received, the children, the parents and even the parting blessing of the young ladies all united to make me feel thankful to God that my labour spent in tears was taking hold, that it was rightly appreciated by all. May it be like the mustard seed. . . .

I noticed some of my dear friends weeping. It is hard to break a thread so gently woven. Shall we not all meet again? They have proven their fidelity to me by being extremely kind to Mother who is here to visit me. . . .

What Grandfather felt and wrote about his work was part of the almost universal testimony on the eagerness and aptness of the freedmen for education. "If knowledge elevates, then this people is destined to rise," reported J. W. Alvord, a Freedmen's Bureau inspector, of that period. "They have within themselves an instinct which anticipates this; a vitality of hope, coupled with patience and willingness to struggle, which foreshadows with certainty their higher condition as a people in the coming time. . . . They may often be seen during the intervals of toil, when off duty as servants, on steamboats, along the railroads and when employed in the streets of the city, or on plantations with some fragment of a spelling book in their hand earnestly at study." The same observations were made in a report of General John Pope, Commander of Military District No. 3, which included Georgia, Alabama and Florida, to General Grant in the summer of 1867. Wrote General Pope: "It may safely be said that the marvelous progress made in the education of these people, aided by the noble charitable contributions of Northern societies and individuals, finds no parallel in the history of mankind. If continued, it must be by the same means, and if the masses of the white people exhibit the same indisposition to be educated that they do now, five years will have transferred intelligence and education, so far as the masses are concerned, to the colored people of this District."

One of the pupils who attended Grandfather's school closing that summer of 1867 was a ten- or twelve-year-old boy named Willis Wilkerson. I could not fully grasp the significance of Grandfather's work until I shook the hand of this centenarian in 1954 and found in his calm self-possession the reason for Robert Fitzgerald's deep emotion when he came to say good-by to those whom he had started along freedom's way. A man more than one hundred years old, white-haired, with beetling white brows and snowy mustache accenting his strong bronze face, standing almost erect despite his century of living, still strong of voice and clear of memory, he was the last survivor of the pupils listed in Grandfather's enrollment book in 1867. Mt. Zion Church was a pile of rotting logs in the woods by now and little Freedman's Chapel had long since disappeared, but Willis Wilkerson stood a monument to that period of deepest effort. He recalled that "Mr. Fitgiles" was one of his first teachers at the Chapel and that he learned to read from an almanac. He said that what he had learned so many, many years ago in the freedmen's school had helped him do business on his own account because he could read and write and figure. That he had succeeded was evidenced by the fact that he had owned and farmed his own land until a few years ago when he became too frail to continue, had to board up his little house and go to live with a relative. Standing before this venerable man and looking down the perilous ascent over which he had come, I felt awe, and my own tears started as I said good-by.

14

GRANDFATHER FITZGERALD returned home from Virginia a crusader for settlement in the South. He talked of little but the need for more missionaries and teachers among the freedmen, the need for putting vacant land under cultivation and starting new business enterprises. There were limitless opportunities for anyone who was willing to work hard and make sacrifices, he felt. He was anxious for his family to buy a farm and move there to live.

Great-Grandfather Thomas listened reflectively to his son's enthusiastic accounts. He was nearing sixty and wanted to settle down quietly, but his sons were restless and ready to go wherever they could find a better life. After the war the family had moved to a larger farm down in West Nottingham Township, close to the yellow clay pits of Nottingham Barrens. It was a fine location for brickmaking and when Richard Fitzgerald came home from sea he started his own brickyard. Great-Grandfather Thomas continued to farm his two places, but with his sons no longer working with him it was difficult. Richard had had a bad season that year and lost five hundred dollars on his brick business. He was so discouraged that he thought of returning to the sea or trying his luck in the West. Perhaps a new start in the South might keep his family together. It was worth thinking about.

For the first two or three weeks after Grandfather's return, his diary read like a cashbook. He noted his profits and losses and expenditures. His pig died, a loss of $20; he sold the oxen which he owned in common with his father for $230, of which his share was $169.50. He had earned $325 teaching school for fourteen months. With these assets he paid off his own notes with interest, loaned his father money to liquidate some debts, bought clothing for himself, his mother and sisters and then commented wryly, "After assisting all a little, my Bank looks small; but it is my duty & I do not regret it." Of Richard he wrote, "I shall try to have him train for usefulness in the South and both [of us] return there. I shall devote my time and talent to that people."

He had arrived home in time to attend the Colored Union Camp Meeting at Media, Pennsylvania, with his mother, Richard and eleven-year-old Mary, who had grown into a studious girl full of adoration for her schoolmaster brother. In spite of the fourteen years' difference in their ages, they were great pals. Grandfather had invested $60 of his savings in a fine rosewood melodeon and they loved to spend time practicing and singing together at home. They all had to get up before daylight to catch the excursion train to Media, which brought ten thousand people to the camp, about half of whom were white. Grandfather observed that it was set up in the suburbs "on the edge of a fine tall oak forest, surrounded by fields of the most beautiful green with the neat white cottages of farmers dotting the landscape here and there." After the devastation he had seen in Virginia, it was a welcome sight. In contrast to the exile and ostracism he had experienced in the South, he noted, "I saw white and colored shouting together. Perfect union prevailed."

The camp meeting gave him an opportunity to circulate among friends, relatives and acquaintances and to carry on his crusade. He found willing listeners. The only drawback to his good work was that he was violating a Presbyterian rule against travel on Sunday. "I have felt a check of conscience for traveling on the Lord's Day, but I trust that God will make all things work together for good, and that the effort to do good may be blessed." Grandfather had not yet met Grandmother Cornelia, who had no such Presbyterian squeamishness about doing necessary things on

Sunday and would have said simply, "When the ox is in the ditch, pull him out!"

It was good to be home again, and how much his parents needed him! He threw himself into the farm work, cleaned out the well, hoed vegetables, harvested oats, threshed wheat, hauled grain to the warehouse and took the wagons to the wheelwright's to be repaired. In the evenings he reviewed his studies in preparation for entering college and admitted, "Find myself quite rusty on them."

When Lincoln University opened, Grandfather received "a hearty welcome back to the 'Alma'" from President Rendall, was assigned to the Freshman Class, "the highest being Sophomore," and noted, "I expect heavy work this session as I intend to make it my last term at school." He plugged away at algebra, bookkeeping and history, reminding himself that he had "not a moment to lose," but before long a steady trickle of letters from his former students in Virginia asking help and advice began to distract him. In a month he was ready "to give up my studies and go South to engage in the great work of educating millions. . . . I have been sick ever since I have [been] home. Mr. Rendall is not willing that I should go from here till the close of the term at which I can get a certificate of honour."

In the end Grandfather decided to forego the coveted certificate. He went home to spend Thanksgiving week and while there wrote to Rev. Logan for a commission to return to the South. One drizzling damp morning in late November he made his decision. "I have concluded to go South and have given up the study of Algebra with Mr. R[endall's] and Mr. W[escott]'s reluctant consent. They do not think it a wise course to leave before finishing at least the studies of my class but . . . I have concluded to get a position as a teacher in one of the many large schools in the South where I can study & teach at the same time. May God guide and assist me in the course I have adopted." He left school on December 3 "with many blessings and hopes for my success. As the brown walls of the University grow small in the distance my heart grows sad, very sad when I think that I leave without having properly qualified myself for the work. My health has been so bad that I have been compelled to take a more active employment in the hope that I may have a change for the better."

He had been negotiating with the Presbyterian General Assembly's Committee on Freedmen for a teaching post in Tennessee, but meanwhile received a letter from the Friends Freedmen's Association in Philadelphia that "there is a possibility that the service of a well recommended teacher may be needed in one of the North Carolina schools. . . . thou will oblige by sending for consideration by the Cmtee in charge testimonials from some reliable person in relation to thy qualification and ability as a teacher. . . . please state thy age and how much teaching experience thou has had." In early January, 1868, the F.F.A. wrote that "the testimonials were satisfactory" and that "it was the decision of the Cmtee to offer thee an appt. as associate teacher at Hillsboro, at a salary of $20 per month, expenses of board, washing and travelling provided by the Assn."

Two weeks later Grandfather Fitzgerald set out for North Carolina. It was a sad leavetaking. "Dear Mother seemed very much affected and wept, dearest to me on earth and next to God the truest friend and the one above all others. To my dear parents I owe a debt I feel I can never discharge," he wrote.

Part of Grandfather's own sadness arose from the fact that he was starting his mission alone without too much hope that his family would join him. Great-Grandfather Thomas had not committed himself about selling out his farm and Richard was still unwilling to try his hand at business in the South. Before leaving home, Grandfather had written to Hampton Institute "to ascertain whether Richard could get admission," and they had another long talk about it while Richard was driving him to Port Deposit to catch the Baltimore train, but the brothers parted with nothing decided. It was up to Grandfather to prove the wisdom of settling in the South.

He made the trip to North Carolina by slow stages, stopping off in Baltimore to stay overnight with an old classmate and to buy himself a suit of clothes, a hat and a pair of glasses. In Richmond he found the Virginia state constitutional convention in full swing and attended one of the sessions. Richmond also held a romantic interest for Grandfather, who, while in Virginia earlier, had overcome his shyness enough to court a young woman named Pattie Robinson. His diary was filled with references to her "auburn ringlets," "her youth, innocence and modesty" and "the pain at heart when I came to say goodbye." He had lunch with young Pattie, and, helped along by the kind landlady who provided cake and wine for them, he must have gotten up enough courage to propose, for he later wrote, "We are to alter our relation in September which time I wish were here. For my love for her is pure as the crystal. Returned to my hotel and in the evening I accompanied the object of my affection to Church. Enjoyed her society so much and would not exchange the pleasant afternoon and evening in her company for a week of ordinary life."

Grandfather left Richmond fortified with his new dreams and plans and in such high spirits not even the tiresome journey to Hillsboro could dampen his enthusiasm.

He arrived on the evening of January 21. "It was dark and could not see anything but I was fortunate enough to get into a wagon with baggage. . . ." The teacher whom he was to assist, a Miss B. V. Harris, was teaching night school when he arrived, but "came in about 9 P.M. and is a very lively pleasant well educated woman from Oberlin College, Ohio. Mr. Heywood Beverly was the next person to whom I was introduced. He is an enterprising man, a tanner and to his charge I have been consigned. He has been building a house that cost $1600. A fine building. He has a fine family."

Grandfather was very much impressed with the quiet historic town of Hillsboro and the industrious colored families he first met there. They owned neat homes, were engaged in trades and had a fine school going with more than 300 scholars enrolled and an average attendance of 125 in the day session. He was delighted to see the large night class of adults. "They are some of them ciphering in compound arithmetic," he noted. His favorable first impressions were not unfounded. Twenty-six-year-old Heywood Beverly, the tanner, was a free-born mulatto, and worth $1,700, which made him wealthier than Washington Duke, a poor tobacco farmer of Orange County who traveled about the country after the war peddling his products from a mule-drawn wagon. In 1870

Washington Duke was worth only $1,400. Two generations later his sons would be worth millions.

Little by little Grandfather learned how the colored people had weathered the war and the first years after Appomattox. In 1860, North Carolina's population was close to a million, one-third of whom were slaves. She also had thirty thousand free persons of color, many of whom owned land, had some education and some of whom had voted before 1835. At the end of the war the state was bankrupt, the banks were closed and the great masses of the people, white and black, were in a starving condition. Thousands of Negroes had followed Sherman's army into the state, whose population was already swelled by white refugees from South Carolina and Georgia. Prices had gone up so high that it was almost impossible to buy food. A barrel of flour, which had cost about $18 when the war began, cost $500 in 1865. Sugar was $30 a pound; molasses, $25 a gallon; meal, $30 a bushel; coffee, $30 a pound. Bacon jumped from 33 cents to $7.50 a pound. Smallpox and yellow fever swept over the state. But for rations distributed by the federal garrisons, the Freedmen's Bureau and huge shipments of grain and provisions from northern philanthropic groups, large numbers of the people would have perished from 1865 to 1867.

Now better crops were under way and some of the suffering was relieved, but many of the colored people were still homeless and going from place to place to get farm work. Those who did not work on shares earned from $6 to $10 a month as farm laborers. Many received no money at all, only their keep.

While Grandfather found some of the Orange County families very poor, "the general class have bought land and built houses though very small. They are charged $3 to $8 for the poorest cottages. The mechanics are the largest class here and they are putting up cottages in every direction." He was quick to note that land values were very cheap in comparison with those in Pennsylvania and when he saw the old Hillsboro Institute where the well-to-do sons of Orange County had once gotten their education, he remarked that it was "rapidly going down and could be bought for $1500. It would do for some Northern Educational Association to buy and use it as a normal school."

Young Beverly and he hit it off very well. Robert began help-

ing him with the carpentry on his house after school hours.
Beverly knew the tanner's trade and Robert had some business
experience and knowledge of northern firms, so the two of them
entered a partnership. They went about the town looking at
tannery plants to get a design for their building and arranged to
buy three acres of land on the edge of Hillsboro for their own mill.

They had hardly got started on the project when Grandfather
received an urgent letter from George Dixon, then heading up the
North Carolina schools under the Friends Freedmen's Association's sponsorship, requesting him to proceed at once to Goldsboro to take over a school which had lost its principal. Goldsboro
was known as a "states' rights" stronghold which had been the
scene of a statewide conference to promote the Secession movement before the war. It was now one of the twelve military posts
under the military government of the state where the 40th U.S.
Infantry troops were garrisoned. Their commander was Grandfather's old leader on the Petersburg assault, General E. W. Hinks,
who had authority to supervise civil officers and elections. Anti-
Negro feeling was high and only the presence of these troops
prevented serious outbreaks.

Grandfather had begun his work in North Carolina just as the
state constitutional convention was meeting in Raleigh. Once
before a constitution had been drafted which based representation
on the white population only and provided that only white people
were eligible to vote and hold office. In 1866, this constitution was
rejected by a majority of less than 2,000 out of a total vote of
41,000. The Negroes had a nucleus of informed leadership after
the war, aided by those who had escaped to the North and later
returned and northern Negroes like Grandfather who migrated to
North Carolina. They asked for equality before the law and opportunities for education.

North Carolina was now trying to find a way to return to the
Union. The state had been under various provisional forms of
government for nearly three years while it wrestled with the problem of what to do with the Negro freedmen. The present constitutional convention had been called in accordance with the
Congressional plan of reconstruction. Of the delegates who met in
Raleigh on January 14, 1868, only 13 were Negroes and 16 so-

called "carpetbaggers." The remainder of the 107 Republican delegates were native whites. Thirteen Conservatives, violently opposed to granting suffrage to the Negroes, completed the representation.

Several months earlier, registration of voters under the Congressional plan was completed and resulted in 72,932 Negro voters out of a total of 179,653. Nineteen North Carolina counties had substantial Negro majorities and in several others the white majorities were less than 100. Since the Conservatives had lost their fight to prevent a convention, the struggle now was based upon which political faction would control the Negro vote. Lines were tightly drawn between Conservatives, who opposed adoption of the Fourteenth Amendment, and Republicans led by former provisional Governor W. W. Holden, a man whose zigzag political career resembled that of a knight on a chessboard. This struggle was to overshadow Grandfather's every effort to establish schools among the colored people for years to come.

His Goldsboro assignment gave a foretaste of the mounting difficulties he would face. He arrived by stage in a violent snowstorm, found the mission house and schoolroom out of wood and supplies because his predecessor "was not careful in keeping up with his bills." He suffered a chill and contracted a heavy cold. His funds were always low and there were many delays in receiving his salary and expense money. It was several days before he could buy enough wood to keep the place warm, and then he wrote, "Today is fine and I feel much better than I have for several days. The winter sun shines brightly on my ice-bound soul." The wood problem was a chronic one and the wood disappeared faster than he could replenish it. It was some time before he discovered the reason. "Some kind person has been getting into our schoolroom every night right after the night school is out and burning our wood. Sgt. Kelly has detected him in the act of getting out in the morning."

Little wonder that homeless folk sought any place to keep warm. The winter was a severe one and school attendance was very irregular. "How dreary I am sitting alone in the Mission House," he confided to his diary. "I went to see a number of old scholars who had stopped coming on account of want. I found them with their parents engaged in clearing off woody land & building houses for themselves for which they get homes for two years. Some of them are so poor and destitute. I carried a number of tracts and religious papers which I read to them. I find most of them hopeful Christians."

There was never enough of anything to go around. He spent his own funds to buy lamp chimneys and oil so that the students could see their books at night. The mission barrels of wool and cotton cloth and other supplies reached only a few of the needy families. He kept scrupulous records of books on hand, of every cent he collected and every item of expense, but constantly he dug into his own salary to keep things going.

Sometimes the federal troops proved to be an embarrassment. "Mrs. R. & Miss G. [two teachers] were insulted in town by a Drunken soldier of the 40th U.S.T. The soldiers have been paid and to their disgrace many of them have been indulging in drinking and frolicking."

Then there were problems of keeping up the morale of fellow teachers in surrounding schools. "Walked down to Dudley 9 miles. Stopped to visit several plantations on the way. Talked with the poor freed people and left papers and tracts with them; find them working mostly for low wages, 7 and low as 6 dollars per month in hopes that times will get better. Arrived in Dudley where Miss Jennie Allen used to teach. Miss Collins has a small school of 16. I examined her school. They are all in the preparatory class. There are a number of families in this town who own their places."

The Dudley school had been a source of great concern to Grandfather. Several weeks earlier Miss Jennie Allen had to close down her school and leave "on acct. of not being paid. She was to be paid by a committee of citizens, but they proved to be too poor." After Miss Allen left, two members of the school committee, "came to see if I could not secure the patronage of some Educational Association as they are not yet able to support their school, and are [not] willing to have their children grow up as ignorant as they. Noble men! but what source shall I try? I have written to several and have not succeeded but I will try again; I feel that it is something terrible to have our people grow up with the additional evil of ignorance upon them, shut out from the world on account of the many prejudices, esp. against their ignorance."

During these days Grandfather made many references in his diary to the Psalmist's words, "They that sow in tears shall reap in joy. He that now goeth on his way weeping, and beareth forth good seed, shall doubtless come again with joy, and bring his sheaves with him." For what kept him going was that no matter how irregular, how poorly equipped, how piecemeal the process of education was, there was always that hunger among the people to learn whatever little they could.

The sheer effort to keep the work alive made it impossible for him to study on his own account, but he never lost his intellectual curiosity about the world in which he lived. "In my walk I came across one of the famed fossil-beds. It had been excavated to a considerable depth and the lower down the pit extended the more numerous and varied the species of shells became. I gathered a specimen of coral perfect as though just taken from the ocean, and to my curiosity I found several pieces of lava thrown up probably by some of the Blue Mountains before the flood. The impression of the flow was still upon it and had imbedded several small stones and shells, and the impression of waves was still upon its surface."

By March 27 the constitutional convention had completed its work and the political campaign to adopt the constitution got under way. The proposed document abolished slavery and property qualifications for office; it set forth a bill of rights proclaiming the equality of men, ordered a system of public schools and universal suffrage to be established and pointedly omitted any reference to compulsory separation of the races in education. The thirteen Conservative delegates voted against it and refused to sign it. It would be presented to the voters for ratification on April 21.

Grandfather now found himself head over heels in politics. He could not avoid it. Being a teacher and natural leader among the freedmen, he was intensely interested in the outcome of the vote although he could not vote himself. He was a subscriber to *Harper's Weekly*, which he read avidly, and was by conviction a Radical Republican. How he felt about Andrew Johnson's policies was summed up in the terse entry: "Feb. 27th—Pres. Johnson impeached. Good!"

The Republicans brought their campaign to Goldsboro in early March and Grandfather had an opportunity to hear their candidate for governor, W. W. Holden, whose speech he found "radical and plausible, but was not well taken by the whites in general." The Conservatives immediately organized a counter meeting, "but their sentiments expressed to the colored people whom they desired to convert, were so repulsive, that I walked away," he wrote.

The campaign was a bitter one. The Conservatives ridiculed the proposed constitution, declaring that the issue was whether the Negro was the social equal of the white man, and that while the Negroes would control the election, most of them had no property and the majority of those who paid taxes in the state were the white people who were disfranchised. They claimed the Reconstruction Acts were unconstitutional, and that the present constitution would bring about Negro supremacy in the state. They affirmed their determination, however, to protect the Negroes in their rights and allow them such privileges as were not inconsistent with the welfare of both races. It is not at all surprising that Grandfather walked away in disgust.

Tuesday of the scheduled vote dawned gray and threatening in Goldsboro after several days of heavy rain. It was the first vote that Grandfather had witnessed among the freedmen and he jotted down his impressions.

April 21. Let the Republicans have the school room for speaking and in which to form their lines of voters. So earnest and desirous of peace [were they] that they formed into columns of two's, marched to the commanding Gen'l. Hinks' Quarters. Gave three times three cheers—deposited their votes at the Ballot Box and went home. Stern men—

P.M. After morning duties were over I went down to the Polls and seeing several who had registered in other parts of the state and whom the Conserv's were trying to make lose their vote I had them put an oath of affirmation and thus secured their votes for the Republican Cause—

April 22. Pleasant weather today. There is quite an Enthusiasm among the colored voter though the Conservative is ramming us close there being only about 180 votes ahead in favour of our Party. A Gus

Bryant (colored) in defiance of his friends voted the Conservative ticket. While I stood at the Polls the vote averaged 5 colored Repbn. votes to 1 white Conservative. But I heard a white man say today is the Black man's day. Tomorrow will be the white man's. I thought— Poor man—those days of distinction between colors is about over in this (now) free country.

When the official vote was announced, the constitution had been ratified by a vote of 93,084 to 74,015.

A white observer in Concord, North Carolina, confirmed Grandfather's impressions in a letter to *The Friend*, dated May 9, 1868. Wrote Victor C. Barringer:

I have been a close observer of the freedmen since surrender, and I must testify to their general commendable conduct. I witnessed for the first time, recently, their deportment in the exercise of the elective franchise; and, on all hands, the evidence comes up that they carried themselves with patience, propriety, firmness, intelligence, and good order, under many temptations and trying circumstances. True they generally voted all one way, but this only evinced their intelligent appreciation of the main issue in the election, which involved their own right to the suffrage. What I would have you particularly mark now is, that they cast their votes without uproar or disorder. Hundreds of them came into this quiet village early in the morning, and, having voted, they did not loiter about the town, but returned immediately to their labor. This is proof of some capacity for self-government. In general, I may say, they are law-abiding and industrious—quite as much as our white population. . . .

Grandfather joined a victory celebration the Saturday night following the election. "I marched in torch light procession from Wilber[force] School to General's Headquarters accompanied by the Regimental Band to give him 3 cheers, after giving three more for the adoption of the New Constitution, marched 500 in number to Gen'l. Brogden's house; he being our Radical Candidate to the House—he gave us a fine speech late as it was and then after marching around town and frightening the Conserv's and Rebels out of their senses we dispersed near 12 mid.—"

Reprisals came swiftly. In fact, on the same night Grandfather was parading victoriously about Goldsboro, at Little Washington in near-by Pitt County, "a fatal affair came off . . . between a

band of guerrillas and a party of U.S. Troops. Two colored soldiers
were killed and their officer wounded and several Conservatives
killed and their Castle, a frame building which they had fortified,
was burned down and they burned up in it, an affair which will
teach this Section how to behave under military authority. Several
had driven their employees off because they voted the *Republican*
ticket."

Violence had answered violence, but there was no heart in
victory. When the two men were buried, "the whole Regiment
paraded through the town with a cart upon which the dead bodies
of the colored soldiers lay. It was quite a mournful affair."

The planters had other ways of striking back and not even a
garrison of 250 troops could protect the victims of this kind of
warfare. A week after the vote, Grandfather wrote, "An old man
staid at the Mission House last night who had been driven away by
his Conservative employer and his dogs because he voted for the
New Constitution. The rest of the hands had been forced to vote
with their Employers, there being no protection nearer than 30
miles. He came in last evening very worn and weary—and left this
morning. He has a family to get away."

This was the first of many sorrowful tales. A few days later he
wrote, "Yesterday an old man neatly dressed came to ask charity
or to borrow till his crop came off—he says that the destitution in
the country is very great—that it would not be so much so but the
Rebel will not let the colored people have anything unless they
pay cash for it because they voted the Republican ticket. Few of
them get cash for their labor and the result is that many colored
families on the plantations are in a starving condition. I gave him
what change I could spare—.35. I have given away a considerable
[amount] to these poor men and today I have just had to turn off
an old man because I had no meal in the house."

There were heartening signs. The Sunday school increased and
he received a barrel of meal and some books for his normal class.
And about this time he got a letter from Richard which "infers
a willingness to come South." He made a brief trip to Hillsboro
and "found my partner Mr. B—— in fine spirits as our house for
Mill, Bark and Finishing Room is up and the vats partly and pipe
for water conduction in process of erection. . . . We have 20

cords of bark in." It was a week-end trip but he delayed his return to Goldsboro until Monday. The evening before he noted, "I could not travel today as I feel it to be wrong. I shall start early tomorrow."

As soon as warm weather reached Goldsboro, Grandfather put into operation what he considered a cardinal principle of the ABC's—cleanliness. He had the students scrub down the school-house until the boards shone. Then he marched the older boys of his normal class out to the banks of the Neuse River to take baths, although "the river is rather cold yet." Once a week he repeated this ritual, joining the boys in their swim. "The river is about 300 yards wide and 20 deep and a very rapid current," but he persevered against all kinds of weather. This practical method was not without its disadvantages. "Last evening while bathing a storm came up and before we could get back to town (a mile distant) it burst on us and soaked my linen well. We presented an imposing spectacle as we double-quicked thro the village." The result of this adventure cost Grandfather $2.30 of his meager earnings to buy another pair of linen pants.

In mid-May the Wilberforce School held its anniversary exercises. Grandfather and some of the older students built an outdoor platform on the banks of the Neuse River. Five hundred people attended the program. The 40th U.S. Infantry Band played "America" and J. E. O'Hara, former principal of the school and delegate to the recent constitutional convention, delivered an address. Grandfather was so busy making lemonade and providing dinner for the band that he had little time to circulate among the people, but his impression was that they all had a grand time at the picnic which followed the program. The only misfortune of the day was that they had chosen as their picnic grounds a neck of land extending far out into the Neuse. "While we were being pleasantly entertained [by the band], the river rose and surround the point upon which the picnic was and we had to bridge it and leave at 3 in the afternoon."

Grandfather stayed on in Goldsboro until July 1, when his school closed officially for the summer. His final entry was a revealing one and typical of him. "Left on the 6 A.M. train for Hillsboro with all my debts save one paid. That one originates as follows—I went one day to Dr. Miller to ask his advice in regard to a breaking out on my skin. He set to work, fixed up a bottle of wash and some salve composed of blue stone lard and charged me a dollar for the preparation and $1.50 for the advice—$2.50. I told him it was too much. I would make a pay't when I got well and I'll do so."

15

GRANDFATHER was so convinced his future lay in North Carolina that, in spite of occasional outbreaks of violence and intimidation of the freedmen, before he left for his summer vacation in 1868 he sent home for his melodeon. It was the only piece of furniture he owned and it was a symbol of home to him. He had it varnished, tuned up and shipped to Hillsboro. He also ordered a bark machine from New York for the tanning business he and Beverly had set up, and left a sum of money with his partner to develop the work while he was gone.

He had some reason to be encouraged. The North Carolina legislature had met and ratified the Fourteenth Amendment, and Republican Governor W. W. Holden took office on July 4. A week later North Carolina was officially proclaimed to have fulfilled the requirements of the Reconstruction Acts and was readmitted to the Union. The reports from Rev. F. A. Fiske, Negro superintendent of Freedmen's Bureau's educational work, showed that some sixteen thousand freedmen were attending the Bureau schools and another ten thousand were receiving instruction through private schools or those supported by religious societies. The Constitution of 1868 required that the General Assembly at its first session provide for a system of free public schools for all the children of the state between six and twenty-one years of age. There was every reason to be hopeful about the future.

Back home in Pennsylvania Grandfather began to wonder. Political war clouds gathered while he worked away on the farm, harrowing corn, cutting oats and hay, helping his father put a roof on the barn and binding, hauling and threshing wheat. Storm warnings grew more ominous as the time neared for him to return to his teaching post. The Rebels had recovered from the first shock of their defeat and were now engaging in the undeclared War of Reconstruction under the cloak of the Democratic party. Wrote Grandfather:

Aug. 31. I saw an extract from a Missouri journal declaring that the Rebellion had recommenced in that state and that the Democrat Rebels had armed themselves and gone to Wayne and other counties and closed all the civil and government offices and driven the officers off. That the sheriff with a detachment of soldiers had to go out to interfere and that a collision was expected. So much for the Democratic Party. . . .

Sept. 4. . . . The colored members pronounced ineligible in the Georgia Legislature, and therefore expelled. The feeling upon this piece of treachery (from the white Democrats) is of deep well settled conviction of the deception of the Democrat Party.

None of his kinsfolk could understand why he was so dead set upon returning south. He was much too frail to stand the hardships of that Godforsaken country, they felt. Robbie had always been the kind of fellow who threw himself into things and worked too hard. That summer working in the harvest he had almost collapsed from the heat several times. Once he was laid up with fever and had to have the doctor in to see him. He got better from the fever but was left somewhat deaf. And they all knew his eyesight was getting worse. He was now helpless if he went anywhere alone after dark. Often he came home long after dawn, his clothes covered with mud or wrinkled from his taking refuge in a hayloft.

As Grandfather explained it to his parents, he was a soldier in a "second war," this time against ignorance. Unless the freedmen were educated they would lose the rights they had gained at such great cost. In North Carolina alone there were one hundred thousand Negro children who could not read and write, to say nothing of the grown folks. These children were the "seed corn" of the future. Until the common schools were established the Freedmen's Bureau and religious groups must fill the breach. There were only about five hundred teachers in the field and Grandfather felt it his duty to join them, for every school kept open even for a few months was a tremendous gain.

Looking at it that way, his parents could say nothing against his going, but they hated to see him go alone. They were not yet ready to sell out and follow him. Sorrowfully they watched him pack his books and clothes the Sunday before he left home, noting how carefully he had cleaned and polished his army pistol and laid it among his things. Great-Grandfather Thomas offered a special petition at family prayers for his son's safety and guidance and that he might have "that wisdom and understanding that the world knows not of." And Great-Grandmother Sarah Ann slipped him fifty dollars of her butter-and-egg money to help him with his new venture.

Yet the gloom which hung over the household that Sunday affected even Grandfather. He wrote: "Mother and Mary are baking a cake and other little necessaries for my journey. Oh, how endearing is the love of a mother. Evening cloudy and portends rain on tomorrow the day I start for Hillsboro, North Carolina. It makes me feel sad and superstitious of evil to leave home on a cloudy or wet day."

Grandfather's premonition of evil became a reality before he had been away from home twenty-four hours. It happened while he was making the trip from Washington to Richmond by boat down the Potomac. It was one of those sudden incidents which descend out of nowhere and always catch their victims unprepared. It shocked him so that he set down a full account of it in his diary:

Sept. 22nd—Tuesday: Took the steamer *Key Port*, Capt. F. Hollingshead command'g. When about 8 or 10 miles from Acquia Creek he came to collect the fare & ordered us (another young man of Richmond, Va.) to go below to the low dark place under the fore-castle. My feelings were hurt very much as well as my friend's, but to make matters worse, on feeling for my transportation papers they were not to be found. I felt quite sure that they had dropped in the saloon while taking a paper from my pocket and I said to the captain, "Sir, I had transportation papers through to Hillsboro, N.C. I must have dropp'd them in the saloon, and if you will have the kindness to let one of the waiters enquire through the saloon and cabin they will very likely be found." He replied, "Damn your papers, go right away down to fire room and go to pitching coal. You have no papers, I don't believe you."

I then showed him a letter stating that I had an appointment at Hillsboro, N.C. and confirming the statement that I had them, and told him that if the papers were not found after an enquiry, that I was willing to go to the fire room or to make it allright with him, but if he would not make an enquiry that I did not feel duty bound to pay him. He said there should be no enquiry made and ordered me to go below which I did, he followed me cursing, the exact words I cannot repeat as I did not wish to have words with him and went out of hearing as much as I could, but I heard him say I was a D——d ——. I did not care to know what, and that he would put me ashore.

He soon after came to me and said: "I will put you ashore unless you give me your watch, or leave it with my clerk." I said, "Captain you have treated me like a dog; you have ordered me from the saloon; you will not have an enquiry made for the papers which I am sure some of your passengers must have; you treat me as though I was not a man because I am colored. And now sir, you can put me ashore, I will not pay my passage twice."

He then had the steamer's course altered, and she ran over to [a] bleak place on the Maryland side called Smith's Point. When the vessel came near the pier the officer came to me as though he would do me violence and before the board was down I leaped ashore, (on the pier). He was cursing at me when I turned toward the vessel, and being provoked by his [dis]courtesy toward me, I said, "Sir if you had been a gentleman which I am sorry to see you are not, I would have lost my transportation willingly, and paid you out of my own pocket. I have got money enough to do so," and I showed him the money. With an oath upon my black soul, he threw a wooden billet at me which I had the exceeding good fortune to dodge. He then told some one to get him an axe to throw at me and he ran as close as he could toward me to pitch it, but he did not have the misfortune to receive—and the poor Negro-hater took his finale by telling some citizens who stood on the pier to correct me, but they scampered away from the pier as though an African lion had been liberated in their presence. I regret the whole affair, but more sincerely that vessels are allowed to leave and return daily to the national Capital commanded by men who delight to insult and maltreat passengers merely because they are colored. And I would suggest to the thinking minds of this company that gentlemen be placed in command of their fine steamer, the C. Vanderbilt running between Acquia Creek and W[ashington]. . . .

Some of the passengers told me they did not approve of his conduct. P.M. A steamer came along about noon and took me across to a point 10 miles below the Va. side. Charged me one dollar. Place called Chatham or Chatterton. I saw Gen'l. [O. O.] Howard on board this boat and he was surprised and gave me his advice about it. I hired a small boat to take me 9 miles up the river and then being sick and weary walked across the country to Acquia Creek landing.

That Grandfather believed injustice should be challenged on the spot is shown by his next entry:

Wednesday, Sept. 23rd—In Washington. I came up last night in the 1 o'clock boat. Feel quite unwell. Misty this morning with some rain. Saw Gen'l. Howard and laid my case before him or his aide and left the matter in his hands. While strolling in the Capitol Park, I came upon an old army comrade who is now a government police at the capital with a salary of $1,700 and uniform a year. He took me through the senate chamber, the Rotunda, the various halls in which there are some of the finest paintings in the world. 7 P.M. Left in the Acquia steamer for Richmond, Va.

A year earlier Grandfather had written in his diary that he and Miss Pattie Robinson of Richmond would "alter our relations in September." From Grandfather's brief stopover in Richmond, his pointed silence about the event and his reference to having gone to see "my treacherous little sweetheart," it seems clear that the young lady had grown tired of waiting and that the engagement was off. "I left my Richmond friends," he wrote sadly, "to make my lonely way to the dreary dominions of the 'Old North State.'"

The one bright spot of his journey was his hearty welcome in Amelia Court House where he stopped off briefly on his way to Danville and North Carolina. "I saw several of my sincere old friends after more than a year's absence. I seem to be at home. . . . I visited the school at this place and a great many of the people up several miles in the country. They almost carried me off in transports of joy and made me eat 3 dinners and about 4 suppers in the short piece of a day I am with them."

Grandfather found that "everything is lovely" in Hillsboro and that the people were delighted to have him back. He opened school immediately, made an inventory of the books on hand and school furniture in the Hillsboro mission and plunged himself into his work. He had little time to think of the unhappy turn in his personal affairs because he had sixty-five scholars to take care of. And there was work at the tannery after school, putting up the office, installing the tanning vats and buying hides.

Eight days after his arrival he made a significant entry in his diary, the only event he reported for that date:

Oct. 6. Formed the acquaintance of a Miss Cornelia Smith, a fine looking octoroon of Chapel Hill.

And indeed she was fine looking. Grandfather never forgot how she looked on that first meeting. She was dressed in her best, a beautiful woolen suit which she had made herself, a high ruche about her neck trimmed with soft white lace, a fringed scarf tied in a bow and pinned with a large oval breast pin. She wore no other adornments and she did not have to. She was the most strikingly beautiful woman Grandfather had ever seen. She wore her hair brushed tightly back in long black curls down her back, with a forelock cut into boyish ringlets which fell over her brow. She was extremely modest with young men, he noted, but there was a fire about her which communicated itself immediately to him.

She was down from Chapel Hill on a visit to Mr. and Mrs. Abel Payne, an elderly couple whom he had met and who reminded him a bit of his own parents. He used to stop by and pass the time of day with them. In fact, if it had not been for the Paynes, I doubt that he would ever have got married. He was so extremely timid in matters of the heart he might have remained a bachelor for life. He saw Grandmother just once and did not mention her in his diary again until about two weeks before they were married. She lived twelve miles away and he had no horse to go courting her. Their courtship was conducted "in absentia" through the Paynes, who acted as willing emissaries. He'd drop in to see them and always ask about "Miss Smith from Chapel Hill." This gave them a chance to tell him all about her, her people and her talents. Months before, they had done the same thing with Grandmother Cornelia about the handsome, refined young "foreigner" who had come to teach at the Hillsboro school. To them everybody was a foreigner who was not born in the South.

Meanwhile, Hillsboro, though a tiny town of only several hundred residents, was caught up in the fever of the Presidential election. For the first time the freedmen in six of the southern states would cast their ballots in a national election and much was at stake. For the next few weeks after his arrival, Grandfather devoted much of his spare time to politics.

Oct. 24. Today is my birthday. I am just 28 years old, and today my hopes are brighter than at any other birthday of my life. . . .

I wrote several resolutions for the U.L. [Union League] of which I became a member on the 17th inst. . . .

30th—Friday. Quite a stir about the election.

31st. Went gunning today and we got 9 squirrel.

Nov. 2nd—Monday. Everybody anxious about the election. I went to Durham and took the votes or the tickets for the Grant and Colfax voters—400—was watched very closely by the conservatives.

3rd—Tuesday, Nov. 3 1868. The Great Epoch in the history of our race has at last arrived, and today the colored citizens of these Southern [states] are casting their votes for the presidential candidates U.S. Grant and Schuyler Colfax. The citizens of Hillsboro are jubilant and their votes are going in like snowflakes, silently and surely. Everything is quiet and there seems to be the best feeling all around.

11 P.M. Grant and his ticket's maj. 56 in this town.

4th. Rep. Maj. 160,000 by telegraph and the Reps. are jubilant. Our Union League of Hillsboro have met and appointed committees in each precinct to look out for the interests of the Republican Party. They have also made arrangements for a grand torch light parade in case we elect Grant.

5th—Thursday. Quite a stir in the political element and a number of Rep. Gentlemen have requested me to write a song for the Republicans to sing if we are victorious & I have consented to do so tonight for tomorrow night.

Grandfather sat up until midnight composing the song of four verses with a chorus after each verse and adapted to the tune of "We'll Rally Round the Flag, Boys." He reported that his "humble attempt has met the approbation of the League and it was enthusiastically received and endorsed by all." The final count showed Grant's popular majority to be around 360,000. Since the Negro freedmen had polled more than 700,000 votes, their ballots had decided the 1868 election. Grandfather described the celebration in Hillsboro:

Nov. 6th—Friday night 12 M. Tonight has truly been a grand one for the Republicans of Hillsboro. We met (I with the rest) at the hour of 8, with fine torches some red, some blue, some white, and with a drum corps; marched and filed and wound through almost every Avenue in the town; cheered for Grant, for the Great American Republican Government, for U. Republicans, for the Freedmen's Bureau and for that other man, and ended with a fine supper and speeches. Everything peacable and quiet as could be wished or expected. . . .

Yes, it had been a grand celebration and peace at last had come to this part of the South. The Republicans went ahead with their organization of the county ticket and a few weeks later Grandfather reported that they had nominated him to run for the office of county magistrate's clerk. "All the rest of the ticket are white. I appreciate the confidence the people reposed in me, and if elected shall endeavour with God's help to discharge faithfully the duties of my office."

Grandfather never got to test his political potentialities. Although he wrote to Governor Holden inquiring about the duties of a magistrate's clerk and his salary, and went about printing up the county ticket and circulars, a short time later he received a letter from the Friends Freedmen's Association expressing their disapproval and he declined the nomination immediately.

After that he settled down to his schoolwork and the tanning trade. Shortly after the election he had a surprise visit from his brother. Richard liked the town and the people and upon his return to Pennsylvania he wrote that Great-Grandfather Thomas now proposed to sell his farm and come to Hillsboro. Grandfather was so elated that he redoubled his efforts to get established. He watched the newspaper advertisements for the sale of farm land

and answered many of them. As soon as he had completed the little one-room office he and Beverly had been building near the tannery, he bought himself some furniture, pots, pans and dishes, fitted it up as a little home and moved in.

Feb. 25 [1869]. . . . Today has been an important era in my life. I have moved into my own little "Cottage by the Stream" and though it is small, a humble one, yet in it I feel as comfortable as a King on his throne.

I moved from Mr. Beverly's with the assistance of his horse and wagon, and tonight I have cooked a part of my supper, which consisted of cofee, eggs and sweet potatoes. My little boy Charley is with me & have played "Home Sweet Home" [on the melodeon] by way of initiating myself into my home & and after giving him a lesson, reading a chapter in my Bible we will go to bed to sleep, "perchance to dream . . ." May the kind and merciful Parent ever keep me, and bless my little home.

Some time earlier Beverly and Grandfather had taken the boy, Charley, who had no home, in to live with them to grind bark and work about the place for his board and room. He also accompanied Grandfather when he had to go out at night. The new venture worked out very well. Grandfather furnished his home with purchases at auction sales and proudly reported his progress from time to time. Once he wrote, "I made the first biscuit I ever made, did it well."

The year 1869 marked the end of Freedmen's Bureau work and the gradual decline of philanthropic support of schools among the freedmen. Earlier in the winter Grandfather received a visit from a delegation of Friends Freedmen's Association officials who expressed themselves as much pleased with his school. They had examined several white schools "but none is under better discipline or making more progress than the Hillsboro school." The Quaker officials informed him, however, that they were making a drive to develop self-sustaining schools and instituting a new pay regulation. If the monthly fee imposed upon the parents of each child attending the school was not paid, the child must be sent home.

This procedure, designed to make the freedmen more responsible, only meant that the poorer children dropped out. Grandfather did not want to make his school dependent upon the ability of the children to pay; he wanted it open to all children. He had visited among the people and knew how great were their difficulties. "I have given away to the destitute shoes, groceries, &c to the amount of $3.00. . . . Visited a poor woman who is confined to her sick bed with pneumonia, has 8 small children and in a destitute condition. I gave them some sugar and coffee. I also visited a poor woman who has 5 small children & no husband. He was killed by Rebel Wheeler's Cavalry. Gave her son a pair of shoes. . . . Gave a poor woman some nice calico to make some dresses for her poor children."

He finally hit upon a plan which he thought might meet the situation. "Tonight I called and met all interested in the school and suggested my willingness to relinquish my claim of tuition from them if they would form a Committee of 20 who would insure me $20.00 per month, which they decided to do. . . . It is my object to have an arrangement by which all children may have access to the school; the committee have decided to reduce the monthly tax of 40 cents to 20 cents and reopen the night school as I requested. . . . The Committee have concluded to take the responsibility for collecting & paying me the $20 required."

In early March, Grandfather received the news from Pennsylvania he had been waiting for. "Letter from father and mother and they are coming down to N.C. to live. Have sold their place & are to have a vendue on the 16th of this month. I am so glad they are to be near me." When the 16th came, he wrote, "Today my father away up in the Keystone State sells his farm stock and utensils, with household and kitchen furniture, and I prayed to the kind heavenly Parent, that he would send them plenty of good able purchasers that they may be still abler to come down here to Settle, that His Grace may keep them and us all."

That same month, the firm of Beverly and Fitzgerald, tanners, launched its business:

March 27. . . . Finished Mr. Moore's 3 hides and delivered them to him. He chose the two calf and the large kid's. Place 1 kid and 1 sheep skin at H. N. Brown's Store for sale. Our Hides are all stamped with the name of our firm on them and they look hot. This is an important day in the history of the lives of Beverly and myself. We begin business as men, and with God's blessing on our effort to be useful we hope to do well.

It seemed at last to Grandfather that his life was taking shape—a business, a little home and his family coming to settle in the South. It was now time to think of taking a wife.

16

THE Fitzgeralds stepped off the evening train at Hillsboro in mid-April, 1869. There were four of them—Great-Grandfather Thomas, tall and well built in his custom-made Prince Albert; his wife, white and haughty looking in her black shawl and white-ribboned bonnet (and with one thousand dollars in her shoe); and the two sedate little girls, fourteen-year-old Mary and nine-year-old Agnes. From the five huge packing cases and bale of carpet which followed them everybody in Hillsboro knew these well-dressed Yankees had come to stay.

Grandfather, who had waited anxiously for weeks, almost missed his folks when they arrived:

Apr. 14—Weds. This evening I went down to the station and while waiting in almost breathless suspense for the passengers to land a man said, "Mr. Fitzgerald, there is a lady looking for you." And that lady was my mother, accompanied by sister Mary, Agnes & Father. I will not describe the meeting, more than it was a happy one. They will stay with me in my little "Hall." They come to settle here and have brought about $1500 with them to buy. They met with a very hearty welcome by the citizens of this place. They had a very pleasant trip here being accompanied by Richard as far as Baltimore. . . . I cannot express my joy.

The white folk of Hillsboro were even more curious about these "foreigners" when it was learned that they were looking for a farm and were ready to pay cash for it. At least twenty callers with offers of land came to see them on the third day after their arrival. They hired a horse and drove about the countryside looking at the various farms for sale. In nine days they had found what they wanted and closed the deal.

Apr. 25. Father and Mother bought the plantation called Woodside. I wrote the deed for the plantation which father has purchased from Squire Robert J. Jeffreys containing 158 acres, for which Mr. Jeffrey pays me in tobacco amounting to about $8.50. We get the plantation together with all the stock, farming utensils, household and kitchen furniture for $1200.

Woodside Farm lay near the banks of the Eno River about six miles southeast of Hillsboro and a mile from University Station, a little whistle-stop on the railroad between Durham's Station and Hillsboro. It had been a beautiful place once. The two-story seven-room house stood in a grove of six huge oak trees at the top of a long slope which rolled gently down to the woods. At the bottom of the slope near the road was a little two-room cottage. It had fifty acres of heavy oak timber and another forty of smaller timber; the rest of the acreage was in farm land. There was a fair-sized orchard and when the Fitzgeralds bought it their stock consisted of a fine young mare called Fanny, a yoke of oxen, seven head of beef cattle, three cows and two calves.

Grandfather observed, "What I have seen of it I like very well, though the house is quite dingy." It was one of many farms in the South which had suffered from years of neglect during and after the war. The fields had not been cultivated in several years and the ground was hard and dry. There were large ditches and washed-out gullies everywhere. The house needed cleaning and repairs; the plows needed sharpening; the underbrush needed clearing. To get the place in shape would require a gang of ten or twelve men by southern standards of work, and all the Fitzgeralds had to help them were the mare and yoke of oxen.

When the Fitzgeralds moved in, the white farmers around Woodside didn't know what to make of their new neighbors. They were friendly but minded their own business and asked no favors. They paid cash for what they wanted in a county where

very few people had cash. And when they didn't deal in cash, they
always had something to trade—hides for food and supplies, or the
use of their oxen and their own labor for materials they wanted.
And they all worked like blue blazes. Woodside Farm was transformed into a going concern in a matter of weeks under the white
folks' unbelieving eyes.

The Yankee schoolteacher who looked so frail that a gust of
wind might blow him away finished up his school in Hillsboro,
moved his things down to Woodside and turned farmer of amazing strength. Great-Grandfather Thomas hired a farm hand and
the three men set to work. They mended harness and tools, repaired wheels, sharpened plowshares, hauled wagonloads of stones
and dirt to fill the ditches and gullies, cleared the fields, cut timber,
hauled logs and rails, built fences and brought in a carpenter to
repair the house. They brought in loads of manure and started a
compost. They plowed and harrowed and put in a corn crop. By
late May they had a truck garden of melons, cucumbers, peas,
beans and tomatoes well on the way. They sowed oats and set out
thousands of sweet-potato plants. They cut hay from the front
meadow, made a lovely lawn and a swing for the children from one
of the branches of the tallest oak in the yard. When they were
not grubbing and clearing the fields, they were setting out fruit
trees or hauling in timber from the woods to build another house.
In time they dug a cellar and drilled a well beneath the kitchen
so they would not have to walk to the spring for water.

The news of their successful settlement traveled back to Pennsylvania, and for a while it seemed that there would be a migration
of friends and relatives to North Carolina. That summer one of
their old neighbors from Upper Oxford, Jacob R. Nocho, who was
now in business at Greensboro, came down to visit them at Woodside and wrote a glowing letter to his mother describing their
farm, stock and timber in detail.

    . . . Thomas was telling me that the Scriptures were about to be
fulfilled with him. There is a passage that say that the time will come
when every man shall worship God under his own vine and fig tree,
so he has a very large grape vine and a splendid fig tree both on his
place. . . . They all looked after me as far as they could see me, and
made me promise that I would come soon again—and if I should get

sick or anything I was to be sure and go there and make it my home. Fitzgeralds are very much respected by both white and colored.

The next thing the white neighbors learned was that two more Fitzgerald brothers had arrived and were going to set up a brick-yard on Woodside Farm. About the same time they discovered that "that school teacher fellow" had married Sid Smith's daughter from Chapel Hill. Grandfather had been so busy getting his family settled that he didn't get around to courting Grandmother until midsummer. One day in July he hitched up Fanny and drove over to the Smith plantation to see her.

As Grandmother told it, she got very little chance to do any courting on that first visit. It was not Great-Grandmother Harriet who welcomed him, but Mary Ruffin Smith. She was curious about this Mr. Fitzgerald she had heard Cornelia talk so much about. She had seen as many as fifteen young men at a time on the Smith place, all making eyes at the oldest Smith daughter, but Cornelia had given them all the go by. Yankee or no Yankee, if Robert Fitzgerald was the man Cornelia liked, Miss Mary wanted to know all about him. So right off she invited him into the parlor and sat down to talk with him. What was even more surprising was that Miss Mary invited him to have dinner with her without batting an eye. Her Chapel Hill friends would have thought Mary Ruffin Smith was surely losing her wits—to sit down at the table with a Yankee and a colored man to boot—but Miss Mary apparently enjoyed herself. It was the first refreshing conversation she had had in years. She found this serious young man intelligent, informed, of impeccable manners and not in the least over-whelmed by her unorthodox courtesy. With lawyerlike shrewdness she probed him about his plans for the future, and evidently she was satisfied for during dinner she came out with a surprising remark.

"I'll tell you, Robert, if you're thinking about marrying Cornelia, you'd better know right off that she's got an ungovernable temper and she's hard to handle. You'll have to be firm with her and give her a switching every now and then," she said as if it were all settled.

Grandmother never forgave Miss Mary this bit of treachery, but it certainly helped things along a bit. It was the push shy Grandfather needed and before he left he asked permission to take Grandmother home to visit his people. For all his own reserve, Grandfather admired Grandmother's spirit. She was like a little untamed colt, he said, full of fire but shy on the bridle. The Fitzgeralds fell in love with her immediately, particularly Great-Grandfather Thomas and young Mary Jane. Great-Grandmother Sarah Ann was too possessive a mother to welcome any woman who rivaled her in the affections of her "Robbie, dear boy." But it was Billy and Richard who did most of the wooing for their backward brother. He stood off and watched while they piled her into the swing and pushed her high in the air, teased her by jerking at her long curls. He took her walking sedately with Mary and Aggie in tow as chaperones and called her "Miss Smith" until two days before they were married.

On August 6 he wrote, "Miss Smith and I are on intimate terms and will probably create conversation soon."

Since Grandmother had long ago made up her mind to say yes, there wasn't much conversation to be created. "From the time I first laid eyes on him I loved everything about him," she told me. "I loved the clothes he wore, the pillow under his head and the very ground he walked on."

Grandfather, however, must have thought she might change her mind, for as soon as she consented to marry him he went up to Hillsboro, got a marriage certificate and the ceremony took place the very next day. They were married at Woodside Farm by Squire A. C. Hunter, justice of the peace from University Station, on Sunday, August 8, 1869. Grandfather wrote that there was unusual interest and great thankfulness at family prayers that morning. It was a day of great rejoicing for all of them. Yet if love was the great force which brought my grandparents together and held them steadfast, trouble was a third party to the marriage vows that day and would remain a loyal partner until death dissolved the union fifty years later.

The Fitzgeralds had downed roots in North Carolina at the very moment the Ku-Klux Klan was rising over the state. Orange County was quiet and the white and colored people seemed to be on the best of terms, but there were disturbing rumors from neighboring Chatham and Alamance counties. Folks were saying the Ku-Kluxers meant to drive out every Yankee who insisted upon "teaching niggers and making them equal to white folks."

Rumors meant little to the Fitzgeralds. They had lived too long near the borders of Maryland and threatened kidnaping raids to fear the Ku-Klux Klan. The boys went right ahead digging their pits and wheeling clay for their brickyard. But there were other worries which hounded my grandparents from the start. They did not have a home and there was not even time for a honeymoon. Grandfather had given up his teaching job in Hillsboro in order to help his parents on the farm, but he was determined to have a school so he was putting up a building on the place for a schoolhouse and was rushing to complete it by September. In addition, there were crop troubles which threatened their summer's work. Grandfather wrote, "The drought has dried up most of the streams and the people go ten to fifteen miles to have their grists ground. Many who can are selling and moving out of the country. Our 18 acres of corn is parched up and there will only be little more than half a crop unless there is a great change in the weather."

The night they were married, Grandfather and Grandmother had a long talk and the next day she went up to Hillsboro. "She is to sew for several ladies," Grandfather reported. "She is anxious to do all she can to help me. She is to be away three weeks."

So Grandmother sewed in Hillsboro while Grandfather divided his time between putting a roof on the little schoolhouse and working on the brickyard. On Sundays he went up to take his bride to church and everywhere they went they received "quite a shower of congratulations" upon their marriage.

But on the very day little Woodside School opened, the Ku-Klux Klan struck in Orange County. Said Grandfather:

Weds. Sept. 1st. The infamous Ku-Klux Klan has visited our posttown Hillsboro and kill'd a black man who was supposed to have burned a barn. They have also marched or paraded in Chapel Hill & are committing depradations on Union men all around. They are unwilling to be governed by law and should therefore be considered outlaws and dealt with accordingly.

Grandfather's school had only eight scholars at first. When he went out around the country to visit some of the families he found that parents had been warned to keep their children away from that Yankee school. And every time he went up to Hillsboro he noticed the closed faces of white men who lounged about the store watching his every movement.

"I hear you got a school going on your farm," one of them said to him.

"Yes sir, I have," said Grandfather cheerfully.

"Well, I hear the Ku-Klux don't like schools for niggers round these parts and aim to close 'em up."

"I'll keep my school open if I have only two scholars," Grandfather replied as he walked away.

The white men scratched their heads and pondered. These Fitzgeralds didn't scare easy. But they tried it again when Billy Fitzgerald came to town.

"Say, Fitz," said the local storekeeper in front of the usual Saturday-afternoon crowd of farmers, "what'll you folks do down there if the Kluxers pay you a visit?"

Uncle Billy hitched up his suspenders and laughed a bit. "Well," he drawled, "I don't reckon there's much we can do. We don't have more'n nineteen or twenty guns and a few rounds of ammunition. But I can tell you one thing, if the Ku-Kluxers do come they won't all go back. They'll leave a few behind."

So the war of nerves went on while the Fitzgeralds turned out forty thousand bricks and Grandfather continued to teach his struggling little school. He brought Grandmother home and together they whitewashed and scrubbed the little cottage down the hill and moved in. Things got more critical. The stock market had taken a plunge on "Black Friday," September 29, that year and a national panic was on. The drought in North Carolina killed most of the crops. The Fitzgeralds had leather and bricks for sale but no takers. Great-Grandfather Thomas even made a trip to Raleigh to sell his bricks without success. When he came back, Grandfather wrote, "We are all somewhat despondent & the boys will probably go home."

About this time Grandmother made one of what was to be many trips back to the Smith plantation to see Miss Mary Ruffin Smith. When she returned with her brother-in-law Richard, who had gone up to Chapel Hill to leave their wool to be carded, she brought home a pig and seven chickens. As long as she lived, Miss Mary never failed to step into the breach when my grandparents were hard up. Grandmother would come back from the Smiths' loaded with tubs of lard, or butter, eggs, chickens, hams, flour and meal. Whatever Miss Mary thought of Yankees in general, Robert Fitzgerald was an exception.

Richard Fitzgerald returned from Chapel Hill reporting that he had seen a number of men "supposed to be K.K.K." and that he was informed "they are to march to take Col. Hugh Guthrie tonight." Grandfather wrote that the family insisted that he and Cornelia "sleep at the Big House to avoid the Ku-Klux who are said to have an ill feeling toward me because of my political opinion." Billy Fitzgerald became so discouraged that he packed his things and went back to Pennsylvania. Wrote Grandfather:

Sept. 29. Billy started for home this morning and left a sad set of individuals, for we have been nightly watching for the Ku-Klux Klan who desire to pay us a visit. Richard took him as far as Durham's. We are in a straitened condition just now, no money but brick and leather for sale; there is scarcely any money in the country. We had to send Billy away with empty pockets and a package of leather.

Richard might have left too, but aside from feeling there was strength in numbers he had a deeper reason for staying on awhile. Grandmother Cornelia had introduced him to one of her best friends, a young teacher from Philadelphia whose father, Rev. Samuel Williams, had come down to preach in the Methodist churches of Orange County. Mr. Williams looked like a Biblical patriarch; he wore a heavy mustache and long flowing beard which came to his waist and grew snowy white as he got older. His daughter, Sallie, was a tall striking young woman with flaming red hair. Grandmother's role as matchmaker was successful. It wasn't long before Richard and Sallie were engaged.

For a while the Ku-Klux Klan disrupted Grandfather's new home. He and Grandmother lived in the cottage and slept at the main house. Night after night the men sat up with their guns in their hands as the masked Klansmen thundered past on the road. In the mornings they found the ground almost cut to pieces from horses' hoofs where the Ku-Kluxers had ridden round and round the empty little cottage and the schoolhouse. Once Grandfather heard the window rattle violently, so he shot into the night with his pistol and whatever was there retreated in the darkness.

It was at this juncture that Abe Valentine came to visit them. He couldn't have come at a worse time for him. Grandfather described his arrival:

Oct. 8. Weather warm. 22 scholars today. Night, 11. Uncle Abe arrived from Pennsylvania. He is in a fine state of health and looks well. He brings a bad report about K.K.K.'s. While coming into the station on the up train 8:30 and just before it stopp'd at University Station, a white man named Ruffin drew a huge knife on a black man and dared him to attempt to defend himself telling him to "Assert his Rights." Ran the black man out of the car & came near making him jump off. The night was dark and it was with great difficulty that Uncle made his way to our house.

Indeed, Abe Valentine looked at only one farm. He heard so much about K.K.K.'s that he left again after a few days, taking Great-Grandmother Sarah Ann and Agnes with him back to Pennsylvania for a visit. The next time they heard from him he had bought "a fine dwelling in Wilmington on Front Street—$2500." They got several letters urging them to come north.

Great-Grandfather's answer to these appeals was a quotation from Ecclesiastes. "He that observeth the wind shall not sow; and he that regardeth the clouds shall not reap." Whether it was prayer or whether it was the rumor that the Fitzgeralds were good shots, nobody knows, but after a while the Klan left them alone. And by December Grandfather's enrollment at Woodside School had climbed to nearly fifty. He was indeed blessed. In adjoining Alamance County that November, four masked men attacked Alonzo B. Corliss, a lame teacher employed by the Friends Freedman's Association. They went to his home, dragged him out of bed in his nightclothes and out of the house without his crutches. His clothing was torn from his body as they pulled him through the bushes. When they got him to the woods, they flogged his naked body with raw cowhide and green hickory sticks—thirty lashes. Then they cut off the hair from one side of his head and painted half of his face and shorn head black. They kicked him in the side and left him lying unconscious in the cold November night air. He lay there for three hours before he came to and tried to crawl home. A colored man brought him his clothes and his wife met him with his crutches and together they helped him to his house. But when his wife fainted at his bedside, his colored students, braving the threats of the Klan, slipped in and dressed his wounds. When he had asked his tormenters what harm he had done they told him, "Teaching niggers."

Down in Orange County the day after this outrage, Robert Fitzgerald announced in his diary:

Nov. 30. I am going to make my school free—and it begins tomorrow. A free school for Rich and Poor, Black and White, high & low, supported principally by myself, the rental being paid by the F.B.

He had written to Dr. H. C. Vogell, the new superintendent of Freedmen's Bureau educational work in the state, and gotten a promise of ten dollars monthly for rental of the school building together with a blackboard, some books and slates for his pupils. Dr. Vogell sent him second- and third-grade readers, "18 Spellers, 12 Geographies, and 12 Grammars." Grandmother Cornelia helped him all she could through her sewing and quilt-making. He proudly reported, "I can now say that my wife has picked the wool, spun the yarn, woven the cloth & cut out and made me a suit of heavy wool clothes and I appreciate them on her account."

It was a brave effort, but he soon found out that you simply couldn't run a school and support a family of two on ten dollars a month, so he appealed to the local school committee for help. A school law had been passed and a poll tax had been levied on all men between the ages of twenty-one and fifty to help build the school fund. There was no reason why colored children of Orange County should not receive some of its benefits. The town school committee could give him no satisfactory information, but since he knew there was a school fund he decided to qualify as a public-school teacher and receive a salary from the state. His first experience with southern school authorities was one which has since become an old story, but in 1870 it was shocking enough for him to describe in some detail:

jan. 25th—Tuesday. I rode up to Samuel Hughes', the Examiner of teachers for this the County of Orange, but he said that he could not examine any teacher or teachers till after he had advertised for 10 days to give notice according to the School Law. He said that no teacher had been examined or employed by the State as the fund had been squandered by "Littlefield," the railroad bills and those in high authority, and that all sent for the use of the schools of this county was 50c to the scholar, the said 50c to support the scholar for 4 months; that there was $2951.00 sent to defray the expenses of teachers, and there were about 5902 [white?] children, about 2235 colored children—allowing but fifty cents per scholar. He was of the opinion that colored children would have to be taught on Sundays and the funds concentrated, that I could do better in the field. I told him that I had taught free school since September 1, 1869, that I did not do it for the hope of gain but from a principle, & that I thought it was a duty; the whites of the South would have to lay aside the prejudice of color and unite in educating the black race for their own future welfare—and make them good citizens, to prevent their prisons and poorhouses from being full, and I asked him as a favour to examine me to enable me thus to come at the small pittance allowed by the state. He asked me why I did not apply to some benevolent association in the North for aid. I told him I did not wish to impose on charity. I would have done so but for the school appropriation made by the Legislature of the state; that I was willing to take my share of that fund though small, rather than apply to a charitable fund, and that he would confer a favour on me if he would assist me in getting my share of the teachers' fund small as it was. I am to meet him on the 2nd Saturday of February to be Publicly examined as this is the only way I can secure my share of the greenbacks.

It is my opinion that Mr. H—— is somewhat biased by prejudice— and he will not put himself to any inconvenience to further the cause of education among the colored people.

Grandfather's restrained estimate of Mr. Hughes was borne out by events. He tried on several occasions to see that worthy gentle- man on his Saturday trips to Hillsboro, but Hughes could never be found. In fact, Grandfather did not catch up with him until one Saturday in August, eight months later. He rose early in the morning and headed him off in the road above Hillsboro. Hughes reluctantly came back to town, examined him orally and pre- sumably found him qualified to teach for the state.

During the intervening months, however, Robert Fitzgerald found that what was to have been a mission of usefulness was rapidly turning into a bitter struggle for personal survival. The presence of seventy-five United States troopers in Chapel Hill quieted down the Ku-Klux Klan somewhat, but the problem of earning a living increased. Woodside School now had sixty-two scholars but he could not afford to teach for nothing. He fell back on his Yankee trading instinct and his business knowledge. Some months after he came to live on the farm he had dissolved his partnership with Heywood Beverly and taken his share of the hides. He now used his hides sparingly, swapping them whenever he could make a good trade—"two kid skins for a fine pair of boots, $6.00," he recorded. He killed pigs, cured hams and traded the hams at Brown's store in Hillsboro for stockings, cloth and groceries. He mended shoes and even tried making a pair. His price was $3.50 and he took payment in flour at five cents a pound. He tore down the little office he had built at the tanyard, hauled the logs, lumber, door and window sashes down to Woodside and traded them to the local wheelwright for part payment on a buggy.

The first glimmer of hope came when "Buck Strayhorn, Capt. of the 'Irregular Train' ordered 4,000 brick to deliver to parties along the line. He thinks of taking a contract and having us make the brick," Grandfather wrote. Then he went down to Raleigh to see if he could not get more contracts. "The morning was dark and rainy & there being no station or platform we had to make a fire along the road in the darkness & rain, & when the train came in sight to stand on the track and wave a light to & fro across the track." The first trip yielded no returns but on the second he got a contract "to make the 4,000,000 brick for the penitentiary."

Grandfather was almost delirious with joy. He went into action at once, and wrote to his brother Richard, who had gone back to Pennsylvania, urging him to come down and take charge of the job. He recommended that Richard bring along Billy. Richard needed no further encouragement since he wanted to come south again and marry Miss Sallie Williams. Billy Fitzgerald said he'd give the South one more try so he brought along his wife, Lottie, and his little daughter, Annie.

The brickmaking job got under way that spring. Grandfather hired a young man to teach his school, and the Fitzgerald brothers got together a crew of men, took them down to Raleigh, put up shanties and went to work digging and leveling the kiln floors while waiting for the brickmaking machine to be repaired. From the start they were delayed by a lack of carpenters and bad weather. It rained continuously, keeping the yards damp and saturating the bricks. Nature seemed arrayed against them. They had just fired one kiln and were setting the brick in another when a flash flood descended upon them. They worked frantically in the drenching rain to get a roof on their kilns but it was no use. "We didn't have the boards to cover our work on the kiln and so sudden was it that the wind and rain prevented our gathering what split boards there were lying around." Each diary entry grew more disheartened. "The flood has covered the yard and destroyed thousands of brick," Grandfather wrote disconsolately. "The flood has extended out several hundred yards & everything is overflowed. . . . The kiln near the bridge is on fire and the flood has reached within six inches of the fires. It has washed down the sheds and destroyed all the bricks in the sheds and on the drying floors."

When the skies cleared months of work had been washed away, but Billy Fitzgerald had already thrown up his hands in disgust. He left in June. Grandfather said sadly, "He is so discouraged by wet weather and loss of time that he is going back to Pennsylvania. I went up the road with him as far as I could. He shed tears at the discouraging prospects. We parted in a shower of rain."

This was the parting of the ways for the three Fitzgerald brothers. Billy had neither the idealism of Robert nor the business tenacity of Richard. Nor had he the capacity for enduring the lot of the Negro, which, after a brief triumph, grew more uncertain in those postwar years. Back in Pennsylvania, he eventually divorced his wife and so far as anyone could tell was finally absorbed into the white race.

Lizzie Fitzgerald, the oldest sister, also made the choice to remain in the North. She made a brief visit to North Carolina, but Grandfather wrote of their farewell, "Bade Lizzie goodbye this morning, perhaps for the last time in years. I don't know. She wants to come out here but her husband is afraid to embark what capital he has in such a barren uncertain country as this."

So it remained for Robert and Richard Fitzgerald to carve a life for themselves on a new frontier. Richard had few of the idealistic notions of his brother, but he had a genius for making a dollar and a pugnacious stubbornness which overrode hardships. He was a gambler for high stakes. He left the Raleigh job just long enough to go down to Woodside and marry Sallie Williams. "I let him have $5.00, went to the Depot and saw him off," his brother wrote. "I hope that God will bless him and make the change in his life a blessing to him as well as a beneficial one to both—the lady I think is a very estimable young girl of 18 summers."

Richard was back on the job in four days and together the brothers salvaged what they could of their contract. When they settled up, they had burned 525,000 usable brick at eight-five cents a thousand, and by the time they paid off their crew of workmen, their profit for four months' work was $83.10. But while they came out of this first contract with little money, they had established the reputation in Wake and Orange counties that the Fitzgerald brothers were reliable brickmakers and good business-men.

That August of 1870, when Grandfather finally got his chance to vote, he found the polls tense with a showdown between the Republicans and the ex-Rebel Conservatives. Troops guarded the election and he observed that Kirk's Militia, organized by Governor Holden to deal with the K.K.K., had rounded up some five hundred men who frankly admitted their membership in its ranks. While waiting to vote he witnessed one of the disturbances which characterized the vote throughout the state that year. "Watson and 2 of his friends attacked Col. Guthrie, knocked him down and jumped him—didn't hurt him much." He added that he "voted the Republican ticket straight through," but when the votes were counted the Conservatives had won control of both houses of the state legislature. The brave dreams of five years died a-borning.

Shortly after the election, Grandfather qualified as a teacher and received his first appointment from the county school committee to teach in a state-supported school at a salary of twenty-five dollars a month. Several weeks later, very early one Sunday morning, September 25, 1870, he pulled out his diary and engraved a box on the page. His eyes were dimming and he could scarcely see what he wrote. He was more weary than he could ever remember having been in his entire life and his hands trembled as he tried to guide his pen:

. . . Went up to Hillsboro after some things. Medecine, &c. When I returned there was a little stranger on hand named

Mary Pauline Fitzgerald

. . . May Sunshine cheer this little traveler on her way through the checkered scenes of life—and may she be a light to others are the wishes of her father.

Grandfather's entry about his firstborn was both a prayer and a prophecy. Whatever other hopes were crushed in those troublous decades to follow, this wish at least would be fulfilled.

17

FROM the moment of birth Aunt Pauline was a bone of contention between Grandmother Cornelia and the Fitzgeralds. As the first grandchild born in the South, she embodied the hopes of a stubborn clan which had chosen to swim against a terrific backwash of history and yet refused to go under. She was blessed with a remarkable physical constitution and a practical wisdom which became more evident as she grew older. Her Fitzgerald elders idolized her, and often Grandmother Cornelia had to raise a row to get control over her own child.

There had come to be much backbiting between Grandmother and her younger Fitzgerald in-laws. They were free born and had a mite of northern education while Grandmother had to admit she was born in slavery and could not prove her parentage. Such things made a great difference in those days and only made Grandmother work the harder at impressing her children with the fact of their Smith forebears. In line with her own training, she was determined to bring them up as Episcopalians although Grandfather was Presbyterian. She won the first round when she had her first child christened Mary Pauline Fitzgerald at the white Episcopal Church in Hillsboro by Dr. Curtis, its rector.

Aunt Pauline's happiest memories of her early childhood were the times she spent with Great-Grandfather Thomas at Woodside Farm. Not long after the family settled in North Carolina, Great-

Grandmother Sarah Ann, with an unfailing eye for business, opened a restaurant in Hillsboro across the street from the courthouse and catered to lawyers, judges and businessmen who came to town. Mary and Agnes helped her and Great-Grandfather Thomas ran the farm alone, except for the aid of Grandfather Robert and Billy Clark, who had come south with the family. Aunt Pauline was Great-Grandfather Thomas' constant companion; she followed him about the farm asking countless questions and he patiently answered each one. He took her with him when he made his trips to Durham in the big two-horse wagon with a load of vegetables, fruits and dairy products. She said he'd tie the horses to a rail across from the railroad station, and when she'd hear the train or see it coming down the track she was terrified for fear it would run right over them or that the horses would bolt and run away. In the evenings her grandfather would rock her to sleep in his arms while he read his Bible.

There were also memories of conflict, of watchfulness, of the time when her father's saber and pistol held equal importance with his Bible on the shelf above the fireplace. There was talk of Rebs and Ku-Kluxers, of floggings and killings, of barns being burned and men being hanged. She would never forget the story her father told of Wayne Garrett, meanest Reb about the county, who rode a speckled gray horse and went about cursing and threatening colored people as if they were still slaves. One cold stormy night Grandfather and Grandmother were sitting by their fire with their two babies when Garrett came to their house. The rain poured down in torrents, the wind howled and lashed the trees and every minute they expected their little cottage to be blown over. They could hear somebody shouting above the storm and when Grandfather went to the door with his lantern, there was Garrett on his speckled gray horse, drenched to the skin and chattering with cold.

"Open up, you white darkies, and lemme in," he yelled.

Grandfather closed the door and got his saber from the shelf. When he opened it again he was swinging the saber.

"I wouldn't keep anybody outdoors on a night like this," he said, "but no man will come into my house who cannot conduct himself like a gentleman in front of my wife and children. If you can behave like a gentleman, put your horse in the shed and come inside. But I warn you, one insulting word and I'll run you through with this saber."

Garrett knew that he meant it, but he preferred the restraint of silence to the storm so he put away his horse and came meekly inside. Grandfather, still holding the saber, handed him some dry clothing and a quilt and pointed to a chair in front of the fireplace. All night long the two men sat facing each other across the room without a word between them—Garrett crouched in his chair and Grandfather sitting with his saber across his knee watching Garrett's every move and stirring only to put another log on the fire. When dawn came the storm had died down and Garrett's clothes were dry. He put them on and slunk out of the house, got on his horse and rode away, but he was very careful how he addressed Grandfather after that.

Aunt Pauline never knew Great-Grandmother Harriet. When she was a toddler that poor woman died, a figure of violence and tragedy in death as she had been in life. During a summer storm she was stunned by lightning which struck her cabin and killed a boy named Dennis who was sitting in front of the fireplace. Great-Grandmother Harriet never recovered from the shock; she was paralyzed and died not long after that. The circumstances of her death made such a deep impression on our family that all activity at home stopped whenever a thunderstorm came up. The windows and doors were closed; nobody dared sit in front of a fireplace or open draft; no one touched anything metal. The whole family gathered in the lower part of the house and sat praying silently until the storm had passed.

When Aunt Pauline was two, Grandfather used to carry her back and forth on his shoulder to school with him. At four she could read and write and recite pieces.

"I was practically born and bred in a schoolhouse with a piece of chalk in my hand," she told me.

At seven she came under Miss Maria Spear's tutelage. My grandparents let her stay with Miss Mary Ruffin Smith for a while and Miss Maria Spear, who had returned to live at the Smith home, volunteered to tutor her.

"Miss Maria was a dear little old lady who wore black dresses, white collars and cuffs and a little white muslin cap on her head.

She was very careful with my training and had set times for my lessons each day. She also taught me to sew. Every night before I went to bed, she'd have me sit at her knee and read my Bible.

"I was the only child on the place but I never got lonely. When my work was done, I could roam and play. I loved to wander about the yard where there were hundreds of chickens, ducks, turkeys and even peacocks. I'd crawl up under the henhouses and cribs to look for nests and gather eggs. I'd watch the little pigs feeding, play with the kittens and try to catch the flying squirrels which built their nests behind the window blinds up in the great old attic. I'd gather bunches of flowers from the rare flower garden to put about the house. I liked most of all the trips to the Chapel of the Cross on Sundays with Miss Mary and Miss Maria in the family carriage."

The child quickly learned, however, that there was one etiquette at the Smith household and another at the Fitzgeralds'. If she was the apple of the Fitzgerald eye, she was an eyesore at times to Mary Ruffin Smith. It was the same story repeated in a different generation. Everyone who came to the house took for granted that little Mary Pauline was a Smith, and there was nothing about her appearance to make them think otherwise.

"Child, you certainly look just like your Granddaddy Sid," the townfolks said.

This was gall and wormwood for Miss Mary. It set her off, and she'd scream out at the child, "Get out of my sight, you little nigger!"

"I'm not a nigger, Miss Mary. I'm a Fitzgerald!"

"You're nothing but a nigger and don't answer me back. I'll beat the tar out of you," the irate woman stormed, but the first time she raised her hand to strike the little girl, the old governess intervened.

"Don't, Mary," Miss Maria said. "Never strike anybody's child. It's not right."

The child would slip away into the garden, frightened and tearful and unable to understand why a fighting word at home like "nigger" was used so freely by Miss Mary. Nor could she understand why she must call one aunt "Aunt Mary" and another "Miss Mary." She could not fathom why the servants called the queer old man she saw hobbling about on a cane mumbling to himself "Marse Frank." They warned her to stay away from him because he'd had a stroke and lost his mind. They said that when he had the stroke, they laid him out for dead and while they were putting on his burial clothes he sat right up and opened his eyes.

She went home talking about "Marse Frank" one time and Grandfather Robert overheard her.

"What did you say?" he roared with unaccustomed violence.

"Marse Frank. The servants say he's crazy."

"Don't you ever let me hear you call anyone 'Marse' as long as you live. You can call him 'Mr. Smith' or 'Mr. Frank,' but if I ever catch you saying Marse again, I'll whale the daylights out of you."

Death ended the confusion of those years. Aunt Pauline saw Miss Maria Spear slowly climbing the attic stairs with a mysterious bundle in her hand one afternoon. She followed her and came upon Miss Maria bending over an old trunk.

"What are you doing, Miss Maria?"

"I'm putting away my burial things, child," was the reply.

Not too long after that when she was sent to say her customary "Good morning" to Miss Maria, the old governess did not answer. She had died in her sleep during the night. After Miss Maria died, Grandfather came for his daughter and never let her go back. While he and Miss Mary Ruffin Smith remained on good terms— she wrote to him often and sent him oil paintings from time to time —he kept his children at a safe distance. Those years at the Smith plantation made an ineradicable mark upon Aunt Pauline's life. Miss Mary had taught her the power of cruel words, and she was exceedingly careful during her many years of teaching never to hurt a small child's feelings. Miss Maria had taught her kindness and thoroughness. She never flinched from duty or even death when it came. She had remembered Miss Maria's example even to laying away her own burial garments.

As the oldest of six children, Aunt Pauline carried heavy responsibility from an early age. Grandfather was fighting on several fronts at once; getting food to eat was uncertain and education was haphazard and piecemeal. It was a time when the idea of a public-school system supported by taxes was not popular in North

Carolina. Half the population was illiterate and at least a third was strongly opposed to paying taxes for education. The system of free schools guaranteed by the Constitution of 1868 was just getting started. Local officials in charge of selecting teachers, fixing salaries, choosing textbooks and maintaining school buildings were often indifferent or downright dishonest. The minimum term was four months a year, but it was widely ignored as a mandate and there was no way of enforcing it. Often a school term lasted only ten weeks.

In the year of Aunt Pauline's birth, only one out of every ten children of school age was enrolled. The Conservatives had wrested control of the state legislature from the Republicans that year, and systematically began to whittle down provisions for uniform education. The distribution of school funds was removed from control by the state board of education and placed in the hands of the legislature. The law which provided for allocation of funds among the counties in proportion to their school population was repealed.

Without a proportional system, it was easy to starve the colored schools. Indifference and hostility marked the attitude of officials. The state superintendent of public instruction had no interest in Negro education and stated that he doubted "any system of instruction will ever lift the African to high spheres of educated mind."

Under the state system of schools, Grandfather found little of the crusading spirit against ignorance which had pervaded the denominational schools and Freedmen's Bureau work. There were few schoolhouses and fewer teachers. The schools were generally log cabins or abandoned houses without desks or tables and only split logs for benches. Supplies and textbooks were a rarity. A school would spring up, last a few months and die out because there were no funds to pay a teacher or to build, repair or furnish a schoolhouse.

Grandfather was an itinerant teacher in those days. Before a school term opened, he'd walk miles about the country, find an empty township house most centrally located and take possession of it for his school. If enrollment was poor he'd have to move on to another locality. The outlook was often discouraging. He'd begin classes in August and just get his work organized when the children had to leave to pull fodder and gather in the crops. The local school committee gave him little co-operation unless he prodded them. He was nominated on the Republican School Committee for Chapel Hill Township in 1871, but was defeated in the election so he had to carry on his fight outside the policy-making sphere. He had no organized public opinion to help him and it was a lonely battle. Common sense was his lawyer and stubbornness his only weapon.

For a while he had carried on his own free school at Woodside Farm. When he first started teaching in the state-supported schools of Orange County in 1870, he was the only teacher assigned to three school districts covering many miles and serving 139 colored children of school age. Only two scholars appeared on the first day of the term. After two weeks the enrollment had risen to ten. Grandfather went out to visit families and find out what was keeping the children away. He wrote:

I teach for 3 districts and in order to be near the other two I have to cross the creek and teach in a house on the south side of New Hope [Creek] while nearly all the children are on the north side and too far from the New Hope building, and the creek is an obstacle there being no log across it. . . . Went to ask . . . chairman of the school committee to allow me to change the school across the creek.

When the committee failed to act, Grandfather took the matter into his own hands. He visited a number of families and discovered they wanted the school transferred across the creek to Woodside. On the first day after the change his enrollment tripled. When the committee learned of his action, they summoned him to Chapel Hill. He was prepared to meet their objections with facts, figures and visual aids.

Sept. 17. Made out my report for the month. . . . Had to go to Chapel Hill to meet the committee in council. They commenced to censure me for moving the school without their advice. [I told them] that I had taught three weeks and one day with an average of 2½ scholars a day and gained 22 scholars the first day of the change. . . . I showed them a map of the locality of New Hope School—that there are no roads leading to N.H., that further, more than thirty of the children had to come . . . for more than five miles through a woody country and cross New Hope Creek on jutting rocks and could cross only when the water was low; . . . further that the house they had assigned to me had neither desk, table, nor bench.

I told the Committee I thought the object was to have the school where it could accomplish the most good—if so, Woodside was the place for it—also we had desks, slates and a blackboard at Woodside— so they decided to let me remain at Woodside.

Grandfather's monthly salary ranged from twenty to twenty-five dollars when he was teaching, but since he was paid only for the time school was actually in session, he had to earn his living the rest of the year through farming, brickmaking, contracting on the roads or whatever he could do to turn a dollar. During school sessions, he'd rise at four o'clock each morning, milk, pick apples, plow a field or haul hay; then he'd bolt his breakfast, walk five miles to school, teach from nine to three, walk home and plunge into his farm work again to get as much done as he could before nightfall. When the local school closed for lack of funds, he'd have to leave his crops in the middle of a season and take another assignment—in Mocksville, Raleigh, Laurinburg or Salisbury—and Grandmother and the children would have to carry on the farm work.

"At six, I climbed up on a stool and washed clothes and cooked meals," Aunt Pauline told me. "By the time I was eight I was doing a woman's work. Father was often away from home teaching and there were four other children to look after—Maria, Tommie, Sallie and your own mother, Agnes, who was just a baby. Little Roberta didn't come along until 1885."

As soon as the children were big enough, they went to work with Grandfather in the fields or, later on, on his brickyard. He never let the fact that he had five daughters and only one son dismay him. What his daughters lacked in brawn they made up for in zeal and agility. They could plow, load hay, work a farm and lay brick as well as their brother Tommie. While Grandfather was conservative in many things, he had very advanced ideas about the training of women. He felt that there were four things every woman should know how to do: ride, shoot, drive a horse and handle a boat.

He knew how to get the most work out of his children; if he had a field to hoe, he'd line them up like soldiers on several furrows, taking the middle row himself. Then he'd hoe along with them while he told them stories, and keep them so interested they'd have the work done in no time. Or he'd recite poetry to them as they worked or teach them recitations and Bible quotations.

In matters of discipline, Grandfather was the sternest of fathers and had no favorites. Aunt Pauline chuckled as she recalled the worst whipping of her life when she was around eight or nine. Grandfather sent her to a private school on Fayetteville Street in Durham taught by a refined young woman from Brooklyn, New York, who had been trained and sent south by the Episcopal Church. The teacher was invited to spend a holiday at my grandparents' home and while she was there the two oldest girls, Pauline and Maria, had charge of making her bed and cleaning her room.

To their amazement and uncontrollable glee, they discovered the northern schoolmarm's secret habit when they found her tiny snuffbox on a table beside her bed. The mischievous youngsters cut themselves some twigs for snuff mops and proceeded to dip snuff as they had seen the old folks do.

"We got drunk from it and were so sick we crawled out to the stable and lay down in the horse trough," Aunt Pauline said. "We knew Father would skin us alive when he found out, so we put on three or four coats apiece. Pretty soon we heard Father calling and the next thing we knew he was standing there with his horsewhip. He got to me first, but my coats weren't as heavy as Maria's. I can still feel those awful licks. Maria did a lot of yelling, but she got off easy. Her four coats saved her."

Great-Grandfather Thomas died the summer Aunt Pauline was nearly nine. He was conscious to the end and told his family he was going to a happier place. He even said he could see the angels around his bed waiting for him. He found death a friendly thing, but it was a great blow to the family. Aunt Pauline remembered how Great-Grandmother Sarah Ann, who was never demonstrative with anyone, screamed her grief.

"What'll I do without my Thomas?" she moaned. "Why, I don't even know how to pray." And to the devout little Pauline, this seemed the most awful thing that could happen to anyone. It was a tribute to this quiet man who left a brief mark upon the world in which he lived that, although he had been away from Pennsylvania more than ten years when he died and the Chester County newspapers of those days took little notice of doings among colored folk, the county weekly of August 7, 1879, carried the following item in its columns: "Died at University Station, Woodside Farm, North Carolina, June 18, Thomas Fitzgerald; formerly lived near Lincoln; age 71 years, ten months."

Before Great-Grandfather's death, each of his sons had bought small parcels of land adjoining his farm and built their homes. Uncle Richard had a fine brickyard going and Grandfather had a smaller brickyard. With their father's passing, Woodside Farm was too large for Great-Grandmother Sarah Ann to carry on alone, so the brothers pulled up stakes again and moved to Durham. Uncle Richard set up his brickyard near Maplewood Cemetery and Grandfather started one down on Rigsbee Road in the north-east part of town.

By now Grandfather had become so blind he could no longer see the print on a page and had to give up teaching. He could barely read large black headlines and he had learned to write by placing a finger on a sheet and pushing his pen along behind it without the aid of vision. In farming, he chopped down cotton with the weeds, and if he were digging a ditch or cutting wood, he often had to make three blows for one to count. Two went wide of the mark. He had to depend almost entirely upon brickmaking by hiring other men to do the work for him and using his children as guides.

During these difficult years when there was scarcely enough money to keep a roof over their heads, Grandmother undertook to educate her children. She bundled up Aunt Pauline in the spring of 1880 and sent her down to Raleigh to St. Augustine's School, which had been organized in 1867 under the Protestant Episcopal Church. Grandmother had attended there herself for a short time and she had great faith in Episcopal education. It was a daring thing to do; the first morning Aunt Pauline was led into the classroom by Miss Mary Pettiford, everyone gasped in astonishment.

"Where on earth did that child come from?" everybody wanted to know, as the other students were men and women in their late twenties and thirties.

"They brought me every subject they studied," Aunt Pauline recalled. "I read for them, worked problems of arithmetic, answered questions in history, gave the parts of speech, spelled and recited poetry. They said I knew the work all right but I was too young to stay. They sent me home again and told me I could come back when I was ten. My tenth birthday came that September, so Mother put me on the train again and I entered St. Aug's."

For the several years she attended there she was the only child in the school. Grandmother sent down butter, eggs or chickens to help pay her tuition whenever she could, but she had to work her way along most of the time. While she was there, Grandfather made his first application for a pension. His closing statement in his letter to the U.S. Pension Office read:

I have never applied for a pension before for two reasons:
1st. I never intended to ask the government to help me as long as I could help it.
2nd. I valued my Discharge from the U.S. Army as more than money, and would not risk it from me for fear it would be lost as thousands of others were.

After a long exchange of correspondence lasting over many months, the Pension Office rejected Grandfather's application in the spring of 1885. What hurt about the rejection was that it stated "the alleged impaired vision did not originate in the service of the United States but, on the contrary, existed prior to enlistment." The United States Army did not officially recognize the bullet wound Grandfather had received while working in the Quartermaster's Department. The rejection came just a few weeks after the sixth child was born.

Aunt Pauline had to come out of school that year. In September, she put up her hair, put on a long grown-up dress and went to take the county teachers' examination.

"There I was with many men and women twice my age," she recalled. "I was so afraid they'd find out I was only fourteen and send me home again, but they didn't ask me any questions. When the certificates were issued I received a First Grade Certificate, nine days before my fifteenth birthday."

Thus began a teaching career which did not end until Aunt Pauline was seventy-six. Her passion for teaching helped her bear the loss of her husband and two infant children. Always a woman of respectability and moderation with an inner fire, she was "a light to others," spanning the great struggle for education from 1870 to 1955. She was an indomitable force in and out of the schoolroom, motivated by the belief that she had to give an account to God for every child who came under her care. She never felt her job was done. Perhaps my most moving memory of her was the day in her eighty-fourth year when she read the Supreme Court decision on integration of the public schools and said,

"Thank God that I have lived to see this come to pass in my time!"

18

THERE was pride on both sides of the Fitzgerald family, but my greatest inheritance, perhaps, was a dogged persistence, a granite quality of endurance in the face of calamity. There was pride in family background, of course, but my folks took greater pride in doing any kind of honest work to earn a living and remain independent. Some people thought this trait was peculiarly Grandfather's, that Grandmother was flighty and contentious. They did not know the inside story: how she had struggled to keep her home together and bring up six children with her husband going blind and losing ground most of the way. Her tenacity, like that of Grandfather, sprang partly from her deep religious faith and partly from a mulishness which refused to countenance despair.

"There's more ways to kill a dog beside choking him on butter," she used to say.

She was remembering those uncertain years when the children were growing up and Grandfather was fighting for his pension while trying to build a home. He had bought an acre of ground in Durham, planned his house on the edge of his line and used the rest of the land to dig clay for his brickyard. He made bricks by hand, the hard kind used for outer walls and guaranteed to withstand all kinds of weather. It was a slow and costly process full of setbacks and failures. His hired men were often careless and took advantage of his blindness. They'd fire the kilns with raw green wood or go to sleep on the job in the middle of a burning and let the fires go out. Grandfather's bricks would come out crumbling and useless and he'd have to start all over again.

Then there were his lonely pilgrimages from place to place, guided only by his cane and a kind passerby, in search of old army comrades to help reconstruct his war record twenty years after his discharge. His search frequently ended in disappointment and he'd come home discouraged to make bricks for a while before starting out again. It took him almost ten years to prove his eligibility for pension payments.

During those years Grandmother was trying to educate their children. Fortunately, she came into a small inheritance when Mary Ruffin Smith died around 1885. Miss Mary had not forgotten the four Smith daughters. She left each of them one hundred acres of land with provision that a house be built upon it not to cost more than $150. To ensure that the land remained free from their husbands' debts or control, she gave them only a life interest in it and provided that it should pass to their children when they died. She also left her household goods and furnishings to be divided equally among the four.

Grandmother's hundred acres came out of the old Smith plantation near Chapel Hill. She was never entirely satisfied with this bequest; she felt Miss Mary had robbed her of the full inheritance her father had intended for her, and the restrictions of "heir property" which she did not own outright rankled. It served, however, as vindication of her own claims and was Miss Mary's backhanded recognition of their relationship. Aside from a twenty-five-acre gift to their half-brother, Julius, who was not of Smith blood, and a few small cash bequests, the four Smith daughters and their children were the only individuals remembered in Mary Ruffin Smith's will.

Whatever Grandmother's dissatisfactions, which increased as years passed, she made the most of her farm. She lived there with the children and worked the land while Grandfather was building his house in Durham. From time to time she sold off timber to help him in his brick business. She used whatever cash she could raise from her crops and fruit to send the children off to school.

When she had no crops or fruit, she'd sell the chickens, the hogs or whatever else she could lay her hands on.

Aunt Sallie would never forget the time Grandmother sent Aunt Maria to Hampton Institute to take up the tailoring trade. When time came for tuition, Grandmother had no money so she decided to sell her cow. Grandfather was away from home working on his pension, Aunt Pauline was off teaching and Uncle Tommie was away at school. Grandmother had no one to send to market except Sallie and Agnes, who were about twelve and eleven years old at the time, but she was not dismayed.

"Children," she told them, "I want you to drive this cow down to Durham and take her to Schwartz' market. Tell Mr. Schwartz that Cornelia Smith sent her and that she's a fine milk cow. I want a good price on her and I'm depending on you to get it."

It was a huge undertaking for two little girls—Durham was fifteen miles away and the cow was none too manageable—but it would never have occurred to them that they could not deliver the cow. They started out early in the morning on a trip which took all day. The cow strayed off the road from time to time to graze in the meadows or lie down to rest and they had to pull and tug at her to get her started again. They arrived at the market in Durham near nightfall, somewhat frightened, their clothes torn and spattered with mud. When Mr. Schwartz heard all the commotion outside and came to find two bedraggled little girls standing guard over a huge cow, he listened to their story in disbelief.

"You don't mean to tell me you drove that cow all the way from Chapel Hill?" he asked.

"Yes sir, we did."

"Well, I never. And you say you're Robert Fitzgerald's daughters?"

"Yes sir, we are."

"How do I know you didn't steal that cow?"

The little girls stood their ground.

"If you doubt our word, you send for our Uncle Richard Fitzgerald."

Mr. Schwartz finally sent for Uncle Richard, who came, took one look at them and laughed.

"They're my brother's children all right, and if they say their mother sent the cow to market, you can take their word for it," he told Mr. Schwartz. So the butcher bought the cow on the spot and Aunt Maria stayed in school another few months.

It was also part of Grandfather's creed not to coddle his daughters. He expected them to make their way in life as he had done. I found a letter he had written to Aunt Maria on September 25, 1895. She had finished her work at Hampton and gone to Philadelphia to find employment as a dressmaker, without success. She wrote to Grandfather for money to come home. He replied:

You must not depend upon sewing. I'd go into service. You can get $12 to $15 per month and stick to work for two months without taking up your money, and you can come home independent. . . . I find many a fine mechanic tramping through the state because he cannot work at his trade. Too many people make this great mistake. You must do as I did when I first went to Philadelphia, then a boy 16. I couldn't get the kind of employment I sought so I took whatever I could get to do and stuck at it until I had accumulated enough to carry me where I wanted to go with money in my pocket. Now you are young and as able as you ever will be. You can live anywhere on the face of the earth as other people can. Take my advice, getting your board and lodging and $15 per month and you will soon be able to come home.

Thrift was another household god in Grandfather's home. It was not only a strong ingredient of his own children's training but it was expected of all prospective sons-in-law. When young Leon B. Jeffers wrote my grandparents for consent to marry Aunt Maria in 1901, they replied in the affirmative, saying, "From earliest acquaintance with you, you have been held in highest esteem by us. Although you may not have money and riches to bestow upon her now, if you have that pure and undefiled love to present to her, with thrift and good management you can soon accumulate some property."

Only three of my grandparents' children were still living when I was coming along—Aunt Pauline, Aunt Maria (who preferred to be called Marie) and Aunt Sallie—all schoolteachers and all having a hand in my upbringing. Their brother, Uncle Tommie, had left home before he was twenty and was never heard from again. Some thought he was lost at sea and others that he died of smallpox during the Spanish-American War. The youngest sister, Roberta, succumbed to typhoid fever when she was barely nineteen. My own mother, Agnes, who had departed from the teaching tradition to become a registered nurse, died suddenly when I was three, leaving six children and my father, who was ill. I saw him only once after that before he died.

Having no parents of my own, I had in effect three mothers, each trying to impress upon me those traits of character expected of a Fitzgerald—stern devotion to duty, capacity for hard work, industry and thrift, and above all honor and courage in all things. Grandfather, of course, was their standard bearer for most of the virtues, but sometimes they talked of my own mother, who was a woman of beauty and courage and whose spirit became a guiding force in my own life although I was too young to remember her.

What happened on my mother's wedding night seemed typical of her courage. Her wedding to William H. Murray, a brilliant young schoolteacher from Baltimore, was scheduled for nine o'clock on the evening of July 1, 1903, at Emanuel A.M.E. Church on Chapel Hill Road in Durham, after which the reception was to be held at Grandfather's house. Engraved invitations were sent out to numerous relatives and friends and the five Fitzgerald daughters were as excited as if all of them were brides. Will Murray was the most popular of their brothers-in-law. He had come down from Baltimore in grand style, flanked by a troupe of young men to attend him.

Preparations were in full swing; everybody was scurrying about all day long. There had never been such a big wedding in the Fitzgerald household. Aunt Marie Jeffers, who was expecting a child, was putting the finishing touches on my mother's wedding gown. As family modiste, she wouldn't think of letting Aggie get married until her skillful fingers had supervised each tuck and fold.

It had been a stiflingly hot day and toward evening a thunderstorm threatened. The bride was almost ready and Aunt Marie stepped back to survey her handiwork when her face went deadly pale, she screamed and fell upon her knees in her first sharp labor pains. The wedding preparations were thrown into bedlam; everything came to a standstill. People gathered at the church and the groom was waiting impatiently, but there was no bride.

At Grandfather's house Aunt Marie's screams could be heard all over the neighborhood. To add to the confusion the thunderstorm struck with terrifying intensity. It was the worst of all times for a child to be born in the Fitzgerald home, but if my mother was frightened she gave no sign. She slipped quietly out of her wedding clothes, put on her uniform and took her place beside the doctor who came to attend Aunt Marie. She was all nurse, coolheaded and composed. Childbirth was hazardous in those days and for a while it looked as if Aunt Marie would not make it. At the height of the storm, between sharp flashes of lightning and rolls of thunder which shook the house, the baby came. My mother's trained eye saw that the doctor's forceps were askew in the emergency and she quickly readjusted them, saving the baby's life. Even so, his head and neck were severely bruised and cut in the delivery and nobody expected him to live. He was thrown aside while doctor and nurse worked frantically to save the mother's life.

Somebody suggested that Agnes call off her wedding, but she shook her head and stuck to her post. When it finally appeared that Aunt Marie would survive the crisis, my mother turned to the neglected infant, bathed and bandaged him, treated his wounds, hovered over him, smacked him and almost breathed life into him. She did not turn him loose until he let out a lusty cry and she felt that he would live. She then calmly washed her hands, put on her wedding dress once more and went out into a downpour to meet her groom. Everything went off as planned, except that it was several hours later and very much subdued. The reception was switched to Uncle Richard's house and the bride received her guests as graciously as if nothing untoward had happened. The baby, Gerald, celebrated his fifty-second birthday not long ago* and Aunt Marie reached eighty-one before she died.

It was through these homespun stories, each with its own moral, that my elders sought to build their family traditions. In later years I realized how very much their wealth had consisted of intangibles. They had little of the world's goods and less of its recognition but they had forged enduring values for themselves which they tried to pass on to me. I would have need of these resources when I left the rugged security of Grandfather's house and found myself in a

*He lived to be about 70.

maze of terrifying forces which I could neither understand nor cope with. While my folks could not shield me from the impact of these forces, through their own courage and strength they could teach me to withstand them. My first experience with this outer world came the summer I was nearly seven.

19

I WAS at Pratt's well getting water for Grandmother the day they found John Henry Corniggins near Vickers Woods. It's strange how one thing leads to another and how suddenly everything gets mixed up together. I hardly knew John Henry. We inhabited different worlds. He was much bigger than I was and until that day as remote as all the other neighborhood children. If Grandmother hadn't gotten sick I might not have known about him at all. I saw him only once, but his name and face have stuck in my memory longer than all the rest, more real and haunting than those of any other child I ever knew.

John Henry Corniggins was one of the many boys who used to roam through the Bottoms after school, whooping and hollering up and down the branch and making countless trips to the trash pile over in Hesse's field. He lived a short way from my house across Morehead Avenue in a hollow where the Bottoms continued southward through the edge of town. He had a little brother named Leander who followed him everywhere. The boys had no father and their mother worked all day in the factory.

The trash pile in Hesse's field was a great eyesore to my folks—it had the most awful smell of rotted garbage and drew swarms of big green flies—but it was our neighborhood's greatest attraction for children. It substituted for everything—parks, playgrounds, clubs or Scout troops—and it was a mine of innumerable treasures. I'd sit on the front porch after school and watch the children rooting about in the big mound of tin cans, broken bottles and discarded housewares. I'd hear their squeals of triumph whenever they'd fished something valuable from the debris. Pretty soon I'd see them coming back along the road in front of our house loaded with old wheels, wooden boxes, pieces of rope and other stuff. Later I'd catch glimpses of them clattering down Morehead Avenue and careening past our street corner in the lopsided wagons they'd built with various sizes of wheels—fruits of their forays. They'd shout hilariously when the overburdened vehicles capsized and dumped them in the middle of the road.

Grandmother thought the trash pile was the devil's workshop. When she was on the warpath lambasting the neighbors about their shortcomings, more than once she warned them against letting their children run wild.

"Snotty-nosed young'uns, tearing up and down these Bottoms like a spotted-rump bull that belongs to nobody," she'd yell. "You better keep them little urchins home and let 'em learn something that'll do 'em some good. A colt needs a bit and bridle, and if you don't curb your young'uns now, they'll make you wish they'd never been born when they get a little older."

The neighbors were used to Grandmother's dire prophecies and few of them heeded her admonitions. Boys continued to roam the Bottoms and make expeditions to the trash pile. I envied their freedom. From my lookout on the porch steps, the trash pile seemed a mecca of childhood delights. I traveled the straight and narrow path to West End School and back home again. Aunt Pauline, who taught at the same school, kept me in tow both ways. Stopping to play or make detours past the trash pile was out of the question. "Mis' Dame" had been in the school system so many years she was no longer a mere teacher; she was a community institution inspiring an awe which attached to everything in her orbit. My schoolmates scooted past me, keeping a polite distance and leaving me to trail along in Mis' Dame's wake in lonely grandeur.

I don't know how long this isolation would have kept up if Grandmother hadn't come down with pellagra. We first noticed she was ailing when she suddenly stopped preaching at the neighbors that spring. It was a bad sign. Feuding with trespassers was like a tonic to Grandmother and it wasn't like her not to boil up and overflow upon them once in a while. When days passed and the astounded neighbors actually beat a footpath along the ledge in our field next to the road without getting a single sermon out of Grandmother, Aunt Pauline knew something was wrong.

"Mama, I don't like the way you're acting. You don't eat enough to keep a bird alive. Why don't you let me have Dr. Shepard come over here and take a look at you?" she pleaded.

"I don't have much for doctors to do," Grandmother told her. "They're ready to stick you in bed for everything. If I get down flat on my back while you're in school, who's gonna look out for your father? He's just like a little child. Wants his victuals on time and wants to know where I am every minute of the day. I've been catering to that man for nigh on to fifty years. Don't know what he'd do if I give out."

If Grandfather had heard her, he would almost have died of shame. He couldn't bear to think that anybody had to take care of him or that his blindness was a problem. He tried hard to manage by himself, and sometimes I thought he was needlessly harsh with Grandmother 'cause he hated to admit how much he leaned upon her. For all her peppery tongue, she handled him very cautiously not to let him know the hundreds of little things she did to ease his way."

I had grown so accustomed to Grandmother's hollering spells the house was like a tomb when she wasn't shouting to the hilltop. We might as well have been living right inside the cemetery instead of a few steps away from it. The Bottoms was strangely still except when people lit up the hillside on Saturday nights. Aunt Pauline and Grandfather were solemn folk most of the time and there wasn't even Aunt Sallie's sudden burst of laughter or her hymn singing to liven up our place. She had been married to Reverend Small for almost a year and lived across town in St. Titus Rectory on Pine Street.

Grandmother began having vomiting spells and grew weaker and weaker. She got so thin her body had shriveled to skin and bones. Then the skin cracked open between her fingers and we could see the raw angry flesh eaten away almost to the bone. She tried various salves on them but they got worse and sores spread all over her body. She hung on until school was out, treating herself, and then she gave up and went to bed. She could hardly lift her head from the pillow or speak above a whisper. She looked awful. Grandmother was such a whirlwind of energy it was pitiful to see her so silent and still, lying upstairs in the big wooden bed in her miserably hot, low-ceilinged bedroom over the parlor. It was worse to see tears rolling down her bony cheeks when she clawed at her sores.

I had never seen Grandmother helpless before and my universe tottered. She was my buffer at home. She never scolded me and she petted me a great deal. We understood one another. Aunt Pauline and Grandfather were much alike. They issued orders like generals on a battlefield, were inflexible about them and tolerated no weaknesses or excuses. Aunt Pauline had been serious-minded all her life. In times of stress Grandfather's mantle fell upon her shoulders as the oldest Fitzgerald daughter. She was heavy handed and gloomy, but she was cool and dependable in emergencies. She took charge, rode out storms and seemed completely above any human deficiency, I thought.

Grandmother and I were different. We were nervous and excitable, easily stampeded, as vulnerable to imaginary terrors as we were to real dangers. We were the sensitive exposed ones who couldn't stand pressures, took everything to heart, were torn by conflicts and cried out in protest when we were wronged or hurt, whether anyone heeded or even heard us. Grandmother must have known this about me even then. She tried to make it easy for me. She'd slip me little sweets behind Aunt Pauline's back like a fellow conspirator. And she'd make fun of Aunt Pauline's stern ways.

"I declare, Old War Horse, you act more like Miss Mary Ruffin Smith the older you get," she'd tell her.

Aunt Pauline puffed up angrily at this, but I think it gave her a bit of satisfaction. She knew that for all of Grandmother's funmaking it was meant as a backhanded compliment. When Grandmother took to her bed she took charge and sent for Dr. Shepard right away. He had been her physician for years. She doted on him and thought there was little in the way of sickness that he couldn't handle. He was a dapper little man, brown as gingerbread and neat as a pin, who wore gold-rimmed glasses. It was a great shock to Aunt Pauline when he examined Grandmother and said he couldn't take her case.

"I think your mother's got pellagra, Mrs. Dame," he said. "I'd like to treat her but that's out of my line. The best thing for you to do is send for Doc Caldwell in Chapel Hill. They say he's had a lot of success with these cases. And you'd better get him over here right away."

Down our way, having pellagra was only a little less disgraceful than having "the bad disease," as folks called gonorrhea and syphilis. People thought it came from dirt and filth and that only ignorant poverty-stricken country folks got it. They considered it highly contagious and avoided those who had it as they would lepers or smallpox cases. It was a great comedown for us. For folks to know the Fitzgeralds had pellagra at their house was almost as calamitous as the disease itself.

Aunt Pauline was mortified, but Grandmother took the news in stride. She'd had too many troubles in her seventy-three years to get steamed up over pellagra. She actually took heart at mention of Doc Caldwell.

"They don't come no smarter than Wilson Caldwell's boy," she said. "I've known him since he was knee high to a duck. Folks call him a quack doctor, but he's got good horse sense. I'd trust that big, fussikin Doc quicker'n I would all these hifalutin Durham doctors put together. There's no put on to him. He's just a diamond in the rough."

Grandmother was very loyal to her Chapel Hill folks. I'd heard her speak many times of the Caldwells. She said they came from some of the finest stock in Orange County and that their people had helped to build the University of North Carolina. She seldom made distinctions between white and colored families of the same name from Orange County. They were all kinfolks to her.

When Doc Caldwell came back from medical school, he went quietly about the county treating folks without pay, taking cases which stumped other doctors and using methods others of his profession had never heard of. He'd sit up until all hours poring over medical journals his father had slipped him overnight from the University library, where Wilson Caldwell was the janitor.

Folks laughed at him at first when he concentrated on diets instead of pills in cases of hookworm and pellagra which were so prevalent among the rural folk. But when he began curing cases among the colored people, the white folks sat up and took notice. Before long they were sending for him to come to their places after dark, and although they tried to keep it quiet Doc was said to have as many pellagra patients among the white folks around Orange and Chatham counties as he had among the colored.

He drove over the twelve miles from Chapel Hill to see Grandmother one night in his mud-spattered old buggy behind a big rawboned nag. He didn't look much like a doctor to me. He was a mountainous, coconut-brown, barrel-stomached man who had several chins, big calloused hands, a face that was all wrinkles and creases, and he smelled strongly of horses and raw tobacco. He bulged from his ill-fitting clothes that stretched over his bulky frame tight as a ship's hawser in port at high tide. His coat seemed bursting at the seams and his vest and pants had parted company, exposing a vast expanse of rumpled shirt which billowed about his suspenders. From time to time he took out his big dingy handkerchief and mopped the great drops of sweat which rolled down the creases and dripped onto his damp frayed collar. He seemed to fill the room, and when he dropped into a chair at Grandmother's bedside the floor shuddered from the shock and the oil lamp on the mantelpiece trembled violently. But when Doc spoke, his deep gentle voice was so full of reassurance you knew right off everything was going to be all right.

"It's an advanced stage of pellagra," he announced as soon as he had examined Grandmother, "but I think we can get it under control."

"Any danger of catching it?" Aunt Pauline asked him.

"You don't 'catch' pellagra. That's a notion folks have," Doc said.

He explained that pellagra came from eating the same kind of food and having a deficiency in the diet. He said when people ate cornmeal and grits, fatback and molasses over many years and didn't get enough other foods in their system, their bodies lacked nourishment and pellagra attacked. He told Aunt Pauline the best way to treat it was to change Grandmother's diet to plenty of red lean meat, fresh vegetables and milk. He prescribed frequent Epsom salts baths and some powders for the itching and burning but no other medicines.

"I'm depending mainly on your diet and on limestone water to cure you, Mrs. Fitzgerald," he told Grandmother. "Know anybody around here who has a deep limestone well that's kept clean?"

The only one we knew of was Pratts' well at the top of Morehead hill. Doc Caldwell said that was fine because he wanted all of Grandmother's food prepared with limestone water and that she must drink at least two glassfuls of it fresh from the well three times a day. This created a crisis because there was no one to get the water.

"I don't know how we'll manage it," Aunt Pauline said. "I could get it myself but with Mama so helpless right now and Papa not being able to see, I'd hate to be out of the house that often."

"Can't you pay some child to make regular trips? One you could trust not to set the water down and let dirt get into it?"

"When the neighbors find out Mama's got pellagra they won't come near us, let alone send their children."

"You could explain that pellagra's not catching."

"I guess I could, but it's a little more than that. You see, when some of the neighbors walk on Mama's land, she blesses them out and says some mighty harsh things to them sometimes. It's times like this we need friends, but after the way Mama has preached to some of these folks, I'd be downright ashamed to go to any of them for favors."

Grandmother raised up a little.

"Don't be signifying at me. I don't bite my tongue and everybody knows it. I'll do without the limestone water. And if the Lord sees fit to raise me up from this sickbed and folks don't treat me right, I'll tell 'em about it same as ever."

"Now, Mrs. Fitzgerald, don't fret yourself," said Doc. "We'll work it out somehow."

I was anxious for Grandmother to hurry up and get well so I said I could go for the water if Aunt Pauline would let me. She said she couldn't turn me loose to run wild through the Bottoms after all Grandmother's talk about other folks' children and that if anything happened to me she'd never hear the end of it. Grandmother said bless my heart but I was too little to lug water all the way down the hill from Pratts'. Doc Caldwell looked as if he thought it was a good idea.

"How old are you, little one?" he asked me.

"Six and a half going on seven," I replied.

"Oh, then you go to school?"

"Yes, I'm in high second."

"How young are you then?"

"Six and a half."

Doc's rumbling laugh shook the furniture and the lamp danced dangerously near the edge of the mantelpiece.

"You're as quick on the trigger as your grandma. I've caught many a youngster on that one."

"She'll do pretty well," said Aunt Pauline. Like Grandfather, she was very sparing with her praise.

"I wouldn't worry about her if I were you, Mrs. Dame. She can take care of herself. I'd let her get the water."

And so it was settled that I'd make the three trips a day to Pratts' well for the limestone water. I'd take two little lard pails with me so I could bring back a gallon each trip. It was a good thing Aunt Pauline decided to let me do it because there wasn't anyone else to do anything for us. As she said, folks wouldn't come near the house. It was like a quarantine. The postman got away as fast as he could and the newspaper boy stood down in the field and heaved our newspaper over the hedge. Neighbors who stopped past the yard to ask how Grandmother was stood far off from the porch and hurried away again without coming in.

Aunt Pauline was on her feet all day running up and down the stairs, changing Grandmother's bed linens several times a day, emptying bedpans, giving her salts baths, putting on gauze dressings, washing sheets, scrubbing, disinfecting, cooking meals and keeping an eye on Grandfather. He was miserable without Grandmother to fuss at him. He'd sit on the porch all day looking forlorn and hardly saying a word. Aunt Pauline kept me too busy doing chores and running errands for me to read him the morning newspaper. Every evening after supper he'd go upstairs and sit with Grandmother, combing her hair while Aunt Pauline and I worked in the garden. There was nothing Grandmother loved more than having Grandfather comb her hair.

I learned to do many things that summer—to chop kindling, stack firewood, feed the chickens, gather eggs, clean the ashes from the stove grate, fill the kerosene lamps, polish the lamp chimneys and trim the wicks, and hoe weeds from the garden. I also graduated from the porch steps and became a person of affairs in the neighborhood. Aunt Pauline began sending me to the grocer's and the drugstore. Running errands wasn't quite as good as being free to roam and visit the trash pile. I was always in a hurry and had to carry things on my way back, but I learned to play on the wing. Aunt Pauline knew exactly how long each errand ought to take and she expected me to go and come without stopping. On my way to the store, I'd shave off a few precious minutes for a game of hopscotch or marbles and then I'd run all the rest of the way there and back on the double trot. I'd arrive home breathless and covered with fine dust but well within my time limit.

My reward was going barefoot that summer, a privilege which placed me on an equal footing with other neighborhood children. It was a privilege I was allowed to keep. I never associated going barefoot with being poor. It was a significant event, like seeing the first robin or dandelion in spring or going to the parade when the circus came to town. We waited all winter for that memorable first warm spring day when we were allowed to take off our shoes and stockings. We'd rush home from school, discard them and plunge our toes into the soft cool earth. We vied with one another to see who could shed his shoes earliest in spring and keep them off longest in fall. We loved to pick up little blobs of damp sand in our toes, to tramp about in the mud on rainy days and to splash through the branch. We were always running nails in our feet or cutting them on sharp weeds and having our folks worried that we would get lockjaw, but we went about proudly displaying our cuts and bruises like battle ribbons. The child with the dirtiest feet and the most scars had high standing among the others.

I suppose there was so little to brag about in the Bottoms we made a lot of fuss over little things—like my going to Pratts' well. People who didn't have city plumbing carried water all the time, but my trips made me feel especially important. Everybody knew my grandmother had pellagra and that I was carrying water for her. To and from the well I traveled in a circle where I could say howdy to all the neighbors on the two streets which bounded the Bottoms and let them see we were getting along all right over there by ourselves.

It wasn't a very long trip—you could see Pratts' chimney through the trees from our house—but I made the most of it. Every morning before breakfast, at noon and in the evening around sunset, I'd take off down the wagon track through our field, a small lard pail stuck on each shoulder like a pair of bulbous wings and Grandmother's big sun straw pulled down over my ears. I'd cross the road and follow the footpath along the Bottoms to the branch. When the water was shallow I crossed on a log, but when the stream was angry and swollen from rains I'd scamper along the banks to a spot where I could hop across on the flat moss-covered rocks. I had to keep a sharp lookout for snakes in the tall weeds but there was always a chance I'd see a terrapin or a bullfrog near the bank.

Once across the branch, I'd loiter along the cowpath up the hill searching for four-leaf clovers or digging my toes into a mole tunnel. When I looked back across the Bottoms to my house from the pine grove, the cemetery behind our house spread out as far as I could see, but the tombstones had shrunk and did not seem nearly so ready to topple down on us as they did from our back fence at home.

The Pratts lived high above the street level in a two-story frame house with a separate one-room kitchen joined at the back by a shed and a pair of low steps. The wellshed stood in the center of their wide sandy yard and a giant persimmon tree towered above it. Their place was the dividing line between the white and colored families who lived on Morehead Avenue. East of Pratts', the tree-arched avenue sloped gently toward town through "Swellton Heights" and the fine old homesteads and spacious lawns of Durham's oldest families. West of Pratts' were the Negro factory and mill workers who lived in tiny cottages or little unpainted three-room dwellings. Here the street had been widened, leveled off and paved in such a way that the small houses either teetered on a high ledge above it or sank to their rooftops below it. There

were no sidewalks and not a single shade tree. Down in the hollow
where Cameron Street crossed Morehead and ran into Shaw
Street, the back porches on both sides of the avenue faced the
Bottoms.

I envied the Pratts high on their hilltop. Their house faced east
toward the beautiful estates and they could sit on their front porch
at night under the protective glow of the street lamp at their
intersection. They were sheltered from the Bottoms by the pine
grove behind their house. There were no children in their home
but their big persimmon tree drew all the neighborhood children
on the hillside. Their well made them the most popular family on
Morehead hill. Dug fifty feet deep and lined with brick, it sur-
passed all other wells. The water was ice cold and people came
from everywhere to get a drink and pass the time of day. Folks said
limestone water purified the blood. They'd stand about waiting
their turn at the big tin dipper which hung on the wellshed and
gossiping with one another. The Pratts were great talkers, and
through their well they kept up with everything that happened.

If they were busy when I arrived with my pails, I'd roam the
yard hunting ripe persimmons or play marbles with the Wilson
children who lived next door or stand around listening to the
gossip. They never allowed me to draw the water myself because
they were afraid the heavy bucket might pull me down into the
well. I had to content myself with standing on tiptoe and peeping
over the side of the shed down the mysterious, dark hole to the
threatening water below. As the bucket hurtled downward, I'd
peer into the depths looking for stars people said you could see in
broad daylight down a well, but all I ever saw was my own scared
face looking up at me. When the bucket hit the water with a big
plop and sank out of sight, the strange mirror shattered and the
angry water churned against the mossy sides until the brimming
bucket rose to the surface and was pulled up again hand over hand
on the creaking chain.

Miss Sarah Pratt, the oldest daughter, who taught one of the
lower grades at West End School with Aunt Pauline, and Miss
Mary Lawson, a county schoolteacher who lived with the Pratt
family, were usually in the kitchen when I arrived. They were
wonderful cooks and there was always a smell of spices or chopped

onions or frying chicken or ham when I came up. Almost every noon they did their baking for supper. If they were taking it out of the oven around the time I came along, they'd offer me a little sample of hot rolls and butter, or apple pie, blackberry cobbler, peach dumpling, cherry mash or something equally tasty. When it was raining, they'd invite me into the kitchen to wait and I'd sit on a little stool talking to them, my eyes glued to the oven door of the big black iron stove. Miss Mary and Miss Sarah were such jolly souls, always so full of news and merriment, I liked them as much for themselves as for their pies and dumplings.

When my pails were filled, I'd start home again down Morehead Avenue, my head bobbing up and down in continual greeting to all the neighbors. The older folks called me "that Fitzge'l child" and the younger ones "Mis' Dame's girl." Nobody remembered my own name. Everybody would ask me how Grandmother was and I'd keep them posted on her progress. I was especially polite to those folks who never harassed her when they went through the Bottoms. It was my way of thanking them. The others got distant politeness. I never stopped on the way home because I couldn't set Grandmother's water down and I had to hurry to get it to her while it was cool.

I usually came in stuffed with information about all of the neighbors. I knew who was getting married, or had a baby, or was on the sick list, or got sent "to the roads." I'd make a beeline to Grandmother's room as soon as I put down the pails in the kitchen and I'd spill out all my news. I think the gossip I picked up at the well did her as much good as the limestone water. She'd laugh and say I was better than a local newspaper and she'd perk up afterward.

That's how I came to find out about John Henry Corniggins. It was around noon when I made my second trip to the well that day. The Carolina heat poured down on everything and there wasn't a breath of air stirring. It was quiet all over the hillside. It wasn't a day for visiting or trading gossip. The porches were empty. People who weren't at work had gone inside their houses out of the hot sun and the neighborhood dogs had crawled beneath the houses to lie panting in the dust.

The well was deserted when I arrived in Pratts' yard but I saw a thin curl of smoke coming out of the kitchen chimney. I set down my pails at the wellshed and knocked on the screen door. Miss Sarah Pratt came out wiping her steaming face on her apron. Behind her floated the smell of burning sugar, melted butter and cinnamon.

"Hello there," she said. "You're a little late, aren't you?"

"How you, Miss Sarah? I had to help Aunt Pauline wash clothes."

"Don't tell me you can wash clothes."

"I can't do the big things but Aunt Pauline lets me rinse out the little ones and spread them on the grass."

"Mrs. Dame has to do all that washing by herself?" Grandmother would call this "picking you."

"Yes Ma'am, but we're making out."

Miss Sarah let down the bucket. I squashed a rotten persimmon between my toes and wondered what she had in the oven. The sunlight filtered through the persimmon boughs and little rainbows appeared on her coffee-brown face. I wondered why some people were called white and some called colored when there were so many colors and you couldn't tell where one left off and the other began. Some folks were Aunt Pauline's color—strawberries and cream—and some were like licorice. Some were cream chocolate and some were dark chocolate. Some were caramel and some were peanut butter. Some were like molasses taffy after it has been pulled awhile and some were like gingerbread. I'd heard somebody say colored people were like a flower garden but I thought they were more like good things to eat.

Miss Sarah pulled up the bucket and was just pouring my water when Lizzie Jones, who lived on Morehead Avenue just below the Pratts, came running up the back path from her porch. I liked Lizzie. She was a plump, round-faced, smiling girl who reminded me of peanut butter. She had sweet ways and never teased Grandmother. She had always seemed very fond of Aunt Pauline, who had taught her when she was a little girl. Now she was nearly grown.

Lizzie stopped just long enough to dipper a drink from what was left in the bucket.

"Haven't got time to stop, Miss Sarah," she gasped between

swallows. "I just heard something's happened to one of those Corniggins boys out yonder in Vickers Woods."

"Mercy me! Which one? What happened?"

"I don't know yet. I'm on my way out there now to see."

"I'd go along with you but I've got a pie in the oven."

"I'll see if Rosa Hogans will go. Tell you what I find out when I get back," said Lizzie disappearing around the corner of Pratts' house.

The neighborhood houses suddenly came alive. There was a sound of running feet and shouting. I picked up my pails and edged away from the well.

"Much obliged for the water, Miss Sarah."

"You're not coming in to taste my peach pie? I'm taking it out in a minute."

"No ma'am. I better be getting on."

I rushed around the house looking for Lizzie. She was standing on the opposite corner in front of Rosa Hogans' house. From everywhere people were streaking along several paths toward the heavy woods beyond where Arnette Avenue ended abruptly in a dump heap. Many of them were factory workers who had worked a half day and still had on their bright blue hoover aprons with white collars and cuffs. Rosa came out of her door and knelt down to tie her shoes. She was a tall, pretty, hazel-nut-colored girl about Lizzie's age.

I struggled up the slope with my pails to the ledge where Lizzie was standing.

"May I go too, Lizzie?"

"Oh, honey, I don't mind taking you but I don't want to get in Dutch with Mis' Dame. She'd get down on me sure if I took you over there in those woods without her say-so."

"You better go on home, sugar," Rosa told me. "Mis' Dame don't stand for any foolishness."

"Couldn't I just go and see and come right back?"

Lizzie looked at Rosa.

"I'm not telling you to go," she said, " 'cause I don't want to get on the bad side of Mis' Dame. But if you do go, you got to hold my hand every step of the way."

I forgot all about Grandmother's water. I set the pails down under the broiling sun in the middle of the path and took Lizzie's hand.

"Lord, if Mis' Dame ever finds out about this," she groaned.

We started for the woods, half running, half stumbling along the footpath past a big billboard, through a field of sumac and weeds higher than my head and on through a bramble thicket. The heavy weeds struck me in the face, the brambles tore at my clothes and ripped my bare legs and the sharp stones bruised my feet, but I knew better than to cry after begging to go along. I clung to Lizzie's hand and kept up the best I could. From the far side of the field we followed the path through a heavy pine forest. Now we could hear somebody crying, hacking little cries like a child with whooping cough. The woods fell away sharply into a clearing on low marshy ground. We ran down the bluff, waded through black mud to our ankles and joined a little half circle of people who stood transfixed staring at something in the bushes.

Then I saw John Henry Corniggins lying in the tall grass close to a briar patch. I saw his feet first, the white soles sticking out of the grass and caked with mud, then his scratched brown legs. He lay on his side, his legs twisted around one another, one hand flung over his head clutching at a clump of earth, the other crumpled under his body. A dirty cap lay near him and huddled beside him was a little boy no bigger than I in ragged knee pants which swallowed his scrawny body. The little boy cried in jerky sobs.

For one long awful moment there was no other sound except the rending sobs. Everything seemed frozen. Not a leaf quivered; not a bird called. John Henry lay so still he did not even move to shoo away the large green fly that settled on his face and crawled over his cheek. Another lighted on his lips and crawled inside his mouth. Overhead a lone buzzard circled toward earth.

The woods stirred and moaned behind us and a rush of air came down the hill. The bushes swayed slightly and a heavy dark shadow moved across the clearing and fell over the spot where John Henry lay. Thunder rumbled off in the distance. The half circle grew larger and began to babble. Scared questioning voices melted into one another in a single muttering voice.

"It's John Henry, that Corniggins boy. I seen him pass my house with Leander not an hour ago."

"He's dead all right. Deader'n a doornail."

"Oh my God! Pore Mis' Corniggins."

"She know yet?"

"Somebody's gone to fetch her from the fact'ry."

"It's gonna be a terrible blow to that pore woman. She's had such a time trying to raise her young'uns."

"Ain't it a shame?"

"How'd it happen?"

"Say that WHITE man shot him."

"WHITE man?"

"Yeah. The one got that watermelon patch up there back of Vickers Avenue."

"How he come to shoot him?"

"Say he been threatening shoot niggers stealing his watermelons."

"Yeah?"

"Well, say he shot John Henry."

"John Henry stealing watermelons?"

"Can't tell."

"What Leander say?"

"Leander so scared you can't hardly make heads or tails outta what he say."

"Doan Leander know who shot his brother?"

"Leander say they was playing dogs and rabbit and run right 'cross the end of the white man's watermelon patch. He say the white man hollered at 'em and they kept on running."

"What else Leander say?"

"Say John Henry was running when he fell."

"I doan see no watermelon down here near him and that watermelon patch is 'way off up that hill. Looks mighty doggone funny to me. Looks like that white man shot this boy outta pure down meanness."

"Thass what I say."

"Oh, dear Jesus! It coulda been my Rufus. He hangs out with John Henry all the time."

"Thass what I tell these chillun 'bout going round white folks' neighborhoods. I'll be plumb scared to let mine out of my sight after this."

"It ain't right. Shooting him down like a dog. If 'twuz my chile, I'd put the law on him, WHITE man or no WHITE man."

"Now you talking. This ain't no Jawjuh."

"Might not be Georgia, but how's anybody gonna prove the white man done it? No witnesses but Leander. It'll be *his* word 'gainst Leander's and Leander ain't nothing but a chile."

"Doan matter. I'd put the law on him all the same."

"Yeah, me too. It's time *somebody* put a stop to shooting up colored folks."

"Well, if a WHITE man done it, you can betcha bottom dollar that's the end of it."

Somebody screamed in the woods behind us.

"Lawd, that must be his mother now. Don't let her come down here and see him like this."

"Somebody take him up there on high ground."

"Here comes Dick Banks. Let him through."

Tall, amber, gray-eyed Dick Banks, the painter and plasterer, who lived on Shaw Street just above John Henry's house, shouldered through the crowd. Without a word he strode into the bushes, knelt down and picked John Henry up in his arms. He carried him out of the marsh and up the slope. John Henry's skinny arms flopped up and down like a dead turkey's wings. A woman put her arms about Leander's shoulders and urged him forward.

"Come on, honey. I'm gonna take you up there to your mama."

Leander whimpered up the path. A silent queue single-filed behind Dick Banks and his burden. He stopped at the edge of the woods and laid John Henry on his back under a tall pine tree. I saw his eyes now for the first time. They were wide open and staring into the sky. They were fixed and shiny like two glass beads. Across his lean brown face gleamed two livid stripes where his cheek had lain against blades of grass. A small hole blackened about the edges showed on his shirt front over his heart.

The sky was so dark overhead now that it looked like night in the woods. A few drops of rain spattered against the pine needles and the thunder rolled nearer. The screams we had heard grew louder and more piercing. I suddenly felt cold and began to tremble although my clothes were dripping wet from sweat. I remembered Grandmother's pails of water sitting on the path.

"I gotta go, Lizzie," I whimpered. "I left Granma's water and a big storm's coming up."

"Guess we'd better," she said in a queer frightened voice. My hand burned in hers. She had never let go of it.

I could hear Aunt Pauline calling me as I hurried down Morehead hill a short while later. She was walking the porch when I came up.

"Where on earth have you been?" she began. "I'm almost out of my mind. I heard screaming and thought something had happened to you. Just look at your clothes and that mud on your feet!"

I burst out crying as soon as I reached the steps.

"A WHITE man shot John Henry Corniggins," I sobbed, "and I saw him DEAD over there in the woods."

Aunt Pauline did not whip me when she heard my story. Her face just looked sterner and her thin lips more set. Grandmother's water wasn't fit to drink and we had to boil it. But I could think of nothing except John Henry Corniggins. It was the first time I could remember seeing death. All the rest of that day and the next I kept asking the same question over and over again.

"Why, Aunt Pauline? Why did the WHITE man shoot John Henry?"

"I can't tell you, child. There are some things you'll understand better when you get older," was all she would say.

Doc Caldwell had Grandmother up again by fall. I no longer had to go to the well. We never found out who killed John Henry. Somebody later said a colored outlaw from the Bottoms had shot him, but nobody believed that story. Everybody thought it was the white man. Nothing was done about it and after a while people stopped talking.

20

AS I look back on those years at Grandfather's house, I see that I inhabited a world of unbelievable contradictions. There were the disciplines of study, of doing one's duty at all costs, of walking up to fear and conquering it. Against these were the imagined terrors of the cemetery and its dead and the equally disconcerting fear of the living—that unknown white world with which I had little or no contact but which surrounded and stifled me, a great amorphous mass without personality about which I had much curiosity but dared not investigate in the interests of maintaining my dignity and pride. There were the exhortations of Grandfather and my aunts as teachers to bring out the best in people and there were Grandmother's gloomy prophecies warning of the worst. There were competing prides and loyalties—Grandfather's loyalty to his Union cause and Grandmother's to her Smiths—and while each sprang from widely different sources, both, it seemed to me, in the long run ended up in near poverty and isolation between the Bottoms and the cemetery.

For me all this could only end in rebellion. I do not know which generated the greater revolt in me: the talk I heard about the Smiths or stories of the Fitzgeralds. Each played its part. Listening to my elders tell of the old days in North Carolina, it sometimes appeared that the world my aunts and mother grew up in bore little resemblance to the one in which I lived only a few decades later.

When the Fitzgeralds had gone south, there were no rigid Jim Crow laws as I knew them in my time and there was still room to breathe. Durham was a village without pre-Civil War history or strong ante-bellum traditions. In some ways it was like a frontier town. There was considerable prejudice, of course, but there were recognition of individual worth and bridges of mutual respect between the older white and colored families of the town which persisted into the twentieth century. Robert and Richard Fitzgerald were respected as builders of this tobacco center and their families were held in high esteem.

Everyone knew the Fitzgerald daughters and what their families stood for. Uncle Richard Fitzgerald was known as the town's leading brick manufacturer and was considered wealthy. He owned a great deal of property all over town and was president of the first Negro bank organized in Durham. He and his family lived in a fine eighteen-room slate-roofed house of many turrets and gables and a wide piazza, set in a large maple-and-magnolia grove and surrounded by white sandy drives and terraced lawns. Grandfather lived in much humbler surroundings but was equally respected for his integrity and stubbornness in the face of many odds. People sometimes distinguished the two families as the "rich Fitzgeralds" and "poor Fitzgeralds," but treated them all with deference and courtesy. When my aunts went to town men of good breeding tipped their hats and used courtesy titles in their business transactions. They went where they pleased with little restraint and were all grown women before the first law requiring separation on trains and streetcars appeared in North Carolina.

They regarded these laws disdainfully as a temporary evil, perhaps, and often ignored them, but they were never crushed by them. They had known better times and were closer to the triumphs of Grandfather's youth. I could only look forward to a time when I could complete Grandfather's work, which had been so violently interrupted during Reconstruction.

Mary Ruffin Smith had sown seeds of rebellion in disposing of her wealth. She had done what she thought was best according to her lights, but we thought differently. She gave the balance of her estate, which consisted mostly of heavily wooded land worth around $50,000, to the Western Diocese of the Protestant

Episcopal Church in the state and to the University of North Carolina. The University got the Jones' Grove tract with the stipulation that it be converted into a permanent trust fund in memory of her late brother who once owned it. The fund was to be used for the education of students at the University and is known as the Francis Jones Smith Scholarships.

Grandmother and her children owned property almost in the shadow of the University with whose history and traditions they were well acquainted. It did not take her daughters long to ask why she must pay taxes to support an institution which they could not attend. It was a burning issue in our family, kindled as much by feelings of personal injustice as by group discrimination. I heard it so often at home that it was only natural that I should be among the first to hammer on the doors of the University and demand the right to enter.

Then there was the fact of Grandfather's pension check and what it symbolized. I used to lead him to town each month when he went to cash it. He seemed to walk straighter on those days. He was the Robert Fitzgerald of old before blindness and infirmity had slowed his steps and interrupted his work. His check was his government's recognition of honored service and of the disability he had suffered in his country's cause.

But I saw the things which Grandfather could not see—in fact had never seen—the signs which literally screamed at me from every side—on streetcars, over drinking fountains, on doorways: FOR WHITE ONLY, FOR COLORED ONLY, WHITE LADIES, COLORED WOMEN, WHITE, COLORED. If I missed the signs I had only to follow my nose to the dirtiest, smelliest, most neglected accommodations or they were pointed out to me by a heavily armed, invariably mountainous red-faced policeman who to me seemed more a signal of calamity than of protection. I saw the names of telephone subscribers conspicuously starred "(C)" in the telephone directory and the equally conspicuous space given to crimes of Negroes by the newspapers, the inconspicuous space given to public recognition and always with the ignominious and insulting "negro" or "negress."

When Grandfather came south to teach, the little Negro freedmen and the poor white children were more or less on an equal footing, shared an abysmal ignorance and went to log cabin schools. A half century later the crusade against starving the colored schools was a feeble whimper. Each morning I passed white children as poor as I going in the opposite direction on their way to school. We never had fights; I don't recall their ever having called me a single insulting name. It was worse than that. They passed me as if I weren't there! They looked through me and beyond me with unseeing eyes. Their school was a beautiful red-and-white brick building on a wide paved street. Its lawn was large and green and watered every day and flower beds were everywhere. Their playground, a wonderland of iron swings, sand slides, see-saws, crossbars and a basketball court, was barred from us by a strong eight-foot-high fence topped by barbed wire. We could only press our noses against the wire and watch them playing on the other side.

I went to West End where Aunt Pauline taught, on Ferrell Street, a dirt road which began at a lumberyard and ended in a dump. On one side of this road were long low warehouses where huge barrels of tobacco shavings and tobacco dust were stored. All day long our nostrils sucked in the brown silt like fine snuff in the air. West End looked more like a warehouse than a school. It was a dilapidated, rickety, two-story wooden building which creaked and swayed in the wind as if it might collapse. Outside it was scarred with peeling paint from many winters of rain and snow. Inside the floors were bare and splintery, the plumbing was leaky, the drinking fountains broken and the toilets in the base-ment smelly and constantly out of order. We'd have to wade through pools of foul water to get to them. At recess we herded into a yard of cracked clay, barren of tree or bush, and played what games we could improvise like hopscotch or springboard, which we contrived by pulling rotted palings off the wooden fence and plac-ing them on brickbats.

It was never the hardship which hurt so much as the *contrast* between what we had and what the white children had. We got the greasy, torn, dog-eared books; they got the new ones. They had field day in the city park; we had it on a furrowed stubbly hill-side. They got wide mention in the newspaper; we got a paragraph at the bottom. The entire city officialdom from the mayor down turned out to review their pageantry; we got a solitary official.

Our seedy run-down school told us that if we had any place at all in the scheme of things it was a separate place, marked off, proscribed and unwanted by the white people. We were bottled up and labeled and set aside—sent to the Jim Crow car, the back of the bus, the side door of the theater, the side window of a restaurant. We came to know that whatever we had was always inferior. We came to understand that no matter how neat and clean, how law abiding, submissive and polite, how studious in school, how churchgoing and moral, how scrupulous in paying our bills and taxes we were, it made no essential difference in our place.

It seemed as if there were only two kinds of people in the world —*They* and *We*—*White* and *Colored.* The world revolved on color and variations in color. It pervaded the air I breathed. I learned it in hundreds of ways. I picked it up from grown folks around me. I heard it in the house, on the playground, in the streets, everywhere. The tide of color beat upon me ceaselessly, relentlessly.

Always the same tune, played like a broken record, robbing one of personal identity. Always the shifting sands of color so that there was no solid ground under one's feet. It was color, color, color all the time, color, features and hair. Folks were never just folks. They were white folks! Black folks! Poor white crackers! No-count niggers! Red necks! Darkies! Peckerwoods! Coons!

Two shades lighter! Two shades darker! Dead white! Coal black! High yaller! Mariny! Good hair! Bad hair! Stringy hair! Nappy hair! Thin lips! Thick lips! Red lips! Liver lips! Blue veined! Blue gummed! Straight nosed! Flat nosed!

Brush your hair, child, don't let it get kinky! Cold-cream your face, child, don't let it get sunburned! Don't suck your lips, child, you'll make them too niggerish! Black is evil, don't mix with mean niggers! Black is honest, you half-white bastard. I always said a little black and a little white sure do make a pretty sight! He's black as sin and evil in the bargain. The blacker the berry, the sweeter the juice!

To hear people talk, color, features and hair were the most important things to know about a person, a yardstick by which everyone measured everybody else. From the looks of my family I could never tell where white folks left off and colored folks began, but it made little difference as far as I was concerned. In a world of black-white opposites, I had no place. Being neither very dark nor very fair, I was a nobody without identity. I was too dark at home and too light at school. The pride I learned at home was almost canceled out by the cloak of shame I wore at school, especially when my schoolmates got angry and yelled at me, "You half-white bastard! You dirty-faced Jew baby! Black is honest! Yaller is dishonest!"

I was a minority within a minority, shoved down by inexorable pressures from without, thrust up by intolerable frustrations from within. Black ancestry brought the shame of slavery; white ancestry was condemned as bastardy and brought another kind of shame. Since there was no middle ground between these two extremes, I sought neutral territory in my American Indian ancestry, a group nonexistent in my community and which could not challenge my asserted kinship. I fell back on Great-Grandmother Harriet and her Cherokee blood. That she too had been a slave subject to all the evils of slavery was submerged in the more significant fact that the American Indians at least had preferred annihilation to enslavement. This seemed to me a worthier trait than acceptance of bondage as the price of survival.

It is little wonder, then, perhaps, that I was strongly anti-American at six, that I hated George Washington, mumbled the oath of allegiance to the American flag which we children were taught in the second grade and was reluctant to stand up when we sang "The Star-Spangled Banner." I was unmoved by the story of Washington's crossing the Delaware, nor was I inspired by his truthfulness and valor. My thin knowledge of history told me that the George Washingtons and their kind had stolen the country from the American Indians, and I could lodge all my protests against this unforgivable piece of thievery.

Every February the lower grades buzzed with activities commemorating the birthdays of George Washington and Abraham Lincoln. I dutifully cut out log cabins to symbolize Lincoln's birth but I invariably messed up the hatchets and bunches of cherries. My folks would have been horrified at my private seditious thoughts if they had known of them. Grandfather and my

aunts considered themselves part of the noblest of professions—
schoolteaching—a profession allied with feelings of deepest patriotism. Aunt Pauline's classroom walls were full of American flags,
pictures of American Presidents, and a print of the famous Spirit
of '76. I regularly attended church every Sunday where prayers
were offered for the "President of the United States and all others
in civil authority." Yet, for all their patriotism, the somber fact
remained that until the three Negro schools of Durham in my
childhood—West End, East End and Whitted—all burned to the
ground mysteriously one after the other, the colored children got
no new buildings.

I do not know how long this lack of patriotism might have kept
up if Grandfather Fitzgerald had not died the summer I was nearly
nine. His last illness came upon him while Aunt Pauline and I
were in Baltimore and we had to cut short our trip and come home
immediately. It was the first time I had ever seen Grandfather
helpless. He looked so still and pale in the big iron bed upstairs.
His eyes were fixed upon the ceiling, his lips were dry and cracked
and his breath came in quick gasps. At first he could talk to us but
he got so he couldn't speak and his lips made soundless movements.

Uncle Richard had died a year earlier but I had not felt his
death. It was the first time in those years of living close to the
symbols of death I was aware of it approaching. Grandmother was
like a wild animal. I had never seen her like that before. She yelled
and stormed so that Grandfather's sisters, Aunt Mary and Aunt
Agnes, did not dare come into the house. They stood at the back
fence and asked how Grandfather was, then went away again.

Aunt Pauline woke me on Monday morning, August 4, while
it was still dark.

"Your grandfather took a turn for the worse during the night. I
don't think he'll last until morning and I've got to send for Aunt
Mary and Aunt Agnes. You're the only one to go. If I stand in the
back door and watch you till you get up the hill, do you think you
could run through the cemetery and get them?"

I was terrified. I had never been through the cemetery alone
after dark, but Grandfather was dying and it seemed that in death
he was to give me the courage I had never found during his life.

I put on my clothes and went out into the crisp cool blackness of early morning. I climbed the fence while Aunt Pauline took her post in the doorway. I sped up the little bricked alleyways, past the ominous Confederate gun, past crazy-leaning tombstones, vaults and marble angels, past the shadowy trees rustling slightly in an early morning breeze, past the mausoleum at the top of the hill where Aunt Pauline could no longer see me and I was on my own.

I outran death that morning and arrived at Aunt Agnes' house in a state of collapse. She was ill and only Aunt Mary could go back with me. It was still twilight and as we started back through the cemetery she took my hand, but I was no longer afraid. I had taken the first step toward walking in Grandfather's shoes. Aunt Pauline took Aunt Mary straight upstairs to Grandfather's room when we got home, but she made me stay outside and I sat on the stair landing feeling lost and alone and wondering about death. When Aunt Pauline came out and started down the stairs crying I knew that Grandfather was gone.

Then the strangest thing happened. Grandmother, who had been like a raging volcano, took charge. She made everybody leave Grandfather's room and locked herself inside. When she came out again some time later she was quiet and calm as if some terrible storm had gone out of her. She had cleaned Grandfather's body, bathed him all over and put on his burial underclothes. She wanted the undertaker to find him as he had lived—everything in order.

I did not see Grandfather again until after the undertaker came and left and a black crepe was hung on our door. He was lying on a bier in front of the fireplace, dressed in his salt-and-pepper-gray broadcloth suit and covered from his chest down with a long dark drape. Out of childish curiosity I slipped into the parlor and looked underneath the drape. Grandfather, who had always been my symbol of strength and authority, now looked tiny and shrunken. He was fully dressed except for his shoes, and his white-stockinged feet turned upward and curled over a bit. I remember wondering why a person was buried without his shoes on. For years I could not go into the parlor without still seeing the image of Grandfather lying in his dark suit before the fireplace with his white-stockinged feet curled up and over.

The family patriarch had gone down in death, and it was like the shock of a great landmark tree crashing in the forest. It was the signal for the gathering of all the relatives from near and far. Most of our blood kinsfolk came together for a three-day period of mourning. The ban on exiles was lifted temporarily, old associations were renewed, family stories embellished by collective memories were retold, and sometimes new business ventures were started. The wake had the solemnity of a high religious observance with an undertone of family reunion. There was subdued merriment among the more distant relatives while the chief mourners stayed in a special room surrounded by only the closest of friends. The atmosphere was hushed most of the time except for the occasional irreverent laughter of children. It seemed to me that I had more visitors and playmates during those three days than I had had in my entire life at Grandfather's house.

But when the day of the funeral came, the only sign of grief among Grandmother and my aunts was their pale, tight-lipped appearance in their long black dresses and flowing black veils. They marched—not walked—in the funeral procession, as Grandfather had always marched before them, and they all sang his favorite hymns as if they were the choir instead of the bereaved. It was a family custom to sing a loved one on his way to the other side and it has been followed to this day.

Once the family patriarch was lowered into his grave, however, and the long black funeral veils were laid away for the future, his mantle of authority fell naturally and wordlessly upon that next member of the clan, man or woman, who had been emerging through the years. Every family must have such a head, it seemed; otherwise it became rudderless and scattered, losing its strength and identity. For the Fitzgerald clan of Fitzgeralds and Cleggs,* that day it became Great-Aunt Mary, the oldest survivor of those who had come south in 1869. In our immediate family it was Aunt Pauline.

Grandfather was buried in the Fitzgerald family graveyard where Great-Grandfather Thomas, Great-Grandmother Sarah Ann, Uncle Richard and other relatives already rested. It was on the west side

*My Great-aunt Agnes Fitzgerald married Robert Clegg.

of Chapel Hill Road next to the old section of Maplewood Cemetery. Only an iron picket fence separated the Fitzgeralds from their white contemporaries who had been early settlers in Durham, but a far wider gulf separated the living descendants. And it was in Grandfather's death that I found a symbol which would somehow sustain me until I grew older and found other ways of balancing loyalty with revolt.

Grandfather died in 1919 and it would be a number of years before the graves of World War I veterans appeared. Meanwhile the white cemetery from our back door to Chapel Hill Road and beyond was filled with Confederate dead. Every Memorial Day or Decoration Day, the cemetery hillside was dotted with crossbarred Confederate flags. As a Union veteran, Grandfather was entitled to a United States flag for his grave, so every May I walked proudly through a field of Confederate flags hugging my gold-pointed replica of Old Glory. I crossed Chapel Hill Road to the Fitzgerald family burial ground and planted it at the head of Grandfather's grave.

This solitary American flag just outside the iron fence which separated it from the Confederate banners waving on the other side was an act of hunger and defiance. It tied me and my family to something bigger than the Rebel atmosphere in which we found ourselves. In time Grandfather would be joined by Grandmother here and we would sell Grandmother's farm and the family homeplace. We would scatter and there would not be one Robert and Cornelia Fitzgerald descendant left in the South. We would become city folk in stifling little apartments in northern cities, far from the land and rootless, and the Fitzgerald name would die out leaving only the Fitzgerald mark here and there. We younger ones would search for something we had lost or perhaps had never had.

But for that moment upon this lone flag I hung my nativity and the right to claim my heritage. It bore mute testimony to the irrefutable fact that I was an American and it helped to negate in my mind the signs and symbols of inferiority and apartness. In those early years there was little identity in my mind between the Union flag which waved over my grandfather's grave and the United States flag upon which I looked with so much skepticism at West End School. It would be a while yet before I realized that the two were the same.

I spent many hours digging up weeds, cutting grass and tending the family plot. It was only a few feet from the main highway between Durham and Chapel Hill. I wanted the white people who drove by to be sure to see this banner and me standing by it. Whatever else they denied me, they could not take from me this right and the undiminished stature it gave me. For there at least at Grandfather's grave with the American flag in my hands, I could stand very tall and in proud shoes.

Acknowledgments

This book is the product of the labor of many individuals: the librarians, archivists, record clerks and government workers who found documents, dug up research materials and answered many requests for information; the knowledgeable residents of many localities who graciously consented to interviews; the countless friends and volunteers who contributed old newspaper clippings, books and pictures not readily available in public libraries; the artists, copy editors, proofreaders and production workers of printing and publishing houses, and the vast number of well-wishers who provided clues, wrote letters containing relevant information and gave encouragement. Many of the individuals who contributed much to the 1956 edition have died but their names are mentioned here in belated tribute. Many others, unnamed, are part of a "cast of thousands" to whom I owe a debt of gratitude.

The 1956 edition was dedicated to four people: Caroline F. Ware, social historian (who, with her husband, Gardiner C. Means, economist, have been my mentors and steadfast supporters since 1942); Edmund Ziman, the psychiatrist who worked with authors and helped me overcome a stubborn writer's block; Marie F. Rodell, now deceased, my literary agent, who introduced me to Harper and supported me through major surgery, the deaths of my three aunts and voluntary part-time employment at odd jobs during the research and writing of *Proud Shoes*; and to the memory of my Aunt Pauline who died one year before the book was published.

Some of the others who made possible the first edition, and its reissue in 1978, are:

Mary Lee Fisher (Morris), my high school teacher of Latin, who taught me grammar and first encouraged me to write.

Lula Burton (Bramwell) and Edna Lisle, my beloved college school-mates whose friendship respectively inspired me to pursue the written word and to meet the challenge of racially mixed origins.

Catherine M. Reigart, my Hunter College teacher of freshman English, whose patience, steady encouragement and high expectations helped me to struggle against a weak foundation in composition and in whose class I wrote the essay which contained the seed of *Proud Shoes*.

Ruth M. Goldstein, my college classmate and student editor who published my first written efforts and whose enthusiasm for the family memoir has been restorative.

Maysie Stone, sculptor, who evoked the family stories while she moulded a bust of me in 1933 and planted the idea of a family memoir.

Stephen Vincent Benét who furthered the idea and nurtured some of the early drafts.

Louis J. Redding, lawyer; J. Saunders Redding, writer; and their widowed father, Lewis A. Redding, in whose Wilmington, Delaware, home traditions of freedom fighting and creative writing combined to light me on my way.

Arthur Schlesinger, Jr., and Benjamin Quarles, historians, whose critical comments and Civil War studies respectively were of enormous aid.

Lillian Smith, whose Southern heritage, Christian convictions and powerful pen were brought to bear upon the manuscript as she guided me through the beginning chapters.

Maida Springer (Kemp), Eric Springer and the late Mrs. Adina Stewart Carrington whose household was a sanctuary and who were my first audience for each chapter read aloud as it was completed.

Helen Lockwood, late head of the Department of English, Vassar College, whose appreciation of enduring American values of liberty, equality and fraternity was a continual source of strength as I worked my way through the writing difficulties.

Betsy Graves Reyneau, pioneer feminist, civil rights activist and painter-critic, whose interpretation of a mutual abolitionist heritage was both inspiring and helpful.

Elizabeth Lawrence Kalashnikoff, my editor at Harper and Brothers (1952–56), who recommended me for the Eugene F. Saxton Award, and never lost faith in me as a writer or in *Proud Shoes* as a contribution to American social history. Her unerring sense of the creative word and the message of the book sustained me through the first edition and the desolate twenty-two intervening years.

Mrs. Edward MacDowell, founder, and the staff of MacDowell Colony (1954–56), Peterborough, New Hampshire, who provided the setting and the relief from the daily grind to permit me to complete the book; and particularly my sister Colonists and writers Henrietta Buckmaster and Helene Hanff whose mutual support through the dark hours of creative chaos before the birth of the inevitable word was crucial.

Irene Barlow, my most enthusiastic champion for reissue during her lifetime and to whose memory this serves as a rededication.

Miss Gertrude Brinckle; Marguerite Prolieau; Myrtle Burris; George B. Stansfield; Dr. Charles F. Romanus; Maj. Gen. Edward F. Witsell; Maj. Gen. William E. Bergin; Dr. Alvin P. Stauffer; Arthur E. DuBois; Lt. Col. C. D. McFerren; Col. Carl T. Hutton; Lt. Comdr. E. W. Irvin, USNR; Lieut. A. A. Cico, USN; Maj. Gen. William H. Harrison; Ernest Barkeley; Dr. Horace Mann Bond; Mr. L. J. Ficcio; The Rev. Eugene L. Henderson; Mrs. Edward A. Walls; Mr. James W.Draper; all of whom helped me with my research for the first edition far beyond the call of their various duties.

Lee Coventry Kessler; Christine Taylor Alston; the Rev. Peter James Lee; June and John Allcott; Mrs. Dangerfield Newby (the former Miss Mary Lawson); Catherine A. Miller; Joan Clegg Brack; Beatrice Fitzgerald Hammond Grevenberg; Agnes Fitzgerald Mauney; Alma Fitzgerald Biggers; and Mr. and Mrs. G. T. Cole, all of whom in various ways have given unstintingly of themselves through research, correspondence, contribution of pictures, reproduction of documents and other labors of love to illustrate and authenticate the 1978 reissue.

The hundreds of friends and readers who have kept up a steady drumbeat of voices and letters through the years to revive this book.

Finally, Cass Canfield, Sr., of Harper & Row; Corona Machemer, my new editor; Frances Collin, my new literary agent; and Charles Kuralt of CBS-TV, all of whom have made the resurrection of *Proud Shoes* a continual experience of excitement and delight.

Sources of Materials
and Documentation

American History Room, New York Public Library, 42nd Street and
  Fifth Avenue, New York, New York.
Chester County Courthouse, West Chester, Pennsylvania.
Chester County Historical Society, West Chester, Pennsylvania.
Durham County Courthouse, Durham, North Carolina.
State of Delaware, Public Archives Division, Dover, Delaware.
Historical Society of Delaware, Wilmington, Delaware.
Lincoln University Archives, Lincoln University, Pennsylvania.
Massachusetts State Archives, Boston, Massachusetts.
National Archives and Records Service, Washington, D.C.
North Carolina Collection, University of North Carolina at
  Chapel Hill.
Orange County Courthouse, Hillsboro, North Carolina.
Peterborough Free Public Library, Peterborough, New Hampshire.
United Presbyterian Church, U.S.A. (successor to Presbyterian
  Church, U.S.A.).
Friends Historical Society, Swarthmore, Pennsylvania.
Cheyney Teachers College, Cheyney, Pennsylvania.
United States District Court, Wilmington, Delaware.
Southern Historical Collection, University of North Carolina at
  Chapel Hill.
The Crisis (official organ of the National Association for the
  Advancement of Colored People), June 1920.
Robert G. Fitzgerald Diary, Part 2d., Vol. 1, May 1, 1864–Sept. 19,
  1864; Vol. 4, June 28, 1867–Aug. 18, 1871.
The National War College, Reference Library, Washington, D.C.
Department of the Army, Office of the Adjutant General, The
  Pentagon, Washington, D.C.
Department of the Army, Office of the Quartermaster General, The
  Pentagon, Washington, D.C.
Department of the Army, Office of the Chief of Military History, The
  Pentagon, Washington, D.C.
Department of the Navy, Bureau of Naval Personnel, The Pentagon,
  Washington, D.C.
Commonwealth of Massachusetts, Adjutant General's Office, J.F.K.
  Building, Boston, Massachusetts.

About the Author

PAULI MURRAY was born in 1910 in Baltimore, where her father was a principal in the Baltimore city schools and her mother was a graduate nurse. After her mother's death she went to Durham, North Carolina, where she was raised by her maternal grandparents and an aunt, a teacher for many years in the Durham city schools. She got her bachelor's degree from Hunter College in 1933. In 1938, she was rejected as a graduate student at the University of North Carolina because of her race. In 1940, she was arrested on an interstate bus in Virginia for violation of the state's segregation law. She got her law degree from Howard University in 1944, graduating at the top of her class with a fellowship to go to Harvard Law School for her master's degree. She was rejected by Harvard because of her sex. Later she earned a master's degree in law from the University of California at Berkeley, and was a tutor in law at Yale, where she received her doctorate in 1965. She also taught law in Ghana, West Africa, and at Boston and Brandeis universities.

There was hardly any part of the struggle for human rights during the 1950's and '60's in which Pauli Murray was not actively involved, notably the civil rights and civil liberties movements and the reawakening of the women's movement. Her experiments in nonviolent creative action in the 1940's anticipated the Martin Luther King movement.

In 1973, following the removal of the bar against women to the diaconate in the Episcopal Church, Dr. Murray was able to consummate her life-long involvement with her church by seeking admission to the ordained ministry. She entered General Theological Seminary in New York to study for Holy Orders in the Episcopal Church. She was made a deacon in 1976 and, in January 1977, was one of three women and three men ordained to the priesthood in Washington Cathedral. On Lincoln's Birthday Sunday, in February 1977, she conducted the service and celebrated the Holy Eucharist in the Episcopal Chapel of the Cross in Chapel Hill, in the same chapel where, church records show, her grandmother Cornelia Smith, "one of five servant children belong to Miss Mary Ruffin Smith," was baptized.